YVOR WINTERS

Uncollected Essays and Reviews

Edited and Introduced by
FRANCIS MURPHY

ALLEN LANE

First published in the United States of America by
The Swallow Press Inc.
This edition first published in 1974

Allen Lane
A Division of Penguin Books
17 Grosvenor Gardens, London SW1

ISBN 0 7139 0740 1

814·008
WIN

Printed in Great Britain by
Lowe and Brydone (Printers) Ltd., Thetford, Norfolk

CONTENTS

II ESSAYS

PREFATORY NOTE

With the exeception of only a few items, this collection brings together the previously uncollected essays and reviews of Yvor Winters listed in the bibliography of his work prepared by Kenneth A. Lohf and Eugene P. Sheehy (1959). Three items omitted from that bibliography have also been included. In the case of "The Cricket", I have not chosen to reprint the "Critical Foreward" to *The Complete Poems of Frederick Goddard Tuckerman* (1965) but instead, Winters' earlier essay "A Discovery" (1950). These essays often served as proving ground for Winters' final judgments, and anyone interested in Winters' career will want to familiarize himself with Winters' later response to many of these writers in *In Defense of Reason* (1947), *The Function of Criticism* (1957) and *Forms of Discovery* (1968). It is hard not to be impressed, however, with how early Winters' judgments were formulated and how much of his critical work, both early and late, is of a piece.

This collection is the result of a conversation with my friend and colleague Dean Flower. He read the manuscript more than once, and a number of his suggestions have been incorporated into the text. If I did not wish to have him charged with my own errors and omissions, I would describe this as a joint effort. But the collection would not have been possible at all without the encouragement of Janet Lewis Winters. Mrs. Winters has made all of Yvor Winters uncollected essays available to me and provided me with material now difficult to come by. Making her acquaintance was one of the several pleasures incurred while completing this book. I would also like to thank Michael Anania of The Swallow Press for his initial help and continuing interest.

Francis Murphy
Northampton, Massachusetts

INTRODUCTION

In "The Critic Who Does Not Exit," an essay written in 1928, Edmund Wilson remarked that what America lacked was not writers or literary parties, but "serious literary criticism": "Works on history are commonly reviewed by historians, and books on physics by physicists: but when a new book of American poetry or a novel or other work of belles lettres appears, one gets the impression that it is simply given to almost any well-intentioned (and not even necessarily literate) person who happens to present himself: and this person then describes in a review his emotions upon reading the book." (*Shores of Light*, 1952, p. 369). Criticism of the literature of our past seemed no more discerning to Wilson than criticism of the literature of the present, and while it was possible to agree on our major nineteenth-century American writers, "yet so far the studies by American hands which have dealt with these American classics have been almost exclusively biographical:"

> We have been eager to expose the weaknesses and curious to probe the neuroses of these ranking American writers, but have found little to say that was interesting in the lack of a criticism which should have undertaken, for example, to show how Hawthorne, Melville and Poe, besides becoming excessively eccentric persons, anticipated, in the middle of the last century, the temperament of our own day and invented methods for rendering it. (Pp. 371-372.)

Confronted by the example of Eliot's *Criterion* (1923), Wilson had every reason to be aware of the shortcomings of American criticism. Stuart Sherman, H. L. Mencken and Van Wyck Brooks, to mention three of Wilson's most prestigious contem-

poraries, were as inadequate in making judgments of the literature of the past as they were inept in handling the new. *Axel's
Castle* (1931) was Wilson's attempt to set a standard for American criticism that was as good as anything one could find in
France: "For there is one language which all French writers, no
matter how divergent their aims, always possess in common: the
language of criticism." (p. 368.) But the curious thing about
Wilson's observations are that they were dated almost the
moment they were uttered. Profiting by the example of Pound
and Eliot, a number of young Americans writing in the late
twenties were to reshape the history of our criticism and make it
one of the chief glories of American literature. In 1956 Eliot
anticipated the current wave of disenchantment when he suggested that the past three decades were perhaps "too brilliant"
an exercise in literary ingenuity. It is hard to know what critics
Eliot had in mind, but in the work of R. P. Blackmur, Kenneth
Burke, Eliot himself, Pound and Yvor Winters, American literary
criticism came of age. It is the work of the last of these critics, a
man whom Frank Kermode has characterized in *Puzzles and
Epiphanies* (1962, p. 47) as "the strangest and in some respects
the most remarkable of all modern American critics," whose work
we encounter in these pages.

Like Empson, Winters' name is identified with controversy.
Everybody knows that Winters preferred T. Sturge Moore to
Yeats, and Edith Wharton to Henry James, or that Winters
thought Tuckerman's "The Cricket" the greatest poem in the
nineteenth century. A lesser number seem to be aware of what
Winters actually said about these writers or to be familiar with
the context in which his judgments were made. Winters has so
often adopted feisty postures that his criticis have responded
with a parallel belligerence, and it must be admitted that Winters
antagonizes almost everybody somewhere along the line. Too
often Winters seems to be on the defensive, but not without
cause. Fewer major critics have been treated with more abuse.
Even Stanley Edgar Hyman, for example, whose discussion of
the major American critics in *The Armed Vision* (1948) is, for
the most part, honest and workmanlike, is especially vulnerable
in his treatment of Winters, a critic who we are informed in the

first paragraph of his essay is "well worth careful study" but who turns out in the last paragraph to be "an excessively irritating and bad critic of some importance." Hyman's chapter on Winters has a number of distortions. I have in mind his remark that "Winters added a fourth deity to his trinity [Bridges, Daryush, Moore]" in 1946, when "without much previous warning" Winters published his *Edwin Arlington Robinson*. Actually Winters had been writing about Robinson for twenty-five years. Robinson was the subject of Winters' first review for *Poetry*, and he served as a standard of comparison for Winters during all this time. Hyman might well have chosen to cite Baudelaire, Dickinson and Hardy as three poets who meant most to Winters did he not choose to emphasize Winters' eccentricity. While deploring the fact that Winters has been misrepresented in criticism, it should be noted he does nothing himself to correct that misrepresentation. How much more useful his essay would have been had Hyman quoted Winters precisely: Winters does call *The Age of Innocence*—the "finest single flower of the Jamesian art," but he adds that neither Mrs. Wharton nor Melville can "equal James in the vast crowd of unforgettable human beings whom he has created": that except in *Billy Budd*, Melville is "scarcely a novelist, and Mrs. Wharton, except in the two novels mentioned [*The Age of Innocence* and *The Valley of Decision*], in *The Custom of the Country*, and in a small group of novelettes, is mediocre when she is not worse" (*In Defense of Reason*, p. 342).

What has made Winters so "irritating" (to use Hyman's word) is that, more than any modern critic—more than any critic since Dr. Johnson—Winters has presumed to judge what he has read, and in doing so, has tested the realm of art by experience. He has asked whether "fictions" prove adequate when they are based on lies. "In knowledge." Frye has written, "the context of the work of literature is literature; in value-judgments, the context of the work of literature is the reader's experience." Frye himself has spoken eloquently (and perhaps one should add, defensively) against value-judgments in criticism, but Frye mostly addresses himself to the matter of taste. "The goal of study is knowledge," he writes, and when "knowledge improves, the sense of value improves too" (*The Stubborn Structure*, 1970, p. 66). Too much of what has passed for criticism, Frye warns, is merely preference for a particular mode or style and it makes for literary fashion. Winters would be the first to agree. His support of Hardy and Robinson when these writers were alien to the spirit of Eliot, o. his more recent inquisition of Yeats, provide some obvious examples of Winters' efforts to rise above the voguish. Frye's judgments are implicit—he values Shakespeare, Milton and Blake because they form a hierarchy of authors who, he believes, affirm the redemptive powers of the human imagination; Winters' judgments have been more explicit, and they are both aesthetic and moral. "The professor of English literature," Winters has observed, "who believes that taste is relative yet who endeavors to convince his students that *Hamlet* is more worthy of their attention than some currently popular novel, is in a serious predicament, a predicament which is moral, intellectual, and in the narrowest sense of the word professional, though he commonly has not the wit to realize the fact." (*In Defense of Reason*, p. 10.) Winters is one of the few modern critics to risk a declaration of principles which tests the end of art. On several occasions he has provided his readers with the assumptions upon which he proceeds. The following is taken from "Problems for the Modern Critic of Literature" (1956):

I believe that a poem (or other work of artistic literature) is a statement in words about a human experience. I use the term *statement* in a very inclusive sense, and for lack of something better. But it seems to me obvious that *The Iliad*, *Macbeth*, and *To the Virgins, to Make Much of Time* [Robert Herrick] all deal with human experience. In each work there is a content which is rationally apprehensible, and each work endeavors to communicate the emotion which is appropriate to the rational apprehension of the subject. The work is thus a judgment, rational and emotional, of the experience—that is a complete moral judgment in so far as the work is successful. . . . we regard as greatest those works which deal with experiences which affect human life most profoundly, and this criterion is not merely one of the intensity of the experience but of the generality of inclusiveness of the implications. In making this statement, I am assuming, of course, that the works in question are sufficiently successful in execution so that execution may be more or less neglected in the comparison. Execution can never be neglected, however, in our judgment of the individual works: a work which is poorly executed is bad, no matter what the conception ...

Winters' credo must not seem naive merely because it is clear. For those of us who were brought up on red wheelbarrows, pseudo-statements and poems that were not meant to mean but *be*, Winters' insistence on evaluation (or moral choice) in art sounded like a call from a Calvinist. We had been mesmerized by Eliot's dicta that "the chief use of the 'meaning' of a poem, in the ordinary sense, may be ... to satisfy one habit of the reader, to keep his mind diverted and quiet, while the poem does its work upon him: much as the imaginary burglar is always provided with a bit of nice meat for the house-dog" (*The Use of Poetry and the Use of Criticism*, 1933, p. 144).

Winters affirmed that there was no art without choice and that choice involved judgment; that even "poetry of the present" (to describe the poetry of Whitman and Lawrence) affects the spontaneous and experiential; that there is no such thing as description without evaluation and that the rhythm of verse is an indication of exactness of feeling. The true concern of the critic is precision of language and the significant subject. As Marshall Van Deusen points out, Winters' position is empirical and unprogrammatic, and in no way denies the validity of the critics' concern with technique. On the contrary, Winters' position provides "a final cause by which the meanings discovered through rhetorical analysis may be evaluated" (*Thought*, vol. 32, 1957-58, p. 435).

Frye is correct, however, when he warns that the one thing that can "kill" literature is "the stock response." The task of genuine criticism "is to bring literature to 'life' by annihilating stock responses, which, of course, are always value-judgments, and regularly confuse literature with life." (*The Stubborn Structure*, p. 66.) Here Frye seems to use the phrase "value-judgments" to mean any *a priori* stance which precludes open-mindedness, and it must be admitted that Winters often proceeds with imperturbable self-confidence in his judgments, although he is perfectly well aware that the danger in affirming absolutes is that the critic will come to feel that "his own judgments are final" and that "he personally has free access to these absolutes." Winters' test of truth to experience can, nevertheless, sometimes harden into dogma. This is particularly true when Winters is dealing with the Romantics, especially Emerson and Whitman. Yet even here Winters' prejudices may have allowed him, as Blackmur put it, "to see what he sees." It is now a critical commonplace to connect Romanticism and modernism, but when Winters was writing about Stevens and Crane it was much more modish to talk about "ideas of order." It was Winters who showed us that the Modern Age was not Augustan but "inescapably Romantic." Harold Bloom, in an essay entitled "The Central Man" (*The Massachusetts Review*, vol. 7, 1966, pp. 23-42) defines the American Romantic tradition in poetry and in doing so makes the following observation about Winters and the role he has played:

Mr. Yvor Winters, with exquisite judgment, pioneered in condemning Emerson, Whitman, the later Stevens, and Hart Crane together. The condemnation, however, little one credits it, has perhaps a value to the man who made it, but the critical insight that first saw these poets as a continuous tradition can scarcely be overpraised. Mr. Winters is perhaps too majestic a moralist to be accepted as a judicial critic. He has, after all, recently offered us *The Cricket* of Frederick Goddard Tuckerman as the best poem written in the English language during the whole of the nineteenth century. But the history of criticism will deal reverently with Mr. Winters; in an age during which a formidable array of minor poets-turned-critics convinced the academies that twentieth-century verse had somehow repudiated its immediate heritage, and mysteriously found its true parentage in the seventeenth century; in so odd and unnatural a time the voice of Winters was heard proclaiming, with perfect truth, that almost all poetry written in English since the age of sensibility, of the mid-eighteenth century, was inescapably Romantic, whatever its contrary desires. Descriptive accurary is the true strength of Winters; no matter that all the Romantics, from Blake and Wordsworth to Emerson and Whitman, to Stevens and Yeats and Crane, have been whithered by the Winters vision. A man who can tell us accurately and powerfully, what he dislikes, does us a greater service than our host of church-wardenly purveyors of historical myths of decline (p. 25).

Winters is more astute than most critics in pointing out some of the inanities of Whitman and Emerson, but his refusal to admit that eventually they saw the errors of their ways is willful and uncharitable. One has the sense that Winters did not (or could not) read further than "Nature" and "Song of Myself." The Emerson of "Experience" and the Whitman of "As I Ebb'd With the Ocean of Life" are closed to him. But in these works Emerson and Whitman are as aware of the "romantic dilemma" as Winters is and show us how impossible it is to have to choose between what Winters calls "abstractions inadequate or irrelevant to experience on the one hand, and experience on the other as far as practicable unilluminated by understanding." This is the Frost that Winters likes in "The Most of It" or the Stevens of "The Course of a Particular," poems in which man recognizes the futility of his desire to merge with the timeless landscape and achieve the sublime. It is the recurrence of this theme in Tuckerman's "The Cricket" that makes the poem so important to Winters:

It is a poem in which are related little by little the poet and his personal longing for death, his realization of the terror of death, his love for the natural landscape as an impersonal thing and hence a symbol of death, his love of the cricket as a small but charming creature, and his realization of the cricket as a timeless part of the non-human landscape, and hence as a symbol of the whole theme (reprinted below, p. 180).

Winters does not object to the Romantic subject. What he objects to is romantic "immersion." T. Sturge Moore's "immersion in sensation," for example, has "actually led to rejuvenation, to an inexhaustibly fascinating freshness of perception: the immersion of other poets has too often led to disintegration." For Winters, Moore defined his "temptation, without succumbing to it." It is unfortunate, however, that Winters offers us Moore at the expense of Yeats. Moore (and Winters' review convinces me) is a fine poet, and his sonnet "Apuleius Mediates," with its Melvillian subject, is equal to any of Melville's poetry on a similar subject. But a greater poet than Yeats? Like most romantics, Yeats is tempted by the visionary, but in his best poems he returns to the actual. It is not so easy to say good-bye to Greece and Rome. Yeats made the same kind of poetic capital out of his conflicting desires that Moore and Crane and Stevens did.

No one seems to forget Winters' pet peeves. Kermode echoed the sentiments of a number of Winters' detractors when he criticized him for being "so much less valuable as a discoverer of neglected talent than as an assailant of temporary orthodoxies" *(Puzzles and Epiphanies*, p. 48). There is, however, more than one Yvor Winters, and as the essays and reviews collected here prove so abundantly,Winters played a large part in sorting out and championing those poets and poems which now have so firm a place in the canon of modern American poetry. As a practicing critic for almost forty years, Winters' enthusiasms have waxed and waned, but his review of *The Collected Poems of Edwin Arlington Robinson* displays a marked continuity in taste. It contains, in fact, the essential Winters: a notable authority of tone, apt comparisons, a pointed wit (Emily Dickinson keeping tidy the room that is her life), a plea for "impersonality" in art carefully aligned to the question of form and rhyme, and an extraordinary combination of passion and detachment. The essay was written when Winters was twenty-one years old and at a time when Robinson was at the height of critical acclaim. It took a certain nonchalance and daring for someone Winters' age to stand apart from the current idolatry and in the most prestigious review in America see Robinson for the great poet he was and at the same time acknowledge Wallace Stevents (who had as yet not published a book) as "this greatest of living and American poets." A remarkable combination of arrogance and genius, followed by what became, unfortunately, an habitual attack on Whitman:

If the tradition of New England seems to be reaching an end in the work of Mr. Frost, Mr. Robinson has at least helped greatly in the founding of a tradition of culture and clean workmanship that such poets as Messrs. Stevens, Eliot, and Pound, and H. D. and Marianne Moore, are carrying on. Mr. Robinson was, when he began, as much a pioneer as Mr. Pound or Mr. Yeats, and he has certainly achieved as great poetry. While the tradition begun, more or less by Whitman, has deteriorated in the later work of Mr. Carl Sandburg, into a sort of plasmodial delirium; and while the school of mellifluous and almost ominous stage-trappings, as exemplified by Poe, has melted into a sort of post-Celtic twilight, and has nearly vanished in the work of Mr. Aiken; the work of these writers and a few others stands out clear and hard in the half-light of our culture. I cannot forget that they exist, even in the face of the desert (reprinted below, p. 00).

Winters' preference over the years has been for the meditative (i.e. retrospective and judgmental) poem in traditional meters, but when Winters wrote his review of Robinson he was writing poetry in free verse and admiring very different poets. The desert he faced was more than a metaphorical one. Because he had contracted tuberculosis he was forced to leave the University of Chicago and live in Santa Fe. He took his modern poets with him and proceeded to educate himself. As his essays and reviews on Marianne Moore, Hart Crane and William Carlos Williams suggest, Winters was the sort of critic Edmund Wilson was looking for, a man who could properly name and appraise the methods for rendering "the temperament of the day." He possessed an exacting ear and an ability to accommodate his taste to poetry in a variety of forms. Winters did not "enact a wholesale holocaust of twentieth century reputations," as Gabriel Pearson claims, nor did he "will himself not to know his own century," *(The Review,* no. 8, p. 8). As these essays prove, Winters knew his age only too well.

xvii

But he did not abandon his mind to it. In his fine "Note on Yvor Winters," Blackmur, commenting on the "experimental school" in American poetry, observed that no reader "will be able to avoid the conviction that the incompleteness, confusion, and ultimate emptiness of that poetry as a *school* are radical, and due to a wrong objective, namely: poetry without subject-matter. No critic has done more than Winters both to restore a sense for the need of objective substance and to indicate the modes by which it may be secured if it is there to secure (*Expense of Greatness*, 1940, p. 170). As for Winters' preference for traditional meters and his argument that "experimental meter loses the rational frame which alone gives its variations the precision of true perception," Blackmur adds:

> Anyone who grew up, as I did, between 1920 and 1930, will appreciate the change in poetic weather which these fragmentary quotations [from Winters] indicate, and will regret, as I do, that the change was not sooner felt. I believe that Mr. Winters is as responsible as anybody that the change has been felt at all (p. 171).

Winters' judgments may seem severe, but they have withstood the test of time. Our compassion for Hart Crane, for example, should not blind us to the quality of Winters' reviews. There is little written on Crane since that has not been concerned with the issues Winters first named, and current critical assessments of *The Bridge* have not reversed Winters' evaluations. His selection of "Repose of Rivers," "For the Marriage of Helen and Faustus," "Recitative," "Voyages II and V," from *White Buildings*, and "The River," "The Dance" and "Cutty Sark" from *The Bridge*, still seems to me to represent Crane at his finest. Winters can tolerate much that is alien to his intellect if he is first struck by the music of the verse. His real instinct is for truth to feeling. Only one who knew the compelling power of the imagination and who must have felt confusion as a physical thing could so warn us against Hart Crane—"because he may easily take possession of us wholly." Evaluation is so infrequent in criticism that any act of judgment seems to most readers harsh and surprising. There is a statement included in the "Foreword" to *In Defense of Reason* (p. 12) which Winters probably should have used to introduce all his work:

> Probably no poem is perfect in the eye of God. So far as I am concerned, a good many poems approach so near to perfection that I find them satisfactory. Some of these I have analyzed both in respect to their virtues and to their defects; others, because of the nature of my discussion, mainly with reference to their defects; but I have dealt with few works which do not seem to me to have discernible virtues, for to do otherwise would seem to me a waste of time (p. 12).

Winters continued to write about his contemporaries and in the years that followed the publication of most of these uncollected reviews, he produced important essays on Eliot, Frost, Ransom and Stevens. Winters taught both the Renaissance and the modern poets at Stanford University, and it was the later poets who most engaged his attention. "They have had to overcome greater problems," Winters wrote, "they have had to think their way, as best they have been able, through a multiplicity of disturbing possibilities: the problems of adjusting their emotional lives to their intellectual lives has thus been greater; they have had to find their respective ways among a greater confusion of possibilities in the matter of poetic style. The poets who have managed at times to surmount these difficulties have achieved in the process a greater knowledge, a greater sophistication, a greater dignity, than one can find in any earlier period. They are more fully realized as human beings" (*Forms of Discovery*, p. 358-59). Winters turned his immediate attention, however, to the major figures in American literature of the nineteenth century. He sought the origins of modern "confusion" and in doing so, wrote his greatest book, *Maule's Curse*. Randall Jarrell said it was "the best book on American literature [he'd] ever read," (*Kenyon Review*, vol. 1, 1939, p. 214) and if one excepts Lawrence's *Studies in Classic American Literature* and Matthiessen's *American Renaissance* there is little written since that does not touch upon its ground.

It would be unfair to both Blackmur and Jarrell, however, if one did not acknowledge their serious reservations about Winters' work as a whole. We return to Winters' preference for Jones Very over Emerson and his qualified preference for Edith Wharton over Henry James. In both cases Winters seems to choose the lesser figure. It is only after making his case for Mrs. Wharton that Winters finally opts for James. Mrs. Wharton may present her moral issues with "greater precision," but James creates the "unforgettable" characters. That return to the more fertile sensibility, Blackmur notes, "is the obligation of the critic as it is the necessity, for survival, of the writer. The point about Mr. Winters is that he returns often enough so that we can afford to dismiss him where he does not: we lose little to gain much." Blackmur's conclusion is worth having before us:

Without the expedience of his principles—the logic of his taste—and without the exaggerations and irrelevances to which they have led him, Mr. Winters could probably have gotten nowhere with the aspects of American poetry and fiction which absorbed his instinctive attention. It may even have been his principles which let him see what he sees. For his subject was confusion, confusion of mode, subject, source, and flux; and the best, or at any rate the quickest way to clarify a confusion is by imposing, as you think, an order upon it which you have derived elsewhere, whether from the general orthodoxy or from your special heresy of the orthodox— your version of the superrational. Actually, of course, you do no such thing, except so far as you fall into error; actually you find, discern, the order which already exists in the confusion before you and of which you form, by sheer egocentricity, the integrating part . . . It is my contention that Mr. Winters knows all this in practice, and that if you will permit yourself to know what he knows you will be able both to ignore and to profit by the mere provisional form of his argument. It is the sensibility, in the end, that absorbs, and manifests like light, the notion of order (p. 174-75).

Winters did know all this. Writing in *Gyroscope* in 1929, he observed that "the technique for dealing with irreducible emotion, for that which cannot be formulated, is not dogma, but art. . . . the *poetic* content inheres in the feeling, the style, the untranslatable, and can be reduced to no formula save itself. It may even, in fact, constitute a complete negation of the logical content: and the moral quality of a poem lies in its poetic content." To impose, as Stevens tells us, is not to discover. At his best, and that is very often indeed, Winters was one of the great discoverers. He brought to criticism, as Jarrell reminded us, "an unusual sensitivity, a rigorous intelligence, and a dismayingly thorough knowledge," and, one could add, an acerbic wit, an unfailing ear for cant, and a lifelong passion for poetry.

F.M.

REVIEWS

A COOL MASTER

The Collected Poems of Edwin Arlington Robinson. MacMillan.

Near the middle of the last century, Ralph Waldo Emerson, a sentimental philosopher with a genius for a sudden twisted hardness of words, wrote lines like:

Daughters of Time, the hypocritic days,
Muffled and dumb like barefoot dervishes,
And marching single in an endless file,
Bring diadems and fagots in their hands.

And it was with Emerson that American poetry may be said to have begun. He was slight enough, but at his best a master, and above all a master of sound. And he began a tradition that still exists.

He was followed shortly by Emily Dickinson, a master of a certain dowdy but undeniably effective mannerism, a spinster who may have written her poems to keep time with her broom. A terrible woman, who annihilated God as if He were her neighbor, and her neighbor as if he were God—all with a leaf or a sunbeam that chanced to fall within her sight as she looked out the window or the door during a pause in her sweeping:

From *Poetry,* XIX no. 5 (1922), pp. 277-88.

And we, we placed the hair,
And drew the head erect;
And then an awful leisure was,
Our faith to regulate.

The woman at her most terrible had the majesty of an erect corpse, a prophet of unspeakable doom; and she spoke through sealed lips. She was greater than Emerson, was one of the greatest poets of our language, but was more or less in the tradition that Emerson began. She and Emerson were probably the only poets of any permanently great importance who occurred in this country during their period.

The tradition of New England hardness has been carried on by Mr. Robinson, in many ways may be said to have reached its pinnacle in Mr. Robinson. This poet, with a wider culture than his predecessors, has linked a suavity of manner to an even greater desperation than that of Dickinson's *The Last Night*—his hardness has become a polished stoniness of vision, of mind.

This man has the culture to know that to those to whom philosophy is comprehensible it is not a matter of the first importance; and he knows that these people are not greatly impressed by a ballyhoo statement of the principles of social or spiritual salvation. A few times he has given his opinion, but quietly and intelligently, and has then passed on to other things. A man's philosophical belief or attitude is certain to be an important part of his milieu, and as a part of his milieu may give rise to perceptions, images. His philosophy becomes a part of his life as does the country in which he was born, and will tinge his vision of the country in which he was born as that country may affect his philosophy. So long as he gives us his own perceptions as they arise in this milieu, he remains an artist. When he becomes more interested in the possible effects of his beliefs upon others, and expounds or persuades, he begins to deal with generalities, concepts (see Croce), and becomes a philosopher, or more than likely a preacher, a mere peddler. This was the fallacy of Whitman and many of the English Victorians, and this is what invalidates nearly all of Whitman's work. Such men forget that it is only the particular, the perception, that is perpetually startling. The generality, or concept, can be pigeonholed, absorbed, and forgotten. And a ballyhoo statement of a concept is seldom a concise one—it is neither fish nor flesh. That is why Whitman is doomed to an eventual dull vacuum that the intricately delicate mind of Plato will never know. Much praise has fallen to Mr. Robinson because he deals with people, "humanity"; and this is a fallacy of inaccurate brains. Humanity is simply Mr. Robinson's physical milieu; the thing, the compound of the things, he sees. It is not the material that makes a poem great, but the perception and organization of that material. A pigeon's wing may make as great an image as a man's tragedy, and in the poetry of Mr. Wallace Stevens has done so. Mr. Robinson's greatness lies not in the people of whom he has written, but in the perfect balance, the infallible precision, with which he has stated their cases.

Mr. Robinson's work may be classified roughly in two groups—his blank verse, and his more closely rhymed poems, including the sonnets. Of his blank verse, the *Octaves* in *The Children of the Night* fall curiously into a group by themselves, and will be considered elsewhere in this review. The other poems in blank verse may be called sketches—some of people the poet may have known, some of historical figures, some of legendary—and they have all the evanescence, brittleness, of sketches. However, there are passages in many of these poems that anticipate Robert Frost, who in at least one poem, *An Old Man's Winter Night*, has used this method with greater effect than its innovator, and has created a great poem. Mr. Frost, of course, leaves more of the bark on his rhythms, achieves a sort of implied colloquialism which has already been too much discussed. But with Frost in mind, consider this passage from *Isaac and Archibald*:

> A journey that I made one afternoon
> With Isaac to find out what Archibald
> Was doing with his oats. It was high time
> Those oats were cut, said Isaac; and he feared
> That Archibald—well, he could never feel
> Quite sure of Archibald. Accordingly
> The good old man invited me—that is,
> Permitted me—to go along with him;

And I, with a small boy's adhesiveness
To competent old age, got up and went.

The similarity to Frost is marked, as is also the pleasing but not profound quality of the verse. It has a distinction, however, that many contemporaries—French as well as English and American —could acquire to good advantage.

Ben Jonson Entertains a Man from Stratford, a much praised poem, seems largely garrulous, occasionally brilliant, and always brittle; and one can go on making very similar comments on the other poems in this form, until one comes to those alternately praised and lamented poems, *Merlin* and *Lancelot.* Remembering Tennyson, one's first inclination is to name these poems great, and certainly they are not inconsiderable. But there are long passages of purely literary frittering, and passages that, while they may possess a certain clean distinction of manner, are dry and unremunerative enough. But there are passages in these poems which are finer than any other blank verse Mr. Robinson has written— dark, massive lines that rise out of the poem and leave one bitter and empty:

> On Dagonet the silent hand of Merlin
> Weighed now as living iron that held him down
> With a primeval power. Doubt, wonderment,
> Impatience, and a self-accusing sorrow
> Born of an ancient love, possessed and held him
> Until his love was more than he could name,
> And he was Merlin's fool, not Arthur's now:
> "Say what you will, I say that I'm the fool
> Of Merlin, King of Nowhere; which is Here.
> With you for king and me for court, what else
> Have we to sigh for but a place to sleep?"

But passing on from this less important side of Mr. Robinson's work to his rhymed poems, one finds at least a large number of perfectly executed poems of a sensitive and feline approach. What effect rhyme, or the intention of rhyme, has upon an artist's product, is a difficult thing to estimate. The question verges almost upon the metaphysical. The artist, creating, lives at a point of intensity, and whether the material is consciously digested before that point is reached, and is simply organized and set down at the time of creation; or whether the point of intensity is first reached and the material then drawn out of the subconscious, doubtless depends a good deal on the individual poet, perhaps on the individual poem. The latter method presupposes a great deal of previous absorption of sense impressions, and is probably the more valid, or at least the more generally effective, method. For the rhythm and the "matter," as they come into being simultaneously and interdependent, will be perfectly fused and without loose ends. The man who comes to a form with a definitely outlined matter, will, more than likely, have to cram or fill before he has finished, and the result is broken. The second method does not, of course, presuppose rhyme, but it seems that rhyme, as an obstacle, will force the issue.

The best of Mr. Robinson's poems appear to have come into being very much in this second fashion. He has spun his images out of a world of sense and thought that have been a part of him so long that he seems to have forgot their beginning—has spun these images out as the movement of his lines, the recurrence of his rhymes, have demanded them. A basic philosophy and emotional viewpoint have provided the necessary unity.

This method inevitably focuses the artist's mind upon the object of the instant, makes it one with that object, and eliminates practically all individual "personality" or self-consciousness. The so-called personal touch is reduced to a minimum of technical habit that is bound to accrue in time to any poet who studies his medium with an eye to his individual needs. The man of some intelligence who cannot, or can seldom, achieve this condition of fusion with his object, is driven back to his ingenuity; and this man, if he have sufficient intelligence or ingenuity, becomes one of the "vigorous personalities" of poetry; and he misses poetry exactly in so far as his personality is vigorous. Browning, on two or three occasions one of the greatest of all poets, is, for the most part, simply the greatest of ingenious versifiers. He was so curious of the quirks with which he could approach an object, that he forgot the object in admiring, and expecting admiration for, himself. And it is for this reason that Mr. Robinson, working in more or less the same field as Browning, is the superior of Browning at almost every turn.

And it is for this reason also that Mr. Robinson's *Ben Jonson* is a failure. For the poet, while in no wise concerned with his own personality, is so intent upon the personality of Jonson, his speaker, that, for the sake of Jonson's vigor, he becomes talkative and eager of identifying mannerism; and the result is, that Shakespeare, about whom the poem is written, comes to the surface only here and there, and any actual image almost never.

The following stanza is an example of Mr. Robinson's work at its best:

> And like a giant harp that hums
> On always, and is always blending
> The coming of what never comes
> With what has past and had an ending,
> The city trembles, throbs, and pounds
> Outside, and through a thousand sounds
> The small intolerable drums
> Of Times are like slow drops descending.

And there is the compact, intensely contemplated statement of *Eros Turannos*, a poem that is, in forty-eight lines, as complete as a Lawrence novel. And the imble trickery of *Miniver Cheevey*, as finished a piece of burlesque as one can find in English. A few of us have feared, in the last few years, that Mr. Robinson was deteriorating; but going through this book one is reassured. If there is nothing in *The Three Taverns* to equal *Eros Turannos*, there are at least two or three poems as great as any save that one Mr. Robinson has written; and there is nothing in these last poems to preclude the possibility of another *Eros Turannos*.

Mr. Robinson, as probably the highest point in his tradition, has been followed by Frost, a more specialized, and generally softer artist. And there is Gould, who, ifhe belongs to the tradition at all, is a mere breaking-up of the tradition, a fusion with Whitman. But in considering the work of a man of so varied a genius as Mr. Robinson, it is interesting, if not over-important, to observe the modes of expression that he has anticipated if not actually influenced; even where he has not chosen, or has not been able to develop, these modes. The resemblance in matter and manner, save for Mr. Robinson's greater suavity, of certain poems, especially the sonnets, in *The Children of the Night*, to the epitaphs in *The Spoon River Anthology*, has been noted by other writers; and I believe it has been said that Mr. Masters was ignorant of the existence of these poems until after the *Anthology* was written. There is little to be said about such a poem as Mr. Robinson's *Luke Havergal*:

> No, there is not a dawn in eastern skies
> To rift the fiery night that's in your eyes;
> But there, where western glooms are gathering,
> The dark will end the dark, if anything:
> God slays Himself with every leaf that flies,
> And hell is more than half of paradise.
> No, there is not a dawn in eastern skies—
> In eastern skies.
>
> Out of a grave I come to tell you this,
> Out of a grave I come to quench the kiss
> That flames upon your forehead with a glow
> That blinds you to the way that you must go.

And Mr. Masters' satire has been forestalled and outdone in these early sonnets.

But a more curious and interesting resemblance to a later poet is found in the *Octaves* in the same volume:

> To me the groaning of world-worshippers
> Rings like a lonely music played in hell
> By one with art enough to cleave the walls
> Of heaven with his cadence, but without
> The wisdom or the will to comprehend
> The strangeness of his own perversity,
> And all without the courage to deny
> The profit and the pride of his defeat.

If the actual thought of this passage is not that of Wallace Stevens, nevertheless the quality of the thought, the manner of thinking, as well as the style, quite definitely is. To what extent Mr. Robinson may have influenced this greatest of living and of American poets, one cannot say, but in at least three of the *Octaves*, one phase of Mr. Stevens' later work—that of *Le Monocle de Mon Oncle* and other recent and shorter poems—is certainly foreshadowed. Mr. Robinson's sound is inevitably the less rich, the less masterly.

In another of the *Octaves* there are a few lines that suggest the earlier poems of Mr. T. S. Eliot, but the resemblance is fleeting and apparently accidental.

If the tradition of New England seems to be reaching an end in the work of Mr. Frost, Mr. Robinson has at least helped greatly in the founding of a tradition of culture and clean workmanship that such poets as Messrs. Stevens, Eliot, and Pound, as H. D. and Marianne Moore, are carrying on. Mr. Robinson was, when he began, as much a pioneer as Mr. Pound or Mr. Yeats, and he has certainly achieved as great poetry. While the tradition begun, more or less, by Whitman, has deteriorated, in the later work of Mr. Carl Sandburg, into a sort of plasmodial delirium; and while the school of mellifluous and almost ominous stage-trappings, as exemplified by Poe, has melted into a sort of post-Celtic twilight, and has nearly vanished in the work of Mr. Aiken; the work of these writers and a few others stands out clear and hard in the half-light of our culture. I cannot forget that they exist, even in the face of the desert.

A WOMAN WITH A HAMMER

The Contemporary Quarry and The Man with a Hammer, by
Anna Wickham. Introduction by Louis Untermeyer. Harcourt,
Brace & Co.

"The most casual reading—if such a thing were possible—of
Mrs. Wickham's work reveals the strength of her candor, the
intense singleness of her purpose," writes Mr. Untermeyer in an
introduction that makes one admire the shrewdness of the gentlemen who chose him for this task. And without wishing to disagree,
the hesitant reader may be permitted to wonder what candor and
purpose may have to do with an art. In the present case, they
seem to resolve themselves into pugnaciously put platitudes, like
the following:

> Am I your mate because I share your bed?
> Go then! Find each day a new mate outside your house.
> I am your mate if I can share your vision.

Nor is one entirely ready to question the possible necessity of this
explanation to the person addressed. It is simply that one, as a
male in general, has a right to sort of hypothetical intelligence; for
a poet is, presumably, addressing the more illuminated of mankind.

Nor, again, should a reviewer allow himself to be too greatly

From *Poetry,* XX no. 2 (1922), pp. 93-95.

piqued by a technical insult to his sex; and the present reviewer
does not purpose to be so. But even perspicuous generalities do
not constitute poetry, and platitudes are not perspicuous; and a
perusal of this sort of poetry in quantities enforces boredom. This
poet like too many others, becomes more interested in the reason
for her unhappiness than in the unhappiness itself; and, having
reasons that are commonplace enough there is no subtle evasion
in her statement, nothing to disguise, however thinly, the barren-
ness of trodden ground.

When she essays a more lyric mode, she is equally stale, and
her staleness is even more obvious to the average eye:

> With other thrift I turn the key
> Of the old chest of Memory,
> And in my spacious dreams unfold
> A flimsy stuff of green and gold.
> And walk and wander in the dress
> Of old delights and tenderness.

In *The Cherry Blossom Wand* she achieves something of a literary
grace, perhaps slightly more than that; and in *Sehnsucht* an epigram that is really very hard and well done; but otherwise there
is little in the book to commend. I quote *Sehnsucht:*

> Because of body's hunger are we born,
> And by contriving hunger are we fed;
> Because of hunger is our work well done,
> And so are songs well sung, and things well said.
> Desire and longing are the whips of God—
> God save us all from death when we are fed.

Mrs. Wickham's handling of sex-problems is too obvious, coming after Lawrence, for serious consideration; indeed, her handling
of all topics, coming after someone or something else, is so. Nothing is so awkward to the mind of him addressed as a belated irony.

"She is, in quick succession, burning hot and icy cold; she is
driven from fiery antagonisms to smoldering apathy; she is acutely
sensitive, restless, harassed," writes our commentator, approaching his climax; and most of us will leave him with the field.

CARLOS WILLIAMS' NEW BOOK

Sour Grapes, by William Carlos Williams. Four Seas Co.

This is, I believe, the fourth book that Dr. Williams has published. *The Tempers,* which came out first, was a bit thin, but contained two fine poems of their sort. Next came *Al Que Quiere,* a hard-bitten book that attempted to create poetry out of urban modernity. *Sour Grapes* develops, more or less, the manner of *Al Que Quiere,* and probably contains a greater number of successful poems. In between these two came *Kora in Hell,* a mass of prose fragments of Flaubertian percision, that as a whole got nowhere. Dr. Williams has a considerable leaning toward the "conceit," and some of his finest poems are examples of it, although at other times he drags this structure in by the heels. By "conceit" I mean an intellectual relationship between two objects physically unrelated, one of which fuses with the sound and takes on an image existence. For example, the poem called *To Waken an Old Lady:*

Old age is
a flight of small
cheeping birds
skimming
bare trees
above a snow glaze.

From *Poetry,* XX no. 4 (1922), pp. 216-220.

> Gaining and failing,
> they are buffeted
> by a dark wind.
> But what?
> On harsh weedstalks
> the flock has rested,
> the snow
> is covered with broken
> seedhusks,
> and the wind tempered
> by a shrill
> piping of plenty.

Such poems as this and *The Nightingales*, as the *Love Song* in *Al Que Quiere* beginning "Sweep the house clean," are as perfect and as final as Herrick; they make a reviewer feel ridiculous. But in *A Celebration* the method is worked to death—perhaps because it was a bit tired before it got under way and then had a long way to go, and in *Primrose* the conceit is superfluous. If we had been given the images without the explanatory yellow, they would have hit harder.

In such poems as *The Widow's Lament in Springtime*, however, one finds the simple physical image—the image without ulterior "meaning" or even metaphor—used with great power.

> Today my son told me
> that in the meadows,
> at the edge of the heavy woods
> in the distance, he saw
> trees of white flowers.
> I feel that I would like
> to go there
> and fall into those flowers
> and sink into the marsh near them.

Dr. Williams concerns himself with certain phases of American life, which he seems to feel acutely; and up to date he is not the dupe of his material. That is, he knows that stenographic reports of snowbirds or hawthornes do not suffice, even when smeared with pretty language. He looks for relations and the sharpest way to get them down.

Despite all Dr. Williams' passion to the contrary, he is greatly influenced by his contemporaries and predecessors by which I do not mean to condemn him, but simply to indicate that he, like any good writer, is inextricably caught in Mr. Eliot's "tradition." His prose is obviously of the school of Flaubert, and his verse has gone through various influences. The poems in this book have, for the most part, worked away from the earlier jagged bitterness, into a certain serenity of manner than one associates with Mr. Pound's Chinese translations—a manner that Mr. Pound (among others) has used consciously and successfully. How conscious Dr. Williams' uses of it may be, I do not know; but if it is used unconsciously, it may be dangerous—the poet may cease to be able to see his material through the sticky haze of his manner. Anyway one has a right to wonder, when so many of Dr. Williams' trivialities *(Spring, Epitaph,* etc.) have become sweet instead of censorable. His grapes are not so sour as they once were, although this may be no great matter.

There are more fine poems in the book than one can mention in a short review, among the most extraordinary being *Romance Moderne,* despite a few low spots. Occasionally a good poem is marred by some unnecessary triteness, as *Overture to a Dance of Locomotives* by its title and last line. Several fine poems have been omitted, among them *Wild Orchard* and *A Coronal.* I choose to end by quoting one poem without comment—*The Nightingale:*

My shoes, as I lean
unlacing them,
stand out upon
flat worsted flowers
under my feet.
Nimbly the shadows
of my fingers play
unlacing
over shoes and flowers.

UNDER THE TREE

Under the Tree, by Elizabeth Madox Roberts. B. W. Huebsch.

Miss Roberts has endeavored to present in verse the psychological spiritual life of a child between the ages, I should say, of about five and ten or eleven. As she appears to have succeeded to a remarkable degree, it is interesting to examine her methods. Her child being self-conscious, analytical, she has chosen to let the child be her own psychologist, and so writes of the experiences recorded from the standpoint of childhood, and not from the standpoint of the adult. This involves a simplification of diction and technique, which bounds her work narrowly, but which she has nevertheless handled in a masterly fashion.

The earliest impressions recorded are of minute observations, sometimes subtle, often very simple, but almost entirely detached from any emotion whatever. They are simply the first stirrings of an hyper-metaphysical mind, which focusses with equal interest upon an optical illusion involving an apparent jerking of the sky or upon the wriggling of a pretty Sunday school teacher's tongue. Or it turns upon itself, the child's home, from the top of the hill, perhaps, with the acute disinterest of a little hill god who has all but found Nirvana:

The church steeple looked very tall and thin,

From *Poetry,* XXII no. 1 (1923), pp. 45-48.

And I found the house that we live in.

I saw it under the poplar tree,
And I bent my head and tried to see

Our house when the rain is over it,
And how it looks when the lamps are lit.

I saw the swing from up on the hill,
The ropes were hanging very still.

And over and over I tried to see
Some of us walking under the tree;

And the children playing everywhere,
And how it looks when I am there.

As the child develops, various emotions become involved in these observations—pleasure, fear, etc. The fear of the imagined, as in *Strange Tree*, of less definitely perceived but more actual terrors, as in *A Child Asleep*. And finally—and most incidentally—appears a more conscious pleasure in beauty for its own sake.

Miss Roberts' art consists most often in juxtaposing simple physical details of a landscape or situation in such a way that they act upon and limit each other definitely and minutely, without being at any point similar or parts of each other. They are simply carefully ordered parts of a whole, and bear in every case an intimate relationship to the sound movement. The lines already quoted serve as an excellent example of this. Occasionally she lets a rhythm that has already been used in this manner carry over its emotion as a sort of superimposed comment upon lines, the content of which is too far removed from the physical to fuse with sound—as in certain lines of *In Maryland*, which I quote intact. It is, of course, an important part of an old art, at least as old as the ballade, but it is here turned to other uses:

When it was Grandmother Barbara's day,
We lived on a hill, and down below,

Beyond the pasture and the trees,
A river used to go.

The river was very wide and blue
And deep, and my! it was a sight
To see the ships go up and down.
And all the sails were white.

And Grandmother Barbara used to wait
Beside the window or the door.
She never was too tired of it
To watch the river any more.

And we could hardly see across;
And the water was blue, as blue as the sky;
And all day long and all day long
We watched the little ships go by.

The poignancy of the poem, the identification of the child with the young grandmother, the distilled nostalgia, scarcely require comment.

Miss Roberts has used other devices, but less consistently, and in a limited discussion there is scarcely room to take them up. This may serve as a key to her method, however.

The fact that the child has been, in this book, her own psychologist is apt to make it, other questions aside, a very popular book with children. But whether or not it ever does acquire this deserved popularity, it is too fine a piece of work to be ignored by the sophisticated adult, whether now or in the future.

A PREJUDICED OPINION

Fringe, by Pearl Andelson. Will Ransom (Chicago).

In a literary civilization that knows the difference between 1913 and 1923 without knowing the difference between good and bad writing, a culture that ignores or patronizes the masterly art of an Agnes Lee or of a Henry B. Fuller, and hurries on to the latest imitation of a possibly excellent billboard, or to the latest acceleration of some particular local cockney—in such a milieu it is not strange that this unusually intelligent and capable book by a member of my own so scorned and condemned generation should be, after an existence of some five or six months, when not wholly ignored, treated casually as a minor manifestation of a minor trend. And yet the book at its lowest ebb is clean-cut and intelligent, and at its highest is extraordinarily fine poetry. It is the common fate of the poet who ignores the prevalent literary minority and endeavors to write like a gentleman—or a lady, as the case may be.

Miss Andelson's chief fault appears to be an occasional tendency to meddle with a sort of neo-metaphysics that is more devious than tangible, and to make an exposition of some such thread the prime or sole excuse for a poem. She does not do this often, however; nor is the sin original or peculiar. It is probably, in her case, simply an instance of failure in the type of poem of which *Excursion* is so

From *Poetry,* XXIII no. 4 (1924), pp. 218-220.

marked a success—a poem that presents certain of the less accessible and more subtly-shaded mental states with extraordinary
precision and beauty. She is also, at times, "dry." Every poet is
unsuccessful a fair part of the time. The two commonest attributes
of abortive effect are dryness and sloppiness.

But fortunately we base most of our final judgments upon a
poet's successes. Miss Andelson has developed and mastered a
compact and beautiful technique that can apparently be made as
simple or as intricate as she desires; and sometimes a cold bitter
passion goes half-way to meet it. The result is *Out of an Early
Snow, To an Erstwhile Loved One,* or *Seaside,* which I quote
entire:

> Steam refrain to rain
> of gravel. Long division
> in the mind
> running about with hods
> carried over. Impossible to find
> an answer true if found.

It is, after all, an excellent poem, and excellent poems are the
things with which we are, eventually, primarily concerned. As
evidence that her work is occasionally more luxurious, here is
the first half of *Excursion:*

> I went from there,
> that place where
> I walked long gray streets
> as one speaks of food, dress,
> down other streets with less elation
> than turning in the conversation
> to other casual conversation.
>
> Gay cottages bloom on hillsides
> of sand near Tamarack.
> Below on the octoroon beach,
> clustering like grapes, the bathers:
> purple, orange, and maroon.

Here are precision, flawless juxtaposition, and an exquisite mastery of end and internal rhyme and of rhythm. In addition to the poems which I have mentioned, *Madonna, Chapter,* and *Connexion* are particularly memorable. The *Ghetto Pieces,* which have been praised here and there, though excellently done, lack universality—depend upon imaginary foot-notes which have nothing to do with the author's personal existence and culture. They savor of the *tour de force.*

If the volume of Miss Andelson's work is yet small, that work appears to have those qualities of intensity and polish which are so admirable, and which are nevertheless comparatively rare; and a certain few of her poems appear to have those qualities to an extraordinary degree.

HOLIDAY AND DAY OF WRATH

Observations, by Marianne Moore. The Dial Press.

This exacting moralist, who enforces with such intricate reso-
nance the profound convictions of her ethical and emotional
fastidiousness, has dumfounded most of those readers whom she
has not completely subjugated; and, in the light of this fact, and
by reason of her having received the *Dial* award for 1924, a brief
exposition of some of the outstanding features of her art by a
professed admirer may be of more or less interest.

I have elsewhere given in considerable detail an analysis of the
known modes of poetic construction, a brief summary of the principal elements of which may possibly clarify Miss Moore's intentions for the hesitant reader. In general plan the lyric may be of
any one of five classes: It may progress from image to image or
from idea to idea *logically* (a common method of Donne, Crashaw,
and others of similar tendencies). Or the images may have a *scattered* relationship to one another, such as one finds in Nashe's
Adieu, farewell earth's bliss—that is, each illuminates a given
central idea or emotion, but there is no logical progress from image
to image. Or the connections of either of these two types may be
reduced to or below the threshold of consciousness, so that we get
what has already been termed a *psychological* progression, such
as one gets from event to event or from place to place in a dream—

From *Poetry,* XXVI no. 1 (1925), pp. 39-44.

Rimbaud's *Larme* is an exceptionally good example of this type. A purely narrative order of parts may be considered, for convenience' sake, to fall under the heading of logical connections. We may also have a single method employed in combination with a rapidly alternating mood, as we find in the work of Laforgue, Gautier, and Mr. Eliot; and we may find a single mood progressing through a double method—thus we find an alternation of the logical and the psychological in Mallarmé's *L'Aprés-midi d'un Faune* and in Mr. Eliot's *Gerontion*.

The emotional unit of the poem may be divided into two general types: the *image*, in which all sound and meaning elements fuse into a single physical whole; and the *anti-image*, in which the relationship of at least one element to the rest is non-physical, which precludes the possibility of the sound-element containing onomatopoeic value for its entire meaning content, as onomatopoeia is obviously a purely physical affair. Symbolic, or connotative value, can, of course, exist simultaneously with imagic value, both in sound and in meaning-content; and that symbol is most intense which, provided it be fresh, sets into harmonious action and reaction the widest possible range of life-connotations in the smallest possible space—it is purely a matter of specific density.

If we confine ourselves to those poets who are masters of the minutiae of style, rhythm, and outline, that poem will be most intense which most fully exhausts the possibilities of the medium —that is, which contains the greatest possible imagic and symbolic intensity. It is possible, of course, that a poem of very great symbolic intensity may outweigh a poem of slighter symbolic intensity and slight imagic intensity, but it is certain that the first poem would be greater with imagic values. It is worth observing in this connection that the metaphysical can attain imagic existence and hence the greatest possible intensity only when expressed in terms of the physical, and this transference of the metaphysical into physical terms is one of Miss Moore's most noteworthy achievements.

In order to fully appreciate the sound effects of Miss Moore's poems one should read them aloud:

Men lower nets, unconscious of the fact that they are

desecrating a grave,
and row quickly away—the blades of the oars
moving together like the feet of water-spiders as if there were
no such thing as death.
The wrinkles progress upon themselves in a phalanx—
beautiful under networks of foam,
and fade breathlessly while the sea rustles in and out of the
seaweed. . . .

The poignancy, the connotative power, of such a passage should need no comment. The emotion is not "worked up"; there is no plea for sympathy, no covert attention to the audience, but the essential emotion remains, complete, profound, self-sufficient, bony, like that of Donne or Emily Dickinson. The balance of the entire poem is as perfect as the balance of any one of its lines.

In general structure Miss Moore's poems usually employ a scattered or logical sequence of images and anti-images, often moving through two sharply defined and alternating moods, one of which is usually classifiable as satirical. By an opposition of symbolic and imagic values, she very often combines both moods in a single passage, and may even maintain this method throughout a poem. And her extraordinary magnificence of phraseology, which Mr. Eliot has already mentioned, is often coincident with intentions purely satirical, so that the satirical, the humorous, attains that which it is supposed to be unable to attain, a maximum of poetic beauty:

I shall not forget him—that Gilgamesh among
the hairy carnivora—that cat with the
wedge-shaped, slate-gray marks on its forelegs and the resolute tail,
astringently remarking: "They have imposed on us with their pale
half-fledged protestations, trembling about
in inarticulate frenzy, saying
it is not for us to understand art; finding it
all so difficult, examining the thing

as if it were inconceivably arcanic, as symmet-
rically frigid as if it had been carved out of chrysoprase

or marble. . . ."

Mr. Eliot has called attention to the inimitable characterization of her animals, and of these her unicorn is no less noteworthy than those in the description of a circus, from which I have just quoted:

> So wary as to disappear for centuries and reappear,
> yet never to be caught,
> the unicorn has been preserved
> by an unmatched device
> wrought like the work of expert blacksmiths,
> with which nothing can compare—
> this animal of that one horn,
> throwing itself upon which head foremost from a cliff,
> it walks away unharmed. . . .

But in reality, this presentation of animals is only one phase of the painfully sharp observation with which she scrutinizes every-thing—animals, persons, and ideas. Her control of what one might call the visual epigram is appalling: "My apish cousins winked too much and were afraid of snakes"; and "the immovable critic twitching his skin like a horse that feels a flea." And her handling of more abstract emotion is no less remarkable:

> Sun, you shall stay
> with us. Holiday
>   And day of wrath shall be as one, wound in a device
>   Of Moorish gorgeousness, round glasses spun
> To flame as hemisphere of one
>   Great hourglass dwindling to a stem. Consume hostility;
>   Employ your weapons in this meeting-place of surging enmity.
> Insurgent feet shall not outrun
> Multiplied flames, O Sun.

The imagic sound-values of this passage are remarkable, especially in the seventh line. Rhythm of this quality is not accidental.

A certain amount of the literary world's ever-ready irritated antagonism has been aroused by Miss Moore's habit of ending a line in the middle of a word. Mr. Thayer has shown that this very often contributes to the accuracy of the relationship between the rhythm and its meaning content, and it is also an inevitable part of the elaborate but exact musical scheme that Miss Moore employs. Her rhythms very commonly run through several lines or even stanzas with no major breaks, and when a minor break falls in the middle of a word she puts it there. Such a break is usually so slight as to offer no difficulty in pronunciation, and should trouble no one who is accustomed to read verse as verse and not as something that it is better not to define. In such a poem as *Black Earth* the sound effects are as tremendous and incessant as thunder, and it is not an empty thunder; the verses are as packed with thought as with sound.

An extended analysis of this poet's procedure is obviously impossible in a brief review, but I hope to have offered a fairly serviceable introduction to a poet whose style, at once intensely cultivated and painstakingly honest, never fails to charm me, and whose mastery of phrase and cadence overwhelms me. It is a privilege to be able to write of one of whose genius one feels so sure.

MINA LOY

Mr. Sacheverell Sitwell once wrote a very long poem, two lines of which stay in my memory:

"My natural clumsiness was my only bar to progress
Until I conquered it by calculation."

As I go through such of Miss Loy's poems as I possess, this seems to describe her. If she has not actually conquered the clumsiness which one can scarcely help feeling in her writings, she has, from time to time, overcome it; and these occasional advantages have resulted in momentous poems. Or perhaps it is not clumsiness, but the inherently unyielding quality of her material that causes this embarrassment. She moves like one walking through granite instead of air, and when she achieves a moment of beauty it strikes one cold.

More intent on the gutter and its horrors than any of the group with which she was allied, and more intensely cerebral, perhaps, than any save one of them, her work ordinarily presents that broken, unemotional, and occasionally witty observation of undeniable facts that one came to regard as the rather uninviting norm of *Others* poetry. (Let me hasten to explain that I do not wish to appear to disparage *Others*, but norms,

From *The Dial*, LXXX no. 6 (1926), pp. 496-499.

27

which are useful only as definite places from which to escape. *Others* seems to me the most interesting single group manifestation that has yet occurred in American verse.) Her unsuccessful work is easier to imitate than that of any of the three other outstanding members of her set—Miss Moore, Dr. Williams, and Mr. Stevens—and beyond a doubt has been more imitated. Rhythmically, it is elementary, whereas the metres of Miss Moore and Dr. Williams are infinitely varied and difficult, and those of Mr. Stevens are at least infinitely subtle. Emotionally, Dr. Williams is no farther from what one might regard as some sort of common denominator than Miss Loy, and he has covered—and opened to poetry—vastly more territory, so that the likelihood of his becoming the chief prophet of my own or some future generation is probably greater. Already, in fact, he is something of this nature, as the Dada movement has added to the principles that he has at one time or another stated, indicated, or practised, nothing save a few minor vices. Of all contemporary poets, he is, I shall say, the closest in spirit to Miss Loy. Miss Moore, on the other hand, as a point of departure, is unthinkable—like Henry James, she is not a point of departure at all, but a terminus. Her work suggests nothing that she herself has not carried to its logical and utmost bounds. And Mr. Stevens, with his ethereal perversity, inhabits a region upon which one feels it would be a pity to encroach.

And yet I think that few poets of my own generation would deny that these writers as a group are more sympathetic, as well as more encouraging, than either the Vorticists or the Mid-Americans. Their advantage over the professional backwoodsmen consists in part, perhaps, in superior intellectual equipment, but mainly, I suspect, in a larger portion of simple common-sense—they have refused from the very beginning to consider themselves in any way related to Shawnee Indians or potato-beetles, and have passed unscathed through a period of unlimited sentimentality. Their advantage over the Vorticists consists not so much in their having superior brains, but in their having used their own brains exclusively. Had their own brains been unequal to the task, this would have been but little advantage, as Mr. Pound, Mr. Eliot, and H.D. are formidable rivals, and, it seems to me, genuinely great poets, but the courage of the Others group appears, by this time, to have been pretty thoroughly justified. It was a hard-headed courage, and little repaid by adulation, and is nearly as admirable as its poetic outcome. One can find little in contemporary poetry of a similar sturdiness except in the work of Messrs. Hardy and Robinson.

Of the four Mr. Stevens and Miss Moore deserve the least compassion for their struggle, if compassion is to be meted out —one suspects that they always knew they could do it; and Dr. Williams, hurling himself at the whole world with the passion of the former bantam-weight champion who bore his name, has achieved a blinding technique and magnificent prose and poetry by sheer excess of nervous power. And indeed compassion is scarcely the proper offering to bring Miss Loy—one feels timorous in bringing anything. She attacked the dirty commonplace with the doggedness of a weight-lifter. Nearly any one might have written her worst poems, and innumerable small fry have written poems as good. Her success, if the least dazzling of the four, is not the least impressive, and is by all odds the most astounding. Using an unexciting method, and writing of the drabbest of material, she has written seven or eight of the most brilliant and unshakably solid satirical poems of our time, and at least two non-satirical pieces that possess for me a beauty that is unspeakably moving and profound. Satires like *The Black Virginity* and the piece on D'Annunzio need give little if any ground before the best of Pope or Dryden, and poems like *Der Blinde Junge* and the *Apology of Genius* need, in my judgement, yield ground to no one. And then there is the host of half-achieved but fascinating poems like *Lunar Baedecker*. One cons them—with the author's pardon—as one might a rosary, and is thankful if the string doesn't break, but most of the beads are at the very least spectacular:

> "Delirious Avenues
> lit
> with the chandelier souls
> of infusoria

. . . . .
Onyx-eyed Odalisques
and ornithologists
observe
the flight
of Eros obsolete"

They are images that have frozen into epigrams. It is this
movement from deadly stasis to stasis, slow and heavy, that,
when unified and organized, gives to her poetry its ominous
grandeur, like that of a stone idol become animate and horribly
aware:

"Lepers of the moon . . .
unknowing
How perturbing lights
our spirit
on the passion of Man
until you turn on us your smooth fool's faces
like buttocks bared in aboriginal mockeries
. . . .
In the raw caverns of the Increate
we forge the dusk of Chaos
to that imperious jewelry of the Universe
—the Beautiful . . . "

Such an apology is in itself a proof of genius—and of a genius
that rises from a level of emotion and attitude which is as nearly
common human territory as one can ever expect to find in a
poet. Mr. Rodker once said that she wrote of the SOUL (in four
capital letters, unless my memory betrays me) but the word
doesn't mean much, no matter how one spells it. One might
substitute the *subconscious* (which Mr. Rodker doubtless meant)
but this word is nearly as frayed. Whatever tag one fastens to
it, and regardless of what happens to her emotion in passing
through her brain (which, being a good brain, is responsible for
her being a good poet) one can scarcely help sensing at bottom
a strange feeling for the most subterranean of human reactions,

of a padding animal resentment, and of a laughter that is curiously physical. This habitation of some variety of common ground, although it may have no intrinsic aesthetic virtue, yet places her beside Dr. Williams as one of the two living poets who have the most, perhaps, to offer the younger American writers —they present us with a solid foundation in place of Whitman's badly aligned corner-stones, a foundation which is likely to be employed, I suspect, for a generation or two, by the more talented writers of this country, or by a rather large part of them. This suggested development is not a call to salvation, nor even a dogmatic prediction, but simply as speculation. If it materializes, Emily Dickinson will have been its only forerunner.

OPEN LETTER TO THE EDITORS OF THIS QUARTER

Like Mr. Aldington I have at last fallen and am writing you an open letter. It is really, however, a review of a review of a revue. I had the pleasure last evening of attending the opening of the Santa Fe fiesta, which was directed by Cadman, the fake Indian musician, at the instigation of Edgar Hewett, Santa Fe's fake archaeologist, who sits on top of a good job, like a lady spider in her web, while a lot of lean scholars roam around the hills and do the dirty work for him. And starve, of course. Hewett was everywhere in evidence, in white ducks with a pink sash about his naturallly florid tummy, looking like an eunuch who couldn't find his scimitar.

He had hired three fake Indian performers, Oskenonton, a young Mohawk artist, whose young wild ways are not so young any more, nor so wild, who appears to have learned his English in the Bowery and has the decency to look as if he were ashamed of himself, the damnable Tsianina, beloved of all Chautauqua audiences; and a nice girl called Te Ata, who may be part Indian, and who calls herself, I believe a Chickasaw princess. I have in the past had the pleasure of seeing the pueblo Indians titter silently at the first two, but Te Alta filled my and their cup to overflowing by reciting Sarett's Blue Duck, and she brought down the house. The Taos delegation wrapped their

From *This Quarter* (Fall 1926), pp. 286-288.

heads in their sheets and tried to strangle themselves, and one fell over backwards. One, in tears, pulled out a handkerchief, but had to give it up for his sheet. Mothers from Tesuque and San Ildefonso tried to smother their infants, and all the little girls from the Indian school were lolling on one another's laps and shoulders from exhaustion. The old men from Tesuque, dressed up for the bow and arrow dance, almost ruined their makeup before they came on.

The poem is obviously a fake, as was performer, but the derision of the Indians was a comfort to me. When the eagle dancers from San Ildefonso, appeared, with their slow rising and falling like huge birds on the ground for a moment only, balancing themselves in half-flight, accompanied by a soft-voiced chorus of five master-singers, the tawdriness of the school-product was overwhelming.

Not that I have any objection to the artist who is able to learn something from the Indians—we can learn from them certain very definite things in poetry, and painting, and probably more in music, though heaven knows I am no musician. One could even borrow a few of their symbols and motifs now and again, and get away with it, provided one had something of one's own to which to apply it. But this notion of interpreting the Indian is too much for me. They are in need of no assistance whatsoever, as anyone is aware who has ever read the really great translations of Frances Densmore, Washington Matthews, Frank Russell, and Jeremiah Curtin—translations that can take their place with no embarassment beside the best Greek or Chinese versions of H.D. or Ezra Pound and which some day will do so. But Sarett and his swarm of little prototypes are like Lamartine in Italy or Symons in a brothel.

The situation had several morals: for Cadman, that he was put in the same category with Sarett; for Miss Monroe, that Sarett was put in the same category with Cadman; for Santa Fe, that Hewett, who studies the Indian and likes Chautauquas, that he was put in the same category as Sarett and Cadman; for you and me, that local color and art colonies are the bunk, and that the only way to emulate the Indian, who is a great artist in a multitude of ways, is to get a job somewhere in a country that we belong to and mind our own business instead of trying to sentimentalize the Indian's or that mind of some other poor devil.

A few months ago, after Sarett's sensational hegira to the north woods in the dead of winter, to escape the Northwestern campus and our mechanical age, a *Chicago Tribune* rotogravure photographer accidentally caught him leaning against a tree, with his axe at his side and his notebook in his hand. Life size. Last night the Indians caught him just the same way. I hope he is still in the north woods when—and if—this letter sees the light. If he isn't he ought to be.

Yours for the advancement of middlewestern realism.

P.S.—Since writing the above, I have encountered a Taos Indian, who has soothed me a little. I asked him what he thought of Oskenonton, et al. He started to laugh, and then stopped and said: "Oh, well, that's their way."

SANTA FE, N.M.
AUGUST 5, 1926

THE INDIAN IN ENGLISH

The Path on the Rainbow: An Anthology of Songs and Chants from the Indians of North America, edited by George W. Cronyn. Boni and Liveright. 1918.
American Indian Love Lyrics and Other Verse, selected by Nellie Barnes. The MacMillan Co., 1925.

Of these two anthologies the former is by all odds the better and larger selection, despite its being saddled with a section of "interpretations". The latter, though containing very few pieces of any interest not to be found in the earlier volume, contains a certain amount of interesting information regarding Indian rhythms, as well as a bibliography for which the layman is grateful. There should be more written on the subject of Indian rhythms, and some of the translators should make a clean breast of the extent to which they were or were not influenced in their choice of verse forms by the work of the Others and Imagist poets, who were very much on the scene about ten years ago. The typography often makes one a little suspicious: nevertheless, the *rhythm* of these translations is fairly constant in its general tendencies and is not very close to the free verse movements of American poets—it is an un-English movement, the achievement of which in English is something of a stunt. If my

From *Transition,* XI no. 4 (1928), pp. 117-125.

reader will endeavor to translate a Spanish *romance* into French or English, he may see what I mean. The typography of these translators is almost invariably fundamental to the rhythm they produce, and the similarity of rhythm achieved by a large number of independent workers leads one to accept it as pretty accurate. Furthermore, it *does* sound like the dance music. The Indian music is often elaborate, and is remote from our European music, and I am not musician enough to analyze it. The beats, however, are curious: there are points in certain dances where one has the feeling that the sound of the drum is being produced by drawing the stick away from the drumhead instead of by the act of striking it, and by drawing it away with considerable effort. It is probably a semihypnotic effect of some of the stranger changes in rhythm which occur. One might describe the rhythm of the translations as being a rhythm based on a considerable degree on suspension of beats and on varying suspensions. If the reader will purchase the Victor record called, I believe, *Pueblo Indian Dance Music* (the two songs are or were mislabeled, but are authentic) he may be moved to accept the translators with less suspicion.

Frances Densmore, in her versions of the Chippewa (or Ojibway) songs, has, it seems to me, accomplished something far more beautiful than any of the versions of Japanese lyrics that have been made in recent years. These poems, so minute in appearance, shrill as the voice of a gnat dying out past the ear, are among the most endlessly fascinating poems of my experience. What they accomplish is beyond analysis. Thus:

> The sound is fading away
> It is of five seconds
>   freedom
> The sound is fading away
> It is of five sounds

Or the exceedingly lovely and often-quoted *Song of Spring:*

> As my eyes
>   search

the prairie
I feel the summer in the spring.

In Mr. James Mooney's versions of the songs of the Ghost-Dance Religion, we find the following stanzas from a Paiute song:

Fog! Fog!
Lightning! Lightning!
Whirlwind! Whirlwind!
Whirlwind! Whirlwind!
The snowy earth comes gliding, the snowy
    earth comes gliding.

And in Mr. Frank Russell's Pima Songs are also some of the most beautiful things in either collection—for instance:

Many people have gathered together,
    And I am ready to start in the race,
And the swallow with beating wings
    Cools me in readiness for the word.

Far in the west stands the Black mountain
    Around which our racers ran at noon.
Who is this man running with me,
    The shadow of whose hands I see?

And the Pima animal songs, though so minute in their evident import (one often suspects some unobvious religious import behind them) are amusing and curious in their exactness. The Wintu *Songs of Spirits*, translated by Jeremiah Curtin, are almost as tremendous as Blake:

The circuit of the earth which you see,
The scattering of the stars in the sky which you see,
All that is the place for my hair.

The finest of the Navajo translations—and they are probably the greatest Indian poetry that we possess in English—are by

Washington Matthews, though a few fine things were done by the late Natalie Curtis Burlin, notably the *Hunting Song*, to be found in both anthologies. Here is the *Magpie Song* by Matthews:

> The Magpie! The Magpie! Here underneath
> In the white of his wings are the footsteps
>   of morning.
> It dawns! It dawns!

And I quote also his version of the *First Song of Dawn Boy:*

> Where my kindred dwell
>   *There I wander,*
> The Red Rock House,
>   *There I wander.*
> Where dark kethawns are at the doorway,
>   *There I wander.*
> With the pollen of dawn upon my trail,
>   *There I wander.*
> Going around with it,
>   *There I wander.*
> Taking another, I depart with it.
>   *With it I wander.*
> In the house of long life,
>   *There I wander.*
> In the house of happiness,
>   *There I wander.*
> Beauty before me,
>   *With it I wander.*
> Beauty behind me,
>   *With it I wander.*
> Beauty below me,
>   *With it I wander.*
> Beauty above me,
>   *With it I wander.*
> Beauty all around me,
>   *With it I wander.*

In old age traveling,
With it I wander.
On the beautiful trail I am,
With it I wander.

And finally, as evidence that the Indian is capable of handling nonreligious and purely dramatic material, I quote this more modern group of Chinook songs, from the Northwest, by Professor Franz Boas:

Songs of the Man

I.
Ya, that is good!
Ya, that is good!
That worthless woman
does not like me.

II.
Very unhappy I was
with my wife
in Victoria.
Nobody
said good-day to us
in Victoria.

III.
Aya, aya!
I have seen
Sitka your country.
Never mind, if I die
now soon.

Songs of the Woman

I.
I don't care

if you desert me.
Many pretty boys are in the town.
Soon I shall take another one.
That is not hard for me!

II.

Nothing shall bother my mind now.
Don't speak to me. I wish I were dead
    with my sister.

III.

Ya, ya,
When you take a wife,
Ya, Ya,
Don't become angry with me.
I do not care.

IV.

I am very glad
    when the steamboat comes here.
I think I shall cry
    when the steamboat leaves.

V.

I broke down! my dear!
Say good-bye!
    to me now.
Always I cry
    for I live far away.

These and other translators, most of them working for the
Bureau of Ethnology of the Department of the Interior, have
given us a considerable body of poetry that is indubitably permanent, and it behooves us to consider it seriously and calmly.
So far, it has been taken, if at all, with a good deal of sentimentality. Any attempt to define the American Indian mind in
terms of some neo-Confucian, neo-Buddhistic, or neo-Freudian
"mysticism" is, I am inclined to suspect, pretty far-fetched. I

am no ethnologist, but I take it that most primitive religion is rather definitely practical in its aims: it consists mainly of scientific formulae for perpetuating the race and for getting three square meals a day. The gods are not spiritual qualities, but natural forces: they are not in any sense abstractions but are things one can lay ones hands on and control. The Indian controls rain and thunder by means of incantation to get crops: the modern scientist controls electricity by other means to construct engines which will make him felt hats in very rapid succession. Now the only essential difference between these two states of mind lies in this, that the first is serious and absolutely fundamental to existence, whereas the second is relatively frivolous. But neither one has any ulterior significance.

In a primitive, non-specialized society, every mind gravitates toward the religious center, by which the race is preserved. All art, therefore, will have a definitely ritualistic nature or will be strongly colored by ritual, and will so be in a greater or less degree comprehensible, or at any rate useful, to all the community. Likewise, as all the community has a practical use for art, and as the individual members of the community are not, as in a modern city, forced to divert all of their energies into narrowly specialized channels, the average taste in artistic matters will be rather high. This is in accord with an opinion which I attribute on heresay to be Kidder, that the average all-around intelligence of the southwestern pueblo Indian is about thirty per cent higher than that of the average white American. My own slight experience substantiates this: I have found the taste of several quite commonplace Indians to be all but infallible in such fields, say, as medieval German art. But the general attitude toward art as ritual and ritual as a practical matter is to be seen at the present moment in those villages which have been interfering with their native participants in the new and non-ritualistic water-color movement which involves the painting of the dances, and which may thus, they fear, diminish in some manner the efficacy of the dances. It is much the same state of mind as that of the protestant who obeys God and shuns the devil in order to go to heaven and play on a golden harp, except that the Indian's is a much more credible and dignified religion and is knit to, rather than divorced from, all the other activities of the community, and consequently results in an ethical standard and practice infinitely higher than anything prevalent in any part of the "Christian" United States. It is a little hard on the painter, who has in some way to evade it or acquiesce to its main principles, but on the whole it is good for the race; and it is the ground work on which all the great Indian artists, known and unknown, have built their art.

The "spiritual" value of all this lies, I believe, in two things: in a sense of the unity of the race and in a sense of the unity of both the race and the individual with the physical (which is also the spiritual, as there is only one) universe, which gives to all phenomena, personal or objective, an immediacy to the perceiver and a vastness of emotional implication, which our own culture, with all its ramifications of causes, explanations, and mystical dualisms, has lost, and which only the occasional artist—a Williams, for instance, or a Walsh—can regain for us. One feels in the unknown composer of the *Magpie Song* a consciousness of an entire race reacting to the freshness of all mornings on an everlasting prairie. In an early painting by Awa-keireh which hangs on my wall—a row of dancers, twenty-five or thirty, grim-faced and working together—is the accumulated thunder of generations of feet stamping an immediate and magnificent earth.

After this, after the stony and savage line of Polelonema, the earthy wit of 'Tonita Pena, after Ma Pe We, with his deer-like sensitivity to deer, come the "interpreters" with their stucco painting, poetry, and music, who take the "symbols" (i. e., perceived and registered facts) of the living Indians and give them a "meaning" and usually, may one suggest, a damned sloppy one. Nothing can be more ridiculous than this self-conscious effort to imitate a metric which belongs to a group of languages and a feeling for music as remote as possible from our own; to reshuffle an imagery and a system of emotional notation that arose from the concentrated effort of an entire race for centuries on problems of which we know nothing. But it is easier to play this game than that played by the Indian—that of mastering one's own universe. Yet the great art remains as art, the statement of valid conclusions. I recollect that a few years ago—and for all I know, it may be true yet, and doubtless stranger things are true—the Indian Fair, held in connection with the Santa Fe Fiesta, used to award a prize for the best exhibition of pottery brought in by an Indian. The prize was a cheap silver cup, of the sort given as prized in dogshows. There are different ways of expressing one's admiration.

STREETS IN THE MOON

Streets in the Moon, by Archibald MacLeish. Houghton Mifflin Co.

It is with certain ineradicable prejudices that I approach this book, and yet I find myself won over. Those writers of my own generation, or of what I take to be roughly such, whose ideals seem to me most definitely related to my own—McAlmon, Carnevali, Cummings—repel me in their verse (despite my tremendous admiration for their prose) by various species of hit-or-miss awkwardness, cuteness, or sweetness. Their attempts to leap clear of literature, to see nakedly, are too seriously modified by these vices to satisfy me. MacLeish, on the other hand, is frankly literary; but his work has at its best a seriousness, a smoothly rolling power, that cannot be denied. And embedded in all his literary loam are living grubs, fat and squirming. I have read two other books of verse that he has published—*The Happy Marriage* and *The Pot of Earth*—that seemed to me not overly happy dilutions of Eliot, Swinburne, and anything else that came handy. The present book contains a few rather tawdry imitations of Eliot—such as *Le Secret Humain*, for example—which rely on the rhymed plop of something damp and ill-smelling but otherwise obvious and uninteresting, a trick in part responsible for the tragic collapse of *The Waste Land*. But for the rest—and the rest is most—the Eliot becomes a vague background, largely and very vaguely technical: the matter is

From *Poetry,* XXIX no. 5 (1927), pp. 278-281.

more richly and immediately perceived than is usual with Eliot, and is all over the book. There is a remarkably high percentage of completely and beautifully achieved poems.

One finds poems with a certain heavy smoky grandeur, that are comparable only to the magnificent and unread master Henry Vaughan:

> Think that this world against the wind of time
> Perpetually falls the way a hawk
> Falls at the wind's edge and is motionless—
> Think that this silver snail, the moon, will climb
> All night upon time's curving stalk,
> That as she climbs bends, bends beneath her—
>
> Yes—
> And think that we remember the past time.

There is a firm and beautiful accumulation of small and common-place details, that, because of the manner of their juxtaposition, eventually take on an enormous significance:

> Under the dry grass stem
> The words are blurred, are thickened, the words sift
> Confused by the rasp of the wind, by the thin grating
> Of ants under the grass, the minute shift
> And tumble of dusty sand separating,
> From dusty sand. The roots of the grass strain,
> Tighten, the earth is rigid, waits—he is waiting—
> And suddenly, and all at once, the rain!

The release in one line of this force, piled up behind it from the very beginning of the poem, is a triumph. There are magnificent grotesques, such as *Some Aspects of Immortality*, and this, *March:*

> Let us think of these
> Winter-stiffened trees
> (Posthumously sucking pap
> From the pores of a dead planet
> Like the bristles on a butchered pig)

Every stalk and every twig
Swollen with delightful sap.

As in *Signature for Tempo II*, one finds a projection into Time
and Space of common things, that, seen anew, suspended, acquire a tremendous and curiously abstract identity. And last,
and possibly least, though not insignificant, is the breath-taking
accumulation of the ponderous vocables of commerce, law, and
professional publicity, to be found in such poems as *Man!* and
Corporate Entity, an accumulation that has no equal in all the
archives of Dada.

Metrically, MacLeish is at his best in rhymed—and short—
poems. His blank verse, using the same heavy movement that is
so impressive in his shorter pieces, becomes monotonous: one
thinks with longing of the more elusive and athletic poems of
Hart Crane. But MacLeish, where he succeeds, succeeds like a
master.

These poems, written, printed, bound, with a luner clarity,
mark for me the advent of one of the very few poets, who, alone
of all the set that have appeared since the Others-Imagist-
Vorticist upheaval of twelve or fourteen years ago, can rightly
take a place beside the most distinguished poets of the preceding generation.

HART CRANE'S POEMS

White Buildings, by Hart Crane, with Foreword by Allen Tate. Boni & Liveright.

When one approaches, with intentions to review, the first book of a poet whom one believes to be one of the small group of contemporary masters, it is irritating to be forestalled by an introduction that is, for once, thoroughly competent. Yet such is my present quandary. The general evaluation and definition of Hart Crane's genius is here so precisely and completely stated, that the reviewer can do little but add footnotes, quibble, and offer helpful hints for beginners.

The first thirteen poems are relatively simple, and most, I believe, are relatively early. They suggest here and there, slightly, T. S. Eliot and Wallace Stevens, but the greater part of them are, as Mr. Tate says, more or less imagistic. The imagism, however, is of the more fragile variety, calling to mind the brittle Parnassianism of H.D. or the thin symbolic flame of Ezra Pound's shorter poems, rather than the packed vitality of a Williams or a Mina Loy. I believe that Mr. Tate goes too far in intimating that the imagistic method is of necessity limited in its possibilities: the possibilities of any method depend not on itself but on the poet who happens to find himself adapted to

From *Poetry,* XXX no. 1 (1927), pp. 47-51.

it, and a great poet is almost invariably hard on pre-existing dogma, not to mention co-existing dogma.

Mr. Crane's faults appear to me to be an occasional tendency to slip into rather vague rhetoric, as in the greater part of *Voyages III* and *IV;* and an attempt to construct poems of a series of perceptions so minute and so thoroughly insulated from each other that little unifying force or outline results, as in the case of *Possessions*. His faults, however, are the least interesting phases of his work.

Sunday Morning Apples, with its anatomy of morning, its curiously dewy geometry, represents his later and more successful method at work on a sufficiently simple theme to serve as a very good introduction to the more difficult poems:

> A boy runs with a dog before the sun, straddling
> Spontaneities that form their independent orbits,
> Their own perennials of light
> In the valley where you live
> > (called Brandywine).

North Labrador presents greater magnificence with fewer complications:

> Cold-hushed, there is only the shifting of moments
> That journey toward no Spring—
> No birth, no death, no time nor sun
> In answer.

In the remainder of the book the two tendencies fuse, and he is at his best when the fusion is most complete: his greatest poems are almost solidly composed of a steely tangible imagery that crystallizes an infinitude of metaphysical and nervous implications—"Striated with nuances, nervosities," as he writes of his jazz-palace. And, in spite of these nuances and nervosities, he maintains a curiously heroic tone, a tone that is comparable at times—as in the conclusion to *Voyages II*—to no one short of Marlowe. We have in him then—a rare phenomenon in these latter days—a poet who accepts his age in its entirety, accepts it with passion, and who has the sensitive equipment to explore it. This book, despite its small dimensions, has already accomplished a remarkable quantity of that exploration.

The greatest poems, for me, are *Repose of Rivers*, *For the Marriage of Faustus and Helen*, *Recitative*, and *Voyages II* and *V*. They maintain almost throughout a level of intensity that seems to me a maximum, and place Mr. Crane—in my own opinion—among the five or six greatest poets writing in English. Mr. Tate has suggested that Mr. Crane's use of the oblique or psychological presentation may hinder his acceptance, but I almost doubt it. The method is not invariably used, and even when it is used, I suspect, is likely to be an advantage in so far as it may hold the reader's attention from line to line. Mr. I.A. Richards has spoken of the strategic value of obsurity, and in the case of a poet whose use of words is so subtly dense with meaning and overtone, whose poems are so free of dead but restful matter, an additional logical obscurity is likely to force the attention upon separate words and lines, and so facilitate at the outset an appreciation of the details as details, which may, in turn, lead on to a grasp of the whole. Such has been, at any rate, the effect upon myself, who make no claim to any especially oracular gifts when I say that I believe myself to have arrived at a partial understanding of this book.

His virtues are more easily perceived if one isolates lines and passages:

> That seething, steady leveling of the marshes.

Or this marvelous appearance and sinking away of turtles at the surface of a swamp:

> And mammoth turtles climbing sulphur dreams
> Yielded, while sun-silt rippled them
> Asunder . . .

And his city

> With scalding unguents spread and smoking darts.

Its inhabitants:

> Brazen hypnotics glitter here;
> Glee shifts from foot to foot,
> Magnetic to their tremulo.
> This crashing opera bouffe,
> Blest excursion! this ricochet
> From roof to roof—
> Know, Olympians, we are breathless
> While nigger cupids scour the stars!

And, as a final example, the last stanza of *Recitative:*

> In alternating bells have you not heard
> All hours clapped dense into a single stride?
> Forgive me for an echo of these things,
> And let us walk through time with equal pride.

The synthesis, implied but not syntactically indicated, of the last line of this last quotation with the first two lines must not be overlooked.

One could take almost any lines from the best poems, set them alone, and be equally surprised by them. In their context the casual reader is likely to overlook them. They are in themselves so dense and are fitted so closely together, they present so shining and uniform a surface, that there is no foothold, no minor charm, no condescension or assistance. It is extremely easy to slide off the surface without having had the slightest idea of what one has been on. I have been watching Mr. Crane's progress for about eight years, with mingled feelings of admiration, bewilderment, and jealousy. My reaction to his poems has always been slow and labored; but now that I have arrived at some degree of familiarity with the book as a whole, I am more than ever convinced that he deserves the careful attention which a comprehension of his work requires.

FUGITIVES

Fugitives: An Anthology of Verse. Harcourt, Brace & Co.

The contributors to this anthology are intelligent enough to be worth damning, or some of them are, to my knowledge, and I give the rest the benefit of the doubt. Allan Tate is very nearly the only writer now regularly practicing criticism in this country who is worth reading. He is also the only poet of any very profound interest in this volume. Robert Penn Warren, however, has made some very acute critical remarks on several occasions, and John Crowe Ransom has written better verse than he has seen fit to include here. He frequently succeeds in being amusing —never, for me, more than that, and not even that on this occasion. Laura Riding remains for me at her best unintelligible, when intelligible insignificant. The elaborate fiddle-faddle of her style might possibly be suspected of concealing something momentous had she not, before discovering Miss Stein, revealed herself in painfully plain prose in a book written in collaboration with Robert Graves and dealing with modernist poetry, whatever that may be. The amount of misinformation, ignorance, and high-power "popular" writing crowded between those two covers, gives one sufficient grounds, I believe, to doubt for the present at least the seriousness of her intentions. Donald

From *Poetry,* XXXII no. 2 (1928), pp. 102-107.

Davidson has written a long poem that has been highly praised by John Gould Fletcher, but which I have not read. The rest of these names are new to me. The book is only one more piece of evidence of the degree to which the poetry of Mr. Eliot is a catastrophe. Being myself a pessimist and no great metaphysician, I am skeptical about the possibility of Mr. Eliot's finding a workable substitute for God. The manner in which he is exploiting his inability to do so as an excuse for his lack of poetic vigor is not worthy of so distinguished a critic. Baudelaire, Thomas Hardy, Emily Dickinson found themselves in precisely the same predicament and maintained their spiritual dignity and vigor. I am aware that they had not read Whitehead, but a few variations in vocabulary do not alter the fundamental nature of the problem that they faced. Baudelaire's Catholicism becomes equivocal almost to the vanishing point if one reads such poems as *Le Gouffre* or *Les Petites Vieilles*. Baudelaire was too busy mastering the data of his own experience to bother much with collecting from other poets. Mr. Eliot, for whom the world will end not with a bang but a whimper, has obviously little to distract his attention from the classics. A denial of tragic emotion means one thing: that one puts little value on life. And that means that one has made only a very limited contact with it. I am aware that Mr. Eliot's essays on the dramatists and the metaphysical poets are probably the greatest that we have in English. They deal, in several cases, with great poets, and always with distinguished poets, and their definitions of the quality of those poets are infinitely precise. But because Mr. Eliot has told how Donne and Marlowe were great, we need not suppose that there are not other ways of being great; nor is there any connection between Mr. Eliot's own verse and the verse of the Elizabethans beyond the passages he has borrowed.

We have in this volume as elsewhere a good deal of what has been known since *The Waste Land* as Websterian blank verse. As a matter of fact, Mr. Eliot's rather loose blank verse is probably closer in structure (though not in content) to that of Fletcher than to Webster's. And that of his imitators is about as remote as possible from either: it is the acme of formlessness.

One hesitates to suggest such a strange juxtaposition as Eliot and Frost, but the influence of the less responsible moments of the latter poet may possibly be fusing here with the influence of Eliot. They present two easy and not profoundly dissimilar ways of writing a species of regular metre. This sort of thing has been received as a boon by the young writers who were raised in the thin "modern" atmosphere and who yet could not stand the actual strain of creating new forms or building on the tremendously energetic forms of such writers as Williams, Pound, and Miss Moore. We hear constant covert hints from the by-now-educated dead that it is more "modern" to be "classical." They mean that the old warriors are tired of howling and that it is now in style to use old forms—well or badly. But it is more "classical" to be alive, regardless of form, and as a matter of actual fact the only first-cla ss metrists since Robinson are using the new metres in some form or degree. The blank verse movement (omitting the very solid blank verse of Stevens and Crane and the best of Frost) has simply provided an excuse to use the old forms a little more badly than they have ever been used before. Ransom, following the lead, perhaps, of Frost, attempts an affected awkwardness; but where Frost really creates a style from it, Ransom is merely awkward. The "Websterians," via Frost, and by rhyming the loosened line, are dwindling rapidly toward Rupert Brooke and the Georgians.

And if one must choose an Elizabethan dramatist for a model, why not choose a great one? Some good might come, for instance, from a general admiration of Chapman or Jonson, as some good has come from Hart Crane's admiration for Jonson and Marlowe. And if one must choose Webster, a greal deal might yet be learned from reading *The Duchess of Malfi* instead of *A Game of Chess*. But to choose Webster, distinguished though he may be, yet still a writer of the decadence, the collapse, spiritual and technical, labels one spiritually, whether it can be helped or not—and it apparently can. There is in these Southern poets an appalling lack or resiliency, of steel springs in mind and metre: we have the physical evidence of a negative attitude. The whole thing has gone soft. Most of it is many removes from Eliot—probably many of these poets consider themselves anything rather than his disciples—but I believe the disintegration starts there. He has in a considerable degree made it respectable to be indifferent, and the indifference has affected the poetic style of an entire generation to a degree that even Mr. Eliot must find distressing.

Allan Tate, in spite of a certain awkwardness, maintains his identity and a very impressive dignity. Such a poem as *Mr. Pope* is impeccable, and *Death of Little Boys* and *Obituary* are very nearly so. He is one of the four or five younger Americans whose poems are worth owning and rereading, and this volume is of value if only because it is the only place in which his best work is gathered together. One regrets the reminiscences of the early Eliot in the *Ode on the Confederate Dead*—a poem that contains some of his best writing—because they are unnecessary and, since Mr. Tate is profoundly unlike T. S. Eliot and in no wise a stylistic gymnast, unassimilated. And one regrets the unnecessary transposition of two lines from Ford to the close of *Procession*. But there is an almost sullen and decidedly powerful sense of tragedy in these poems that is unlike anything else now being produced.

The formlessness of the younger poets seems to have taken two directions: we have on the one hand the group here represented, who have, one suspects through inertia, continued the process begun by Mr. Eliot, of breaking down the pre-Restoration dramatic line, and of breaking down other lines in a related manner; and on the other hand the group, more energetic but scarcely more successful, who, through an admiration for Whitman and Sandburg and other belated and by them unrecognized forms of Rousseauism, and through a misconception of Williams, are throwing themselves about the world and the printed page in a manner that can have only one conclusion— annihilation through meaningless exhaustion and waste. It should be borne in mind by these last, the core of the group that appeared in *This Quarter*—though I make exception of Ernest Walsh, whose last poems seem to me very remarkable, and to some of the prose of Carnevali, and to all of the thoroughly amazing prose of Morley Callaghan—that Rimbaud was destroyed by a metaphysical vision and not by exasperated nerves, and that tragedy, to be interesting, should be due to something more dignified than the inadequacy of former spankings. There is a certain impressiveness in Racine, let us say, that I fail to find in such a book as *Wuthering Heights*.

If the younger Americans are to achieve anything of the first importance it will be due to one of two reasons: the Grace of God, or the Grace of God coupled with a recognition of the spiritual value of five poets—Charles Baudelaire, Tristan Corbière, Thomas Hardy, Emily Dickinson, and Gerard Hopkins; and of the spiritual *and* formal value of two poets—Hart Crane, and, especially, that of the most magnificent master of English and of human emotions since Thomas Hardy, William Carlos Williams.

THE POETRY OF LOUISE BOGAN

Dark Summer, by Louise Bogan. Charles Scribner's Sons.

This, Miss Bogan's second volume, includes the best poems from her first, so that a reading of it offers a complete view of her talent to the present time. The chief stylistic influence discernible is that of E. A. Robinson, and that only here and there. Two of the early poems reprinted in this book—"Portrait" and "The Romantic"—close on a typically Robinsonian epigram; and there are a good many similar passages in her first book, "Body of This Death." She has either escaped or absorbed this influence in her later work, progressing toward a more purely lyrical mode that culminates in "The Mark," "Come break with time," and "Simple Autumnal"; poems that demand—and will bear—comparison with the best songs of the sixteenth and seventeenth centuries, whether one select examples from Campion, Jonson, or Dryden. One might quote, as examples of her style at its purest and most intense, this quatrain from "Simple Autumnal":

> The measured blood beats out the year's delay.
> The tearless eyes and heart forbidden grief,
> Watch the burned, restless, but abiding leaf,

From *New Republic,* LX (October 16, 1929), pp. 247-248.

The brighter branches arming the bright day.

Or the final stanza from "The Mark":

The diagram of whirling shade,
The visible, that thinks to spin
Forever webs that time has made
Though momently time wears them thin
And all at length are gathered in.

But these fragments are parts of closely organized wholes and it is really unjust to tear them off in this fashion.

She has certain technical limitations. She apparently has little or no understanding of free verse, and her more regular un-rhymed verse (one hesitates to call it blank verse), though extremely interesting from a purely metrical standpoint, divulges an inability to treat the long line and the long poem as such—she treats them rather as a series of stylistic and perceptive incidents that would probably have gone into short rhymed lines had they been able to gather about themselves a little more symbolic value. They almost drop from the limb that bears them into separate identity, but never quite; neither, most of the time, are they quite organically necessary to that limb. And the movement of the long unit is hopelessly impeded by—one is tempted to say, made up of—minor, decorative digressions. This, from any standpoint, is an incorrect technique for a long poem, whether narrative or philosophical. One sometimes sees the opposite phenomenon in the lyrics of a novelist, those of Mr. Joyce, for example: the novelist is accustomed to use these minor felicities occasionally and with discretion in prose, but is unable, if he is simply a novelist, to give them poetic intensity when he rhymes them. The result is minute, if sometimes charming, lyrics. But either way there is a failure to comprehend the essential nature of the form.

The intricacy of some of the best of Miss Bogan's poems is, I imagine, an intricacy of feeling, and hence of style, rather than of idea. The basic ideas of her work do not appear to be particularly complex. The writer of our period finds himself tempted, on one side, by the roads to rhythmic salvation offered by the various

sects of tree-climbing mystics, and on another by the faint mori-
bund murmurs of transatlantic, Middle-Western, and middle-
aged Whitmanism: these, and related manifestations of our democratic era and of its Pragmatic Providence, our educational system, have to be avoided. Miss Bogan, one suspects, has avoided
them as a cat avoids water rather than as a philosopher avoids
nonsense—and the result is a kind of instinctive distrust of certain ranges of experience that either might or might not involve
some kind of spiritual looseness. She plays safe and allows no
implications to enter a poem that are not defined in its subject-
matter: she thus achieves the irreproachable mastery of her best
poems, but she also causes each poem to be a sort of insulated
unit, even pushing the quality occasionally, as in "Old Countryside," to a certain dryness. Thomas Hardy, writing a twelve-line
lyric on the passage of time, often seems to involve the tragedy
and the wisdom of the whole human experience; there is a kind
of emotional current passing into the form from the formless
recollections of the man; the gesture, the cadence, the pauses,
indicate a richness of wisdom and experience not defined in the
meaning of the words. In Miss Bogan's poems, as in those of
Jonson or Landor, this is the case, if at all, to a very limited
degree. The poem is a sharply defined segment of experience,
raised to something very near to major power by the sheer brilliance of the craftsmanship. But if the poem deals with the mes-
sage of time, it deals with that and nothing more, in its effect on
an isolated entity as such. To see what I mean, one may compare
"In Time of 'The Breaking of Nations,'" "During Wind and
Rain," or "Afterwards," to "The Mark" or "Simple Autumnal."
Neither poet will suffer particularly by the comparison: the integrity of each is perfect and the execution superb. But the under-
lying wisdom, the experiential reach, of Hardy's poetry is the
greater.

The poet of the present age, in order to free himself from the
handicap of the philosophical misconceptions of the age, has, I
believe, to turn metaphysician in a profound and serious way if
he is not to be victimized by false emotions, as most of our contemporaries in at least a measure are; or if he is not to be, as Miss
Bogan in some degree is, limited rather more than some of his

more fortunate forefathers. Very few contemporary poets seem aware of the difficulty or seem willing to make the effort. I am thoroughly convinced that the effort need not be, as Mr. Allen Tate seems certain that it is, fruitless. The least—and the most —that one can demand of it is that it clear the air once and for all of a great deal of nonsensical doctrine and belief, along with the attendant feelings, and that it justify, and make it possible to assume with a measure of ease, a normal and more or less classical dignity of attitude toward human destiny and human experience, an attitude that at least *seems* natural to Hardy but that is achieved by only a few contemporaries (Miss Bogan among them) and by most of them (Miss Bogan included) only with a good deal of effort, suspicion, and trembling. The means to this end may strike the innocent bystander as unjustifiably complicated, but it is still the only means that will accomplish the end in a thoroughly satisfactory fashion. The short cuts invariably end in bogs, and the avoidance of the labor ends either in bogs or in insecurity.

But Miss Bogan's subject-matter, or rather attitude, if it seems limited in the way I have indicated, is as central, as fundamental, as any attitude so limited could be. It would take only a turn, a flicker, to transform her into a major poet; it is conceivable that the flicker may be taking place as I write, that it may even have occurred in her book, *a mon insu*. The least that the most defamatory of critics can say in her praise is that she suffers no diminution by comparison with the best of the English lyricists, that she is certainly as good in every respect as a great many of the best, and that she is beyond any doubt one of the principal ornaments of contemporary American poetry.

THE POETRY OF
MALCOLM COWLEY

Blue Juniata, by Malcolm. Jonathon Cape and Harrison Smith.

This book covers a period of something more than ten years, and its less successful poems might serve as an outline history of the fashions that have risen and fallen during that period. This is not to its credit. For the styles so adopted have been in nearly every case adopted from the outside with little or no awareness of their organic causes, and they have seldom been mastered. The earliest poems are Laforguian: *Nocture*, for instance, is almost a paraphrase of Laforgue's *Complainte des Pianos*; it embodies the decidedly unsatisfactory adolescent emotion that is the basis of all of Laforgue's work but not the two great Laforguian virtues of style—speed and rhythmic outline. The *Complainte des Pianos* has the dazzling rapidity of a first-rate xylophone performance: *Nocturne* is slow and limp. *Deathbed*, however, a poem of about the same time, escapes the influences of the period and offers a very curious and well-handled emotion. If the first nineteen lines of *Angelica* could be condensed into two or three, one would have another poem nearly as good. The poem does not get started until the twentieth line; from there on it has form and precision; but before that point it is vague, aimless, and

From *Hound and Horn*, III no. 1 (1929), pp. 111-113.

reminiscent of that Laforguian pastiche of Mr. Eliot's, *A Portrait of a Lady*.

Mr. Cowley, having drifted through the Dada days of *Broom*, with a few interesting experiments and a few sound lines, seems to have returned to his native countryside for inspiration, and we have as a result the first section in the book, though some of these poems antedate the rest by several years. The group has a charming feeling as a whole, interesting passages, and perhaps three poems—*The Hill above the Mine, Chestnut Ridge*, and *Laurel Mountain*—that are successful throughout. They share one quality with the more or less similarly sentimental poetry of Francis Jammes: the group as a whole is more moving than any of its parts, the reason being a kind of stylistic dilution of an emotion that is nevertheless quite genuine of its kind, so that the poetry never permits of very close scrutiny of any given point. Mr. Cowley allows himself, for instance, many such unorganized catalogues and progressions as the following:

> only the bones of a house,
> lilacs growing beside them,
> roses in clumps between them,
> honeysuckle over;
> a door, a crooked chimney,
> mud-chinked, a yawning fireplace,
> the skeleton of a pine.

That he is capable of firmer writing is proved by the graceful synthesis that follows:

> I heard a railroad section hand playing on a jew's-harp,
> *Where is now that merry party I remember long ago?*
> *Nelly was a lady* . . . twice . . . *Old Black Joe*,
> as if he laid a hand upon my shoulder,
> saying:
> "Your father lived here long ago;
> your father's father built the house, lies buried
> under the pine—"
> Sing *Nelly was a lady*
> *Blue Juniata* . . . *Old Black Joe*.

This passage, incidentally, is probably the taking-off point for a similar passage in *The River*, by Hart Crane. The more recent poems are for me the most interesting and deserve less reserved praise. *Leonora* is adroit and amusing to a high degree, and *Tumbling Mustard*, the perfection, perhaps, of the same mood, is one of the loveliest, most amusing, and most skillful songs of our time. The meter, especially in the fifth line of each stanza, is astonishingly fine and astonishingly witty. In one of the more serious poems there is this slightly vague grandiloquence by way of a final statement:

> But you shall hear the thunder
> of bursting walls; the gates of night swing wide,
> and journeys will be set against the sunrise;
> your path shall be the empty streets of air.

This is an apparently satisfactory answer to a man who is "waiting without patience to be filled with God." The last stanza of *Tumbling Mustard* says the same thing but evaluates its content more accurately:

> Tumbleweed, tumbleweed,
> riding his velocipede
> easts side, west side,
> all around the moon;
> Denver, San Francisco, Winnipeg and Dallas, maybe if
> the gas holds out we'll get there soon.

This piece might easily pass for a poetic summary of the first three-fourths of Mr. Cowley's career as one has it in the present volume.

In addition, *There is a Moment* is perfectly written and wholly admirable; *William Wilson* is firm and closely organized; and *The Lady from Harlem* is perhaps better than any of these. It is mainly in these poems and in *Deathbed* that the author is endeavoring to study and master himself; elsewhere he too often seems to be seeking some vague salvation in an attempt to reflect his age, or something else, occasionally Laforgue and Eliot; or, as a sort of nostalgic but apparently no better justified alternative, his section of Pennsylvania. He is, on the strength of these, one of the eight or ten most distinguished poets of his generation; he might become, proceeding from these, something more. I quote *The Lady from Harlem* (In Memory of Florence Mills) entire:

> The fetish-woman crossed the stage,
> her limbs convulsed with yellow magic.
> Art is the gratuitous
> shiver that makes the shimmy tragic.
> Obeah, obeah, wailed the saxohones.
>
> Though orchestras play Dixie Dreams,
> never in Dixie field was,picked
> the gun-cotton that swells your breast,
> explodes and leaves me derelict
> amid the wreckage of your smile,
>
> floating over the parterre.
> Your sudden fingers touched my wrist.
> Tell me, did Madam Walker do your hair
> before she died in Tarrytown
> among her butlers, footmen, chefs?
>
> Throned on a tomb of brass you reign
> between the bass and treble clefs.

This is finely felt and closely written; it is an organic, not a sought and theoretically correct emotion. It is to be hoped that its author is aware of its virtues, relative as well as absolute.

ROBINSON JEFFERS

Dear Judas, by Robinson Jeffers. Horace Liveright.

It is difficult to write of Mr. Jeffers' latest book without discussing his former volumes; after his first collection he deals chiefly with one theme in all of his poems; and all of his works illustrate a single problem, a spiritual malady of considerable significance. Mr. Jeffers is theologically a kind of monist; he envisages, as did Wordsworth, Nature as Deity; but his Nature is the Nature of the physics textbook and not of the rambling botanist—Mr. Jeffers seems to have taken the terminology of modern physics more literally than it is meant by its creators. Nature, or God, is thus a kind of self-sufficient mechanism, of which man is an off-shoot, but from which man is cut off by his humanity (just what gave rise to this humanity, which is absolutely severed from all connection with God, is left for others to decide): there is consequently no mode of communication between the consciousness of man and the mode of existence of God; God is praised adequately only by the screaming demons that make up the atom. Man, if he accepts this dilemma as necessary, is able to choose between two modes of action: he may renounce God and rely on his humanity, or he may renounce his humanity and rely on God.

Mr. Jeffers preaches the second choice: union with God, obli-

From *Poetry,* XXXV no. 5 (1930), pp. 279-286.

vion, the complete extinction of one's humanity, is the only good he is able to discover; and life, as such, is "incest," an insidious and destructive evil. So much, says Mr. Jeffers by implication, for Greek and Christian ethics. Now the mysticism of, say, San Juan de la Cruz offers at least the semblance of a spiritual, a human, discipline as a preliminary to union with Divinity; but for Mr. Jeffers a simple and mechanical device lies always ready; namely, suicide, a device to which he has not resorted.

In refusing to take this logical step, however, Mr. Jeffers illustrates one of a very interesting series of romantic compromises. The romantic of the ecstatic-pantheist type denies life, yet goes on living; nearly all romantics decry the intellect and philosophy, yet they offer justifications (necessarily foggy and fragmentary) of their attitude; they deride literary "technique" (the mastery of, and development of the sensitivity to, relationships between words, so that these relationships may extend almost illimitably the vocabulary) yet they write (of necessity, carelessly, with small efficiency). Not all romantics are guilty of all of these confusions, nor, doubtless, is Mr. Jeffers; but all of these confusions are essentially romantic—they are very natural developments of moral monism. And Mr. Jeffers, having decried human life as such, and having denied the worth of the rules of the game, endeavors to write narrative and dramatic poems—poems, in other words, dealing with people who are playing the game. Jesus, the hero of *Dear Judas*, speaking apparently for Mr. Jeffers, says that the secret reason for the doctrine of forgiveness is that all men are driven by the mechanism-God to act as they do, that they are entirely helpless; yet he adds in the next breath that this secret must be guarded, for if it were given out, men would run amuck, would get out of hand—*they would begin acting differently.*

The Woman at Point Sur is a perfect laboratory of Mr. Jeffers' philosophy. Barclay, an insane divine, preaches Mr. Jeffers' religion, and his disciples, acting upon it, become emotional mechanisms, lewd and twitching conglomerations of plexi, their humanity annulled. Human experience, in these circumstances, having necessarily and according to the doctrine no meaning, there can be and is no necessary sequence of events: every act is equivalent to every other; every act is the peak of hysteria; most of the incidents could be shuffled around into varying sequences without violating anything save, perhaps, Mr. Jeffers' private sense of their relative intensity. Since the poem is his, of course, such a private sense is legitimate enough; the point is that this is not a narrative, nor a dramatic, but a lyrical criterion. A successful lyrical poem of one hundred and seventy-five pages is unlikely, for the essence of lyrical expression is concentration; but it is at least theoretically possible. The difficulty is that the lyric achieves its effect by the generalization of emotion (that is, by the separation of the emotion from the personal history that gives rise to it in actual concrete experience) and by the concentration of expression. Narrative can survive in a measure without concentration, or intensity of detail, provided the narrative logic is detailed and compelling, as in the case of Balzac, though it is only wise to add that this occurs most often in prose. Now Mr. Jeffers, as I have pointed out, has abandoned narrative logic with the theory of ethics, and he has never achieved, in addition, a close and masterly style. His writing is loose, turgid, and careless; like most anti-intellectualists, he relies on his feelings alone and has no standard of criticism for them outside of themselves. There are occasional good flashes in his poems, and to these I shall return later, but they are very few, are very limited in their range of feeling and in their subject matter, and they are very far between. Mr. Jeffers has no remaining method of sustaining his lyric, then, other than the employment of an accidental (i.e., non-narrative) chain of anecdotes (i.e., details that are lyrically impure); his philosophical doctrine and his artistic dilemma alike decree that these shall be anecdotes of hysteria. By this method Mr. Jeffers continually *lays claim* to a high pitch of emotion which has no narrative support (that is, support of the inevitable accumulation of experience), nor lyrical support (that is, support of the intense perception of pure, or transferable, emotion), which has, in short, no support at all, and which is therefore simply unmastered and self-inflicted hysteria.

Cawdor alone of Mr. Jeffers' poems contains a plot that in its rough outlines might be sound, and *Cawdor* likewise contains his best poetry; the poem as a whole, and in spite of the confused treatment of the woman, is moving, and the lines describing the seals at dawn are fine, as are the two or three last lines of the apotheosis of the eagle. Most of the preceding material in the latter passage, however, like most of the material in the sections that give Mr. Jeffers' notions of the post-mortem experience of man, are turgid, repetitious, arbitrary, and unconvincing. The plot itself is blurred for lack of stylistic finish (that is, lack of ability on the part of the poet to see every detail of sense and movement incisively down to the last preposition, the last comma, as every detail *is* seen in Racine or Shakespeare); and it remains again a fair question whether a moral monist *can* arrive at any clear conclusions about the values of a course of action, since he denies the existence of any conceivable standard of values within the strict limits of human life as such. In *The Tower Beyond Tragedy* Mr. Jeffers takes a ready-made plot, the Clytemnestra-Orestes situation, which is particularly strong dramatically, because Orestes is forced to choose between two sins, the murder of his mother and the refusal to avenge his father. But at the very last moment, in Mr. Jeffers' version, Orestes is converted to Mr. Jeffers' religion and goes off explaining (to Electra, who has just tried to seduce him) that though men may think he is fleeing before the furies he is really just drifting up to the mountains to meditate on the stars; and the preceding action is, of course, rendered morally and emotionally meaningless.

In the latest volume, the title poem, *Dear Judas*, is a kind of dilution of *The Women at Point Sur*, with Jesus as Barclay, and with a less detailed background. Mr. Jeffers' mouthpiece and hero, Jesus, is little short of revolting as he whips reflexively from didactic passion to malice, self-justification, and vengeance. The poem shares the structural principles, or lack of them, of *The Women at Point Sur*; and it has no quotable lines, save, possibly, the last three, which are, however, heavy with dross. *The Loving Shepherdess*, the other long poem of the present volume, deals with a girl who knows herself doomed to die at a certain time in childbirth, and who wanders over the countryside caring for a small and diminishing flock of sheep in an anguish of devotion. The events here again are anecdotal and reversible, and the emotion is lyrical or nothing. The theme had two possibilities: the poet could have immersed the girl in a dream of approaching death, or he could have immersed her in the sentimental pathos of the immediate situation. There are moments when he seems to be trying for the former effect, but his perceptions are not fine enough and the mass of anecdotal detail is too heavy; the poem succeeds in being no more than a very Wordsworthian embodiment of a kind of maudlin humanitarianism— which is a curious but not an unexpected outcome of Mr. Jeffers' sentimental misanthropy. The heroine is turned cruelly from door to door, and the sheep fall one by one before the reader's eyes, the doors and the sheep constituting the bulk of the anecdotal material; till finally the girl dies in a ditch in an impossible effort to give birth to her child.

The short poems in the book deal with themes that Mr. Jeffers has handled better before. He has written here and there impressive lines descriptive of the sea and its rocks, and of dying birds of prey. *Hurt Hawks II*, in the *Cawdor* volume, is the most perfect short poem and is quite fine; there are excellent lines scattered through other pieces. These poems are, however, limited both in paraphrasable content and in experiential implication: they glorify brute nature and annihilation and are numb to the intricacies of human feeling; they share in the latter respect the limitations of all mystical poetry. Mr. Jeffers' insistence on another of his favorite lyrical themes, his own aloofness, is becoming, by dint of repetition, almost embarrassing; one has the constant feeling that he is trying to bully the reader into accepting him at his own evaluation.

Self-repetition has been the inevitable effect of anti-intellectualist doctrine on all of its supporters. If life is valued, explored, subdivided, and defined, poetic themes are infinite in number; if life is denied, the only theme is the rather sterile and monotonous one of the denial. Similarly, those poets who flee from form, which is infinitely variable, since every form is a definite and an individual thing, can achieve only the uniformity of chaos; and those individuals who endeavor to escape morality, which is personal form and controlled direction, can, in the very nature of things, achieve nothing save the uniformity of mechanism. One might classify Mr. Jeffers as a "great failure" if one meant by the phrase that he had wasted unusual talents; but not if one meant that he had failed in a major effort, for his aims are badly thought-out and are essentially trivial.

FOSTER DAMON'S SECOND BOOK

Tilted Moons, by S. Foster Damon. Harper & Bros.

Mr. Damon's exceptionally impressive work on Blake, and his scholarly and superbly competent essays on other literary subjects, lead one to expect more, perhaps, of his poetry than one is likely to find in it. The present collection contains some very early pieces, and one assumes that the arrangement is in general roughly chronological, for the wavering meters of the first part of the book tend to become more sure of themselves farther on. But throughout there is too great slowness of movement and a too great laxity of statement. Occasionally Mr. Damon seems to suspect his weakness and sets out rather violently to remedy it. The result is a kind of highly engenious intellectual doggerel, as in *Image and After-image:*

> But look!—wavering from my ankles,
> The scattered image of myself
> Flaps and bulges incomplete;
> Knees knock and bandy, head swells to rings,
> Corrupting the surface of the sea
> With visionary anatomy
> In most un-Greek foreshortenings:

From *Poetry,* XXXV no. 6 (1930), pp. 340-342.

While bits of sun skip round its head,
Dancing nimbly, higher and higher,
As though the summer ocean bred
Enormous fleas of white fire.

The fleas are charming, but the line is arbitrary and insensitive;
it has no genuine poetic life.

In *Family Portrait*, Mr. Damon has found a subject that lends
itself more naturally to epigrammatic treatment, and this sort of
verse is not amiss; also, in the latter poem, the verse is better
controlled. *Family Portrait* is probably the best poem in the
book; it has discreet wit, social and historical atmosphere, and
poetic verve. For example:

Aunt Clarissa was not wanted.
She knew it well, but still undaunted
Rode up to Boston, and brought back
(With shocking evidence of her lack
Of what the family called taste)
A portrait of her, powdered, laced
Firm in her most expensive dress,
And not one hint of loveliness!
—Unless perhaps you did not mind her,
But looked away, and saw behind her,
A purple curtain (decorated
With arms not quite authenticated)
Looped back upon a marble column
To show an ocean dim and solemn.
But the painter had no painter's tact:
He was, unfortunately, exact;
Her mouth was shrill and proud and vexed—
You knew just what she would say next.

July, a more purely lyrical and somewhat Parnassian piece
about a water-lily and a statue in a garden, is almost as good.
It is a trifle slow, but is measured and even in movement and is
very effective as a whole. Too often, in the remainder of the book,
Mr. Damon treats his material in terms of a rather arbitrary

allegory and obscures the specific issues; and his allegory has the additional misfortune of having been worn pretty thin before he found it—there is rather too much of peacocks, moonlight on marble, and so on. In spite of the faults, the book is worth keeping and reading, and the best poems may be with us for a reasonably long time.

THE PROGRESS OF
HART CRANE

The Bridge, by Hart Crane. Black Sun Press (Paris); Horace Liveright.

It is necessary, before attempting to criticize Mr. Crane's new book, to place it in the proper genre and to give as accurate an account as one is able of its theme. The book cannot be called an epic, in spite of its endeavor to create and embody a national myth, because it has no narrative framework and so lacks the formal unity of an epic. It is not didactic, because there is no logical exposition of ideas; neither Homer nor Dante will supply a standard of comparison. The structure we shall find is lyrical; but the poem is not a single lyric, it is rather a collection of lyrics on themes more or less related and loosely following out of each other. The model, in so far as there is one, is obviously Whitman, whom the author proclaims in this book as his master.

The book is composed of eight parts, of which two contain more than one lyric. There is a *Proem: To Brooklyn Bridge*, in which the initial inspiration of the book is suggested. Part I, *Ave Maria*, is a monologue spoken by Columbus on his first return to Spain; one receives the impression that Columbus is not only the herald of the new world to the old, but that he is in some way the herald of life to the unborn. Part II, *Powhatan's*

From *Poetry,* XXXVI no. 3 (1930), pp. 153-165.

Daughter, deals with the soil, the flesh of the continent (Pocahontas), and is composed of five lyrics: the first, *Harbor Dawn*,
shows a protagonist, perhaps the author, or better simply man,
awakening not only to day but to life after "400 years and more
. . . or is it from the soundless shore of sleep?"; the second, *Van
Winkle*, gives a kind of fragmentary glimpse of American boy-
hood (the boy is Van Winkle, one gathers, because he is explor-
ing the new world in a somewhat dazed condition after "400
years and more"); the third, *The River*, shows the adolescent
joining the vagrants and coming to his first realization of the soil,
the body of Pocahontas; the fourth, *The Dance*, projects the personality of the author into an imagined Indian brave, Maquokeeta, whose apotheosis at the stake and amid a war dance effects
a permanent and spiritual union with Pocahontas; fifth, *Indiana*,
depicts an old pioneer bidding goodbye to her adopted son, who
is setting out in search of adventure. Part III, *Cutty Sark*, is a
kind of ghost-dance of the old clippers, the early days of American navigation. Part IV, *Cape Hatteras*, is a long prayer to Walt
Whitman, into the midst of which is inserted a brief history of
aviation, beginning with the first flight of the Wrights and ending
with a contemporary crash; the exact relationship of this section
to the book as a whole remains obscure to me, as does the formal
intention of the lyric itself. Part V is composed of *Three Songs*,
which provide an interlude and which deal in a purer and more
condensed form with themes treated elsewhere. The intention of
the sixth section, *Quaker Hill*, remains as obscure to me as that
of the fourth; the poem is prefaced by selections from Isadora
Duncan and Emily Dickinson, both of whom are mentioned in
the poem as "ideals" of the past, the decay of which the poem
indicates; these constituting a combination that is almost enough
to freeze the blood of one with my own prejudices and inhibi-
tions. Part VII, *The Tunnel*, deals with the subway, the modern
metropolitan Purgatory, the trial and purification by fire and
hallucination, in which the ghost of Poe appears to be rather
incidentially entangled. Part VIII, *Atlantis*, is the apotheosis of
the bridge addressed in the poem, in the form of the new Atlantis, the future America. It ends with Mr. Crane's version of
Whitman's "Look for me under your bootsoles":

O Answerer of All—Anemone—
Now while thy petals spend the suns about us, hold—
(O Thou whose radiance doth inherit me)
Atlantis—hold thy floating singer late!

I do not offer this analysis as complete or final, but as the best
I have been able to devise so far; I have discovered in the past
that Mr. Crane's work is likely to clear up in a measure with
familiarity. Nevertheless, it should be apparent from the looseness of the progression—and it will be more apparent after an
inspection of the variety of meters—that the book as a whole
has no more unity than the *Song of Myself;* it must be treated,
as I have said, as a series of lyrics on a theme that is basically
Whitmanian, but that, under the influence of Blake and Mr.
Crane's own inclinations, is extended into regions with which
Whitman did not concern himself.

Now Whitman doubtless regarded himself as something of an
epic writer, and it is possible that Mr. Crane feels that he is one;
the difference between Whitman (who is his own epic) and *pius
Aeneas* is that the latter is not only obeying destiny, he is obeying his mother. That is, destiny, for Aeneas, is not a vague surge
toward an infinite future, it is a deliberate effort to achieve a
definitie aim, and the effort is composed of specific moral duties;
it is the serious attitude toward those duties that made him *pius*
to the Augustan Roman. It is the same attitude that gives to
every one of his acts a definite and absolutely individual value,
as well as a definite bearing on the theme of the book as a whole.
That is, destiny for Vergil was a clear and comprehensible thing
and had a clear relationship to a complete scale of human values.
Whitman found all human values about equal and could envisage
good only as an enthusiastic acceptance of everything at hand;
but if nothing is bad it follows equally that nothing is good—
that is, everything is equivalent to everything else and there are
no values at all; unless one can envisage as good a kind of meaningless and inexhaustible energy, or unless one can face about
with Mr. Jeffers and regard annihilation, complete negation, as
the only good. It is therefore natural that Whitman's poems, like
Mr. Jeffers' should be little save boundless catalogues. Both of

these poets, and Mr. Crane as well, are headed precisely for nowhere, in spite of all the shouting. All three are occasionally betrayed by their talents into producing a passage better than their usual run, but this only goes to prove the fallacy of their initial assumptions. Mr. Crane, since he possesses the greatest genius in the Whitmanian tradition, and since, strangely enough, he grafts onto the Whitmanian tradition something of the stylistic discipline of the Symbolists, most often exceeds himself in this manner. The Whitmanian basis of Mr. Crane's book makes a hero, as I have said, impossible. And the "destiny" of a nation is hard to get at in the abstract, since it is a vague generality, like "the French temperament" or "the average American." It reduces itself, when one comes to describe it—without a hero—to the most elementary and the least interesting aspects of the general landscape, aspects which cannot possibly be imbued with any definite significance, no matter how excited one may get, for the simple reason that no definite significance is available. It is on this rock that *Atlantis* shatters; and on a similar rock, we shall presently see, occurs the wreck of *The Dance*, the other climax of the volume.

There is only one poem in the volume that endeavors to treat clearly of an individual human relationship; the poem is *Indiana*, and it fails miserably—it could scarcely be more mawkish and helpless. The fact is unimportant except that it strengthens one's suspicion that Mr. Crane is temperamentally unable to understand a very wide range of experience, and one's feeling that even his best poems—which, in spite of this limitation, are very fine—have about them something of the fragility of innocence. The two most powerful poems in the book, though they are not the most perfect, are *The River* and *The Dance*.

The River falls into three distinct and unsynthesized parts. The first is a catalogue of the "din and slogans of the year"—prefatory information thrown at one in the raw and absolutely unmastered. The second part, which deals with the hoboes, the intercessors with Pocahontas "who have touched her knowing her without name," is better organized but is still turgid and confused; it has magnificent moments. The third part—each of the three parts is metrically distinct from the rest—though not quite as clean as Mr. Crane's finest writing, carries the epic quality of the Whitmanian vision (the vision of humanity *en masse*, or undifferentiated) to the greatest dignity and power of which it is, probably, capable; the stream of humanity becomes fused, poetically, with the stream of the Mississippi, and the result is a passage of extraordinary poetry:

> Down, down—born pioneers in time's despite,
> Grimed tributaries to an ancient flow—
> They win no frontier by their wayward plight,
> But drift in stillness, as from Jordan's brow.
>
> You will not hear it as the sea; even stone
> Is not more hushed by gravity. . . . But slow,
> As loth to take more tribute—sliding prone,
> Like one whose eyes were buried long ago,
>
> The River, spreading, flows—and spends your dream.
> What are you, lost within this tideless spell?
> You are your father's father, and the stream—
> A liquid theme that floating niggers swell.

The complete passage contains eight stanzas of mounting intensity: it has a few faults of detail, but I cannot read it—much less read it aloud—without being profoundly moved.

The Dance is more even, but chiefly because it is more evenly impure. I have already indicated briefly the theme of *The Dance*. It is in the following stanza that the apotheosis of Maquokeeta begins:

> O, like the lizard in the furious noon,
> That drops his legs and colors in the sun,
> —And laughs, pure serpent, Time itself, and moon
> Of his own fate—I saw thy change begun!

It is obvious from such a stanza that we are analyzing the flaws in a genius of a high order—none of the famous purple patches in Shelley, for example, surpasses this stanza and probably none equals it; so be it. But the flaws in Mr. Crane's genius are, I believe, so great as to partake, if they persist, almost of the nature of a public catastrophe. The most that we can learn about the nature of the apotheosis follows a few lines further on:

> Thy freedom is her largesse, Prince, and hid
> On paths thou knewest best to claim her by.
>
> High unto Labrador the sun strikes free
> Her speechless dream of snow, and stirred again,
> She is the torrent and the singing tree;
> And she is virgin to the last of men. . . .
>
> And when the caribou slant down for salt
> Do arrows thirst and leap? Do antlers shine
> Alert, star-triggered in the listening vault
> Of dusk?—And are her perfect brows to thine?

These lines are in themselves, for the most part, very good; placed in the proper poetic setting and with an adequate ideational background, they might contribute to a wholly sound poem. Here, however, they represent the climax of that poem which would appear to be intended as one of the two climactic points of the sequence. They constitute an assertion of the faith on which the sequence is built; there is no evidence here or elsewhere in the poem or the book that they are merely a poetic and incomplete hint of a more definite belief; and there is a great deal of evidence that Mr. Crane suspects continually the inadequacy of his belief, or at any rate is continually hampered and frustrated by that inadequacy. Mr. Crane demands of his medicine-man to "lie to us—dance us back the tribal morn." Let us examine another passage:

> Spears and assemblies: black drums thrusting on—
> O yelling battlements!—I, too, was liege
> To rainbows currying each pulsant bone:
> Surpassed the circumstance, danced out the siege!

And buzzard-circleted, screamed from the stake;
I could not pick the arrows from my side.
Wrapped in that fire I saw more escorts wake—
Flickering, sprint up the hill groins like a tide.

Any one of these lines is a brilliant performance; but only two of
them, I believe, at the most, are brilliant on a poetic level—the
fourth (possibly) and the sixth. The sixth is worthy of Racine.
The others are brilliant on what I should call a descriptive level.
To make this clear, I offer several others taken nearly at random
from the same poem:

A cyclone threshes in the turbine crest,
Swooping in eagle feathers down your back.

I left my sleek boat nibbling margin grass.

I learned to catch the trout's moon-whisper.

These lines, though they are perceived with great precision, have
no evident connection with the theme except as they are a part of
the natural landscape, and that connection is inadequate for art.
One feels no fluid experience bathing the perceptions and giving
them a significant relation; one feels rather fact after fact, each,
or nearly each, admirably presented but only very casually relevant, being hurled at one by the author in a fine frenzy as if he
were trying to convice one, to hypnotize one, that he might in
turn be convinced himself.

There are moments throughout the poem when the hypnosis
is achieved, and lines of pure electricity occur; but the lapse to
the descriptive is sudden and immediate. The poem is composed
mainly of unfused details, and is excited rather than rhythmic.
The quality which we call restraint, and which is here lacking, is
the result of a feeling on the part of a poet that the motivation of
his emotion is sound and needs no justification, that the emotion
is inevitable; his problem, then, is only to give order to his emotion. In Mr. Crane we see an attempt to emotionalize a theme to
the point where both he and the reader will forget to question its

justification. It is, whatever fragmentary success may result from it, a form of hysteria. In this case the author is endeavoring to evoke a plane of experience higher than that of this world, about which he knows nothing and is able to imagine little or nothing, by the use of details taken from the plane of experience (this world) from which he is trying to escape. The details, as I have said, are good, but they almost never have meaning for the simple reason that the meaning is not available. I do not wish to imply that a wholly concrete statement may not have poetic value— it may, as in some of the best work of the Imagists and the Imagist fringe (Dr. Williams, Miss Moore, and so on), if the author is clearly aware of the value when he writes it; if, in other words, the feeling is definitely implicated in the perception. *Atlantis*, as I have already said, is an attempt to embody another non-existent "destiny" in miscellaneous concrete details. It contains, like *The Dance*, superb poetry; unlike *The Dance*, its low spots are imprecise—in place of exact description we get vague thunder.

The same faults of rhetoric are to be found in *National Winter Garden*, one of the *Three Songs*, but are almost absent from the first of its companion pieces. *Southern Cross*, a poem which very nearly, though not quite, equals the two most perfect poems, to my mind, that Mr. Crane has written, *Repose of Rivers* and *Voyages II*, from his former volume. *The Harbor Dawn, Van Winkle, The Tunnel, Cape Hatteras*, and *Quaker Hill* are too vague in detail and chaotic in form to be worth much; *Cape Hatteras*, indeed in its attitude toward Whitman, strikes me as desperately sentimental. Mr. Crane's estimate of Whitman and his complete failure to understand Emily Dickinson (for which see his charming but uncomprehending poem addressed to her and published several years ago in the *Nation*) are of a piece not only with each other but with his own failures and limitations as a poet.

Cutty Sark is a frail but exquisite and almost incomparably skillful dance of shadows. Its conclusion is a perpetual delight. It is a kind of radio question sent into the past to locate certain lost clippers, clippers the names of which, though apparently made for Mr. Crane's purposes, are historical:

Buntlines tusseling (91 days, 20 hours and anchored!)
                                                      Rainbow, Leander
(last trip a tragedy (where can you be
Nimbus? and you rivals two—

      a long tack keeping—
                                                      Taeping?
                                                      Ariel?

The remaining poems—the *Proem* and *Ave Maria*—are, so far as
I can see, basically sound; that is, I am aware of no earthly reason why Mr. Crane should not write a poem expressing his admiration of the Brooklyn Bridge, or an imaginary monologue
spoken by Columbus. Both poems contain fine things; both,
unfortunately, contain a great deal that is empty. As in *Atlantis,*
the weak portions are composed of inexact poetic verbiage. Those
poems illustrate the danger inherent in Mr. Crane's almost blind
faith in his moment-to-moment inspiration, the danger that the
author may turn himself into a kind of stylistic automaton, the
danger that he may develop a sentimental leniency toward his
vices and become wholly their victim, instead of understanding
them and eliminating them.

Mr. Crane is not alone in this danger; it is one of the greatest
dangers of the entire body of anti-intellectualist literature of our
time. It can be seen in Miss Roberts' latest novel, *The Great
Meadow,* a book in which the dangers potential in the style of her
first two novels have become actual and almost smother a good
plot. It can be seen in a good deal of the latest work of Mr. Joyce,
who, while revolutionizing the word, spends an appalling lot of
detailed revolution telling us how little clouds commit suicide and
the like. It can be seen, I regret above all to add, in the last three
or four years' work of Dr. Williams, whose experiments in perpetual motion are becoming so repetitious as to appear very
nearly mechanical or even static. Dr. Williams, though a writer
of greater range and mastery, in all likelihood, than any of these
others, is a bigot and is bound to be the victim of his own bigotry
just as are the intellectual bigots whom he damns. Mr. Frost, at
the age of fifty-odd, can continue to grow amazingly. Mr. Joyce

and Dr. Williams appear to be disintegrating in their forties, Miss Roberts and Mr. Crane in their thirties. Thomas Hardy could grow in his eighties. Two things would appear certain about the situation: it is profoundly alarming, and it is not inevitable. It is possible that Mr. Crane may recover himself. In any event, he has given us, in his first book, several lyrics that one is tempted to call great, and in both books several charming minor lyrics and many magnificent fragments. And one thing he has demonstrated, the impossibility of getting anywhere with the Whitmanian inspiration. No writer of comparable ability has struggled with it before, and, with Mr. Crane's wreckage in view, it seems highly unlikely that any writer of comparable genius will struggle with it again.

EDMUND WILSON AS POET

Poets, Farewell! by Edmund Wilson. Charles Scribner's Sons. 1929.

If Allen Tate is correct in defining a journalist as one who does not stay long enough with his subject matter to learn what it is about, then Mr. Wilson is too often a journalist when he essays verse. His failures occur mainly because of a delusive facility, which shows itself at its best in such echoes of the later style of Yeats as occur in *A Young Girl Indicted for Murder* and at its worst in his light verse. The poems included in the section called *Nonsense,* and a few others that should have appeared there, might have been amusing enough one by one in manuscript, but, collected in a professedly serious volume, they are mildly exasperating. The power to write light verse that is poetry is a special gift, possessed in all likelihood by only two Americans of Mr. Wilson's generation, Malcolm Cowley and Archibald MacLeish; when Mr. Wilson attempts the genre he merely writes newspaper verse that is not discernibly better than the usual trade article. His facility betrays him again in such a piece as *The Lido,* in which a young girl yields her *frêles faveurs* in a mildly Proustain setting, the entire affair being treated in terms of the atmospheric effects. *Copper and White* is barely more than a newspaper report

From *Hound and Horn,* III no. 2 (1930), pp. 291-293.

of similar material; his short prose pieces are extremely weak, and for more or less similar reasons.

Somewhat more interesting are the group of poems under the title of *Stucco and Stone* and the piece called *Boboli Gardens*, poems that represent Mr. Wilson's contribution to the contemporary adventures in rhymed Parnassianism undertaken chiefly by the professed devoltés—-and revoltées—against the unrhymed Parnassianism of H. D. The first poem under the first title has the enameled suavity that, being meaningless, one can permit without irritation to no one save Gautier; the third poem of the group is looser but more charming. The last three stanzas of *Boboli Gardens* are particularly lovely, though they shade out of something like Samain into something vaguely reminiscent of Mr. Yeats' *Presences*. It is possibly worth mentioning that none of the Parnassianism of the last ten years, fashionable as some of it has been, will bear even a moment's comparison with the bleak choral grandeur of a seldom noted poem by Agnes Lee, a poem called *A Statue in a Garden*, written, I believe, nearly twenty years ago.

One's objection to Mr. Wilson's assumption of the Yeatsian armor is not to the garment as such, for it is a good one, nor to imitation, which is necessary and desirable to a certain extent. But it is not a sufficient discipline for the wearing of that particular costume to admire the grand manner in general and the Yeatsian grand manner in particular. A traditional grand manner, ready for anyone to assume, occurs only when there is a traditional discipline and morality by which everyone is prepared. No such discipline now exists; Mr. Yeats's manner has grown out of his to say the least strenuous and life-long if somewhat idiosyncratic discipline; it is an intensely personal thing. It might conceivably be taken over in a measure by another poet, but only by a poet who had in a sense earned the right, who had performed a comparable amount or kind of moral labor. Mr. Wilson sometimes seems to rattle a trifle loosely in the armor. The fact that Mr. Wilson is intellectually a good many degrees less innocent than Mr. Yeats does not affect this particular situation, or at least not in Mr. Wilson's favor, even though Mr. Yeats's moral (and poetic) results are frequently seriously weakened by their chimeric bases. One of the factors contributing to Mr. Yeats's ultimate stylistic effect is the very sincerity of his innocence, a kind of pathetic nobility, any part of which would be out of place in Mr. Wilson's work.

It would be unfair to dwell on the weak poems in Mr. Wilson's book did they not embody vices that seem in constant danger of invading his best work and cheapening it. He approaches his muse with just a little too confident a swagger and frequently suffers as he deserves; for a secure mastery of style proceeds normally out of an awkwardness that is several stages beyond Mr. Wilson's particular kind of smoothness, an awkwardness that is born of humility before basic difficulties and that is overcome only by pretty heavy labor.

The book, in spite of all one can say against it, has its fine moments. *Infection,* though a shade too dependent on Yeats, is admirable; and admirable likewise is the poem entitled *To a Painter Going Abroad,* despite its slight excess of minor European geography. This latter poem contains a statement so finely phrased as:

> Tell her I know what desperate pastime fills
> The summer's slow defeat—

and it is definite and firm throughout. Best of all is the piece called *Provincetown,* which I quote entire:

> We never from the barren down,
>   Beneath the silver-lucid breast
> Of drifting plume, gazed out to drown
>   Where daylight whitens to the west.
>
> Here never in this place I knew
>   Such beauty by your side, such peace—
> These skies that brightening imbue
>   With dawn's delight the day's release.
>
> Only, upon the barren beach,
>   Beside the gray egg of a gull,

With that fixed look and fervent speech,
   You stopped and called it beautiful.

Lone as the voice that sped the word!—
   Gray-green as eyes that ate its round!—
The desert dropping of a bird,
   Bare-bedded in the sandy ground.

Tonight, where clouds like foam are blown,
   I ride alone the surf of light—
As—even by my side—alone,
   That stony beauty burned your sight.

The poem is, for the present reviewer, one of the best lyrics of recent years; and it suffices, along with a few others, to lift the book from the ruck of a good deal of amateurishness to the intense elegance of the amateur in life and in art at his finest.

RECENT VERSE

Selected Poems of Conrad Aiken, by Conrad Aiken. Charles Scribner's Sons, 1929.
O City, Cities, by R. Ellsworth Larsson. Payson & Clarke, Ltd., 1929.
High Falcon, by Leonie Adams. John Day Company.

I

When there appear the collected or selected poems of a mature poet, the temptation to "place" him with respect to his contemporaries is very great. One realizes, of course, that the attempt is very dangerous, but it may conceivably be illuminating. The best American poets of Mr. Aiken's generation, it should be fairly safe by now to say, are Robert Frost (if his age does not disqualify him), W. C. Williams, Ezra Pound, T. S. Eliot, Marianne Moore, Mina Loy, Archibald MacLeish, John Crowe Ransom, Wallace Stevens, and possibly H. D. It is doubtful if any one of these is a poet of the very first order if we look for the qualities that Arnold found or thought he found in Wordsworth (and Wordsworth was, according to Arnold only of the second order) or that one today can find easily enough in Arnold; but Mr. Frost in six or eight of the lyrics in *West-Running Brook* will come fairly near

From *Hound and Horn,* III no. 3 (1930), pp. 454-461.

the mark, in spite of his deliberate (and not wholly successful) effort to evade certain themes that Arnold would have insisted on his mastering (see his shockingly timid remarks in the lyric called *The Times Table*); and Dr. Williams will come at least as near in a dozen or more scattered lyrics, in spite of the various criteria of good poetry that he has endeavored at different times to establish, which would, if applied to his own best poems, render them of little or no worth. Whatever the spiritual limitations of any of this list of writers, however, they have shown themselves here and there to be, all of them, first rate stylists. The question arises whether Mr. Aiken is their equal as a stylist; it is my opininon that he is not.

Mr. Aiken's debt to Mr. Eliot has been over-estimated; it really amounts to little or nothing. Mr. Eliot's early work, which is supposed to have exerted the influence, employs a line that is based on the standard iambic pentameter; Mr. Aikens' line varies, but it is almost never that. The only resemblance that I can disccver is the similar tendency to wandering rhymes (very common in all of the late French symbolists, from Laforgue to Vielé-Griffin); and in *Senlin* Mr. Aiken made his protagonist philosophize while combing his hair. Like Mr. Eliot, Mr. Aiken has used a kind of stream-of-consciousness method, and like him also has endeavored through the use of that method to deal rather extensively with the spiritual difficulties and the concrete aspects of our period. *The Waste Land* lacks form; Mr. Aiken's long poems in a sense achieve form or at least cohesion—that is, they are not obviously falling apart from line to line. But if one examines them carefully, it is fairly evident that the lines cohere not because they have any common intention or direction, but because they have no intention or direction; there is nothing to force them apart, no group of identities for the poet to weld together. Mr. Aiken has practically no sense of the integrity of the line; Mr. Eliot, whatever his weaknesses, has that sense as a critic, though he often fails to rise to it as a poet, and, when he does rise to it, often fails to get beyond it. If one performs the experiment of opening Mr. Aiken's book at random to two or three passages in any of the long poems or in nearly any of the short ones, one can scarcely help being struck by the almost exact similarity of his work at every point. The following passage is from page nine, *The Jig of Forslin:*

> I heard a story once of one who murdered,
> For what I cannot remember; but he murdered.
> With a knife's greedy edge, or with white hands—
> What does it matter? The swift deed was done . . .
> That was a sombre sea-pool to explore—
> Strange things are on that floor.
>
> And once, the music I was listening to
> Suddenly opened, like a luminous book,
> To one bright page that told of a strange thing:
> A man stepped out in the purple of an arc-light,
> A man I knew—I knew him well—
> And because the harlot he loved had jilted him,
> He held his breath and died.

This is from a short poem on page 301:

> And already the minutes, the hours, the days,
> Separate thoughts and separate ways,
> Fall whitely and silently and slowly between us,
> Fall between us like phantasmal rain and snow.
> And we, who were thrust for an instant so sharply together,
> Under changing skies to alien destinies go.
>
> Melody heard in the midnight on the wind—
> Orange poppy of fire seen in a dream—
> Vainly I try to keep you. How the sky,
> A great blue wind, with a gigantic laugh,
> Scorns us apart like chaff.
> Like a bird blown to sea am I.

Mr. Aiken's heroes commit murder to appropriate music, fall from skyscrapers, or wander in the lamplight in the rain (to steal a cadence from him) in exactly the same frame of mind and in the same colorless vocabulary. Each act (an almost infinite variety of disconnected and meaningless acts, a kind of cosmic drift or milky way of acts, in fact) passes before one; each is mentioned, but none is poetically realized. One cannot think of any one of Mr. Aiken's poems as a unit, but one can think only of his poetry as a vague and perpetual flux. His poems, like his lines, lack bounds. He achieves a momentary illusion of form by abandoning all claim to form; his poems move evenly, but they might just as well stop anywhere; they are simply a record of revery.

Mr. Aiken has expounded at one time or another theories of musical outline that I do not profess wholly to understand. Musical outline in a poem is, I imagine, if it becomes an isolated quality, a vice rather than a virtue. The kind of proportion that involves not only the sound of the lines, but the meanings and connotations of the words as words, of the lines as lines, and of the poem as a whole, is the sum total of poetic style, but it is a very complex thing. It may occur in poems as short as Mr. Frost's *Acquainted with the Night* or Dr. Williams' *To Waken an Old Lady*. It will never be achieved by letting cadences run on indefinitely in a long sweeping wash of sound, for such sound will utterly swamp the other components. To achieve it one must be aware of and control a good many qualities at once. Excessive attention to one quality in art, as in other activities, usually indicates a rather general blindness and seldom results in the mastery even of that quality. Dr. Williams' meter, as pure meter, is incomparably better than Mr. Aiken's, and so is Mr. Frost's. Mr. Aiken's metrical effects are facile and uncontrolled; he succeeds perfectly in achieving second-rate effects that would be mussed up badly by a more critical, even if more creative, mind, such as, say Mr. Eliot's. Swineburne sins the same way, but does not go so far; also his positive virtues are more considerable. One could say the same of Ezra Pound. Aiken, Swineburne, and Pound achieve their varying degrees of success and their uniform smoothness, one suspects, because their respective critical visions are not much clearer than their creative. Mr. Eliot is not so lucky.

Mr. Aiken's place, then, I imagine, is very likely to be in that fringe of contemporary poets who have achieved a kind of frail brilliance through the exaggeration and limited mastery of some one quality. His best poem is *Priapus and the Pool*. It is short, and, though it is a bit diffuse, it says at least as much as any of his long pieces. The cadences are terser and better orchestrated than in anything else he has done; his meter, at least, in this poem, has form—one has a feeling that it is doing fairly definite and interesting things, and one can forecast the arrival of the end before one gets there. The poem deserves a respectable place beside the *Blue Symphony* of John Gould Fletcher, a poet who regarded poetry and music as about the same thing and who thought, for a time, that by naming and suggesting colors in a regulated series one could create a type of music; and beside the *Patterns* and one or two late poems by Amy Lowell, whose nervous preoccupation with leaves and sunlight occasionally took on a brittle charm. Mr. Aiken's place is less among the best poets of our time than among the most interesting poetic curiosities. If one is sceptical about the truth of this conclusion let him compare, say, any of Mr. Aiken's nocturnal reveries with Mr. Frost's *Acquainted with the Night*; the difference is the difference between a formless record of mere fact and a sharply limited and beautifully ordered poetic structure—limited as Arnold used the term, and not in the pejorative sense in which it is often used today, and, though ordered, none the less fearful and haunting—and, incidentally, a poetic structure of vastly more significance than has been so far admitted by any of Mr. Frost's old-guard admirers.

II

Mr. Larsson has metrical habits not unlike Mr. Aiken's; his line is of a different sort, but he uses it the same way. His matter is too seriously dependent upon the later Eliot, and his manner is somewhat dependent upon Cummings. He does to Eliot, however, more or less what the poets of the nineties did to Swinburne. Eliot's matter is no longer felt as something in any way real; it is accepted as a conventional confection. The rain and the rats in the attic become more or less equivalent to the flowers and the flames of sin. Even when Mr. Eliot borrows most profusely he seems to be aware of the reality of the vision of his sources; he is quite simply beaten by it. Mr. Larsson does not appear greatly afflicted by such an awareness of reality—the themes merely present interesting possibilities for rearrangement. His meters are in a sense intricate, but only because like Mr. Aiken's, they run on more or less indefinitely, not because they are genuinely subtle or difficult: the trick is mainly one of arresting, breaking, and impelling to slightly irregular overflow, the iambic pentameter line, and it is a trick that it is harder to avoid than to indulge in, especially when one is throwing in irregular rhymes. Mr. Larsson, like Mr. Aiken, and like a good many other contemporaries who are popularly supposed to be adroit stylists, is in a state of arrested expertness. He is elaborating on effects that the few first-rate stylists of our time have learned through hard work to avoid entirely. The poems, like or even more than Mr. Aiken's, lack individual identity, though Mr. Larsson has plenty of personality himself—more, in fact, than does Mr. Aiken. There is no one poem in the book as good as *Priapus and the Pool*; but there are not two consecutives lines in Mr. Aiken as good as these from Mr. Larsson:

> Sun in an arc
>   and summer dead:
>   the year
> spends itself in windiness and din

That is perhaps as comprehensive a comment as one could make on both books; but at odd moments, anyway, Mr. Larsson really makes the most of something he has observed—he has the capacity to learn how to write. Whether he has the inclination remains to be seen.

III

Miss Adams' first volume, *Those Not Elect*, failed, for whatever reasons, to interest me; her second volume interests me a great deal, partly because it contains at least five brilliantly executed poems and a number of fine passages, and partly because it contains a number of weaknesses, at least several of which are rather common among the better writers of Miss Adams' generation and are in danger of becoming more common. I shall take advantage of the critic's prerogative and begin with the vices.

Two of the faults most common in her work, as well as most irritating, though perhaps not most profoundly important, are a persistent use of certain forms of ambiguous syntax, chiefly the dangling participle and the pronoun of uncertain reference, a use which results in an obscurity in no wise organic to the feeling and hence definitely bad; and a tendency to dilute and expand certain poems (*Windy Way* is one of the worst examples) with pretty literary turns and phrases which bear much the same relationship to poetry that scales bear to music.

More important is her preoccupation with, and exaggeration of the significance of, the feelings attendant upon the fringe of sleep; these feelings are sometimes genuinely curious, but only the most unbridled mysticism can imbue them with any vast amount of meaning. The tendency to take them too seriously is indicative of a tendency to find profundity in the strange simply because it is strange, and this, though it has been a common poetic vice for at least a hundred and fifty years, is decidedly uncritical and is bound to be in one degree or another disastrous to poetry. It is much more difficult to face experience on one's feet and with one's eyes open than in any other condition, and it is hence vastly more necessary that one endeavor to give it order while in this condition.

Miss Adams' mysticism shows itself in another way in two of her most perfectly executed songs, *Time and Spirit*, and *The Mount*, as well as in a few less perfect pieces. The feeling, the experience, in these poems involves certain ideas which most readers, I imagine, will have a hard time taking seriously, and it involves these ideas not by rejecting them nor by regarding them sceptically, but by accepting them with a certain fervor. The reader, to experience the poems, must likewise accept them; but as the acceptance in most cases can be no more than extremely temporary, the poems become momentary luxuries, indulgences, and are scarcely spiritual necessities. This sort of easy indulgence, of facile escape from the real difficulties of achieving spiritual mastery, is altogether too common in modern poetry. Mr. Hart Crane is another serious sinner on this score, and one of the greatest is Mr. Yeats, who exhibits an inordinate capacity for temporarily solving the riddle of life in magnificently written lines, his solution, frequently being something no more considerable than a handful of automatic letters, and the grandeur of his rhetoric on such an occasion leaving the reader dumfounded.

Finally, there are probably not over a dozen poems in the book that are not packed with echoes, general and specific, from Yeats. Mr. Yeats, though he has written poems that are almost certainly of a major order, has a very dangerous habit of striking histrionically noble attitudes when he finds himself in the face of situations that are genuinely hard to understand; such attitudes are at best but very rough estimates of the situations and a very rough substitute for the humble and careful exactness of Hardy or of Baudelaire. They are, being somewhat ready-made and standardized, the most easily imitated aspect of his work; and they are particularly tempting to a generation whose more intelligent members are struggling desperately to reassert the dignity and moral values lost by their predecessors. There is every reason to believe at the present moment that Mr. Yeats may exert as funest an influence in the next five or six years as did Mr. Eliot in the last, and one that may be recognized and abandoned more slowly, for appearing to be something it is not. His weaker moments and methods offer too facile an escape from the too facile collapse of Mr. Eliot: they offer escape via a stylistic formula rather than intellectual and moral effort and hence can lead ultimately only to another collapse or to poetry that, though apparently sustained, is devoid of genuine meaning. They add intellectual unsoundness to the emotional unsoundness of Mr. Eliot, or rather they seem to conceal the latter under the former.

For evidence of this danger one need only examine recent work, not only by Miss Adams, but by Edmund Wilson, Raymond Holden, and Robert Penn Warren, to mention no more, all of them writers of considerable ability. These poets have not sold their souls to Mr. Yeats, but they have all been tempted, and the varying degrees to which the temptation has moved them are indicative of a very real peril.

The most perfectly executed poems, in addition to *Time and Spirit* and *The Mount*, are *Country Summer*, *Song from a Country Fair*, and *The Figurehead*, and to these three one can take, I think, very little exception, whether in the matter of style or of conception. The first is a landscape and nothing more, but is a particularly rich and lovely one; the second one is, in super-ficial appearance, a kind of marginal note, but it possesses very curious and almost terrifying implications; the third, possibly the finest of all, I offer for the reader's consideration:

> This that is washed with weed and pebblestone
> Curved once a dolphin's length before the prow,
> And I who read the land to which we bore
> In its grave eyes, question my idol now,
> What cold and marvelous fancy it may keep,
> Since the salt terror swept us from our course,
> Or if a wisdom later than the storm,
> For old green ocean's tinctured it so deep;
> And with some reason to me on this strand
> The waves, the ceremoial waves have come
> And stooped their barbaric heads, and all spread out
> Their lovely arms before them, and are gone,
> Leaving their murderous tribute on the sand.

There is not only, here, extraordinary beauty of visual imagery, there is a kind of beauty that is possibly more profound and which it is certainly harder to achieve: the fourth line, for instance, especially as it concentrates in its second half, is one of the most deeply moving lines in the poem, and the emotion is not in the least illusory, though it is impossible, perhaps, to give objectively satisfactory reasons for it—it is something in the cadence and it is something more than that.

MAJOR FICTION

Flowering Judas, by Katherine Anne Porter. Harcourt, Brace and Co. Primavera Editions.

Miss Porter's book contains six stories, *María Concepción, Magic, Rope, He, The Jilting of Granny Weatherall*, and *Flowering Judas*, arranged in this order, which is the order of compostion. Of these six tales, three deal with themes that are sharply limited. *Magic*, for example, tells of a prostitute who leaves a brothel because of brutal treatment from the proprietress and returns ostensibly as the result of a charm worked upon her in her absence, actually, one suspects, because of her physical exhaustion. What one has, however, is a static sketch of the brothel, the beating the departure, the charm, the return. It is a good sketch, but it is nothing more. *Rope*, which is composed almost entirely in dialogue presented as indirect discourse, gives the rise and fall of a quarrel between a husband and wife, a quarrel that appears to be wholly the result of nervous fatigue. The timing is skillful; the details are admirable; but the quarrel remains a quarrel, presented in an almost crystalline fashion, indeed, but with no very wide implications. The next story, *He*, deals with a half-wit boy in a family benumbed by his presence; it is moving, but it is primarily a study in disease; one feels of

From *Hound and Horn,* IV no. 2 (1930-1931), pp. 303-305.

this story as of the two preceding that it was intended to be an object of curiosity, a brilliantly executed fictive knick-knack, rather than a general symbol of experience.

Despite this objection, the three stories are written with such skill that they would suffice to give Miss Porter a very respectable place among contemporary fictionists; but they have probably been surpassed in some measure by one or two writers of lesser talents, notably by Mr. Morley Callaghan, who, at his best (*Last Spring They Came Over, A Cocky Young Man, A Girl with Ambition*), displays an irony in handling subjects roughly comparable to those of *Rope* and of *He* that is at once infinitely discreet and cruelly devastating. Mr. Callaghan's irony exists in what one might call a pure state and can be applied to his limited subjects with extreme precision; Miss Porters' irony is inseparable from a very complex attitude, an attitude that is usually intensely tragic (in the most respectable sense of the word), that always, at any rate, involves much more than irony, and that requires a subject capable of carrying a considerable weight of feeling—when her irony is applied to such a subject as that of *Rope*, one feels, slightly, at least, that the irony is dragging a little too much else with it; and that the actual theme of the story is not quite an adequate embodiment of the tension one feels in the atmosphere. There is neither the ironic detachment of Mr. Callaghan nor the complete absorption of the author in the symbol that occurs in Miss Porter's more ambitious tales.

María Concepción, the earliest story included, is much richer than the three which follow it. It is the story of a Mexican girl who kills a rival for her husband's love. Such a story told by one of the contemporary objectivists, of whom Mr. Hemingway is the most popular and Mr. Callaghan the most distinguished representative, would probably have been given as nearly as possible from the point of view of the peasants themselves, perhaps in terms of their bare words and actions. Mr. Callaghan does this in *Soldier Harmon*, the story of a Sadistic pugilist. The norm toward which this sort of thing tends, I suppose, is something like Little Black Sambo or the Sunbonnet Babies. Miss Porter follows the older tradition of treating her characters as important symbols, that is, from the point of view of the intelligent human;

the story actually deals with her own feelings about the feelings of her people. This does not mean that she appears on the stage in person; her relationship to the story is felt in the quality of the perception. She has such precedent as the works of Hardy and Graham, to mention no others. Mr. Callaghan's only contribution, in his own name, to such stories, and it is a contribution he has made rather seldom, is, as I have said, his chemically pure irony.

María Concepción is technically straight narrative, marred a little by over-decoration. The last two stories in the book, *The Jilting of Granny Weatherall*, and *Flowering Judas*, employ a convention that makes for greater concentration, the convention of revery alternating with perceptions of the present. It is, however, a *convention*, rigidly controlled by the author, with no surrender on her part to a psychological flux, no weakening of her selection and arrangement. The perceptions of the present, including a good deal of conversation, give the setting and the actual narrative progression that takes place between the first sentence and the last. The revery provides another dimension, the background and antecedent history. In this manner *The Jilting of Granny Weatherall* presents completely in some twenty-two pages the rich and tragic career of an old woman, along with a portrait of her household as they are gathered about her deathbed. There is no excess of simplification, no summary, no omission. The story is as complete and powerful as a fine poetic drama. *Flowering Judas*, with which most of the readers of this review will be familiar, covers as much ground, quite as successfully, though the actual length of time involved is considerably less. *Theft*, a story unfortunately omitted from this volume, but available in Mr. O'Brien's collection for 1930, raises to intense seriousness a device employed in *Rope*, that of using a simple occurrence as the ineluctable allegory of things much greater than itself, and yet of making that occurrence so real in itself that the obviousness of the allegory, far from being a weakness, is a source of tremendous strength. I can think offhand of no one who has succeeded in doing anything quite like it. *Theft*, again, employs a straight narrative method, but is much swifter and much more intense than *María Concepción*. *Theft* and the last two stories in the book seem to me to be major fiction. I can think of no living American who has written short stories at once so fine in detail, so powerful as units, and so mature and intelligent in outlook, except W. C. Williams; and one can make that exception for but one, I believe, of his compositions, *The Destruction of Tenochtitlan.* Even the Declamations of Mr. Kenneth Burke, if they are to be regarded as fiction, fall short of Miss Porter in firmness of detail and in organic progression.

THE SYMBOLIST INFLUENCE

L'Influence De Symbolisme Francais Sur La Poésie Américaine (de 1910 a 1920) par René Taupin. Docteur es Lettres. Bibliotheque de la Revue de Litterature Comparée, Dirigée par MM.F. Baldensperger et P. Hazard. Librairie Ancienne Honeré Champion. Paris. 1929.

Mr. Taupin's study is of very great value, not only as an account of the French influence on the period of American poetry which he considers, but as a history of that period; as a history, the work is necessarily incomplete, but it is more complete and of greater value in general than Mr. Glenn Hughes's excellent history of the Imagist movement recently published in English.[1] Mr. Taupin, however, is seriously handicapped in several ways, the first of them being in a lack of critical perception. On page 10 he states flatly that the only true poets produced in America during the nineteenth century were Whitman and Poe, and he seems to imply pretty strongly that they were the only literary artists. And if we are to accept literally what he has written on page 108, he believes that poetry was dead in England at the inception of the Imagist movement; and if we are to accept literally the first sentence on page 211, he believes that poetry was dead in English at the inception of the movement. He appar-

From *Hound and Horn,* IV no. 4 (1931), pp. 607-618.
1. *Imagism and the Imagists,* by Glenn Hughes. Stanford University Press.

ently would brush aside as negligible all or most of the following writers: Emily Dickinson, Emerson, Hardy, Bridges, Robinson, and Frost, and perhaps Yeats, T. S. Moore, Hawthorne, Melville, Stephen Crane, and Henry James. This is no indictment whatever of these writers; it is a very serious indictment of Mr. Taupin's judgment. French criticism of American letters and perhaps of English letters as well would seem to be, not only in the case of Mr. Taupin, but in general, at least a quarter of a century behind the times and perhaps more, to exhibit, in short, that same provincialism which which Mr. Taupin deplores in the American literature of the eighties and nineties. Similarly, Mr. Taupin finds the verse of Mr. Pound, H. D., and Miss Moore, unmusicial as compared to that of Swinburne, a fact which tends to discredit many of his judgments from the very outset. The most revealing of his blunders of this kind is a footnote on page 136, referring to Mr. Pound: "Il savait brillamant parler la langue traditionelle:

> I am aweary with the utter and beautiful weariness
> And with the ultimate wisdom and with things terrene,
> I am aweary with your smiles and your laughter,
> And the sun and the winds again
> Reclaim their booty and the heart of me."

But the passage is neither brilliantly executed nor in the least traditional; it is absurdly incompetent apprentice work; it is fortunately not a fair example of Mr. Pound's early writing.

There are certain extremely elusive difficulties that inhere in any such study as this, of which Mr. Taupin seems to be only indifferently aware. What, for example, is an influence, and how do we identify it? When, as in Mr. Taupin's admirable chapters on Mr. Pound, Mr. Eliot, Mr. Fletcher, and Miss Lowell, we find instance after instance of translation, along with the public avowal of influence in critical writings, one can scarcely remain sceptical. But sometimes there appears to be an influence where there is none. Mr. Jules Romains has answered in detail the critics of his early work who traced that work to Whitman; the work has certain general resemblances to Whitman; yet so far as

I know there is not the slightest reason to doubt the honesty and accuracy of Mr. Romains's history of his early poems. It appears to be fairly evident that Poe influenced Baudelaire far less than he was once supposed to have influenced him. Emerson's *Mithridates* and Rimbaud's *Fêtes de la Faim* have the same theme, many images in common, and much similarity in respect to meter and general structure, yet I suspect it might be hard to prove an influence either way. Emerson, long before Mr. Valéry, began exploiting the more or less mathematical concept of the universe, which has provided Mr. Valéry with so many brilliant images, especially in *Le Cimetiere Marin*. Yet considering Mr. Valéry's personal history, one would feel it absurd to suppose that Emerson had influenced Mr. Valéry on that score. Emerson, like the Symbolists, and before them, was experimenting very skillfully and quite deliberately with the great classical line of his tradition (the early or mid-Shakespearian), and endeavoring to reconcile it with certain very personal inventions of his own (see *Days* and *Blight*, for example); like the later Symbolists, he was working with a species of rhymed free verse. I have seen several writers within the last year or so stating that Gerard Hopkins is an important influence in the career of Hart Crane; yet Mr. Crane read Hopkins for the first time somewhere near Christmas 1927, borrowing my copy to do so, and expressing upon returning it the utmost surprise at the nature and extent of Hopkins's stylistic experiments: at that time, Mr. Crane's first book had long been published, and nearly all of *The Bridge* had been written, including *Atlantic*, *The Dance*, *Cutty Sark*, and *The River*. Mr. Crane had quite likely seen quotations from Hopkins here and there, but he gave me to understand that he had never read the book; and to be influenced by Hopkins (not by a misconception of him) one would have to read all of him, poems, and notes, with considerable care. And if Hopkins ever did influence Mr. Crane, the strange thing about the affair is that Mr. Crane nowhere shows a trace of the influence: his meter starts from a strictly iambic movement (Marlowe, and Jonson) and his syntactic disintegration of logic, whereas the apparent syntactic disintegration in Hopkins is the result of a personal system of syntax rigidly adhered to, and nearly every poem rests on a solid logical structure; their philosophies, since Mr. Crane is a mystic of the school of Blake and Whitman, and since Hopkins was a Jesuit priest and despite his tinge of Scotism, are radically different and result in radically different poetic tempers. The metric of Hopkins, on the other hand, does bear a curious resemblance to the systems of Dr. Williams and Miss Moore, but these two poets had formed their systems before Hopkins was published.

To the errors in the preceding paragraph Mr. Taupin nowhere commits himself, but he commits himself to comparable errors. Of Miss Moore he writes: "Il est tres probable que Marianne Moore n'avait lu ni Laforgue ni Rimbaud quand en 1915 elle publia ses premiers poemes, bien que beaucoup aient cru y voir l'influence de ces deux symbolistes; mais c'est encore la langue symboliste que parle sa poésie, et un idiome qui n'est pas eloigné de celui de ces poetes ni même de celui de Mallarmé." Mr. Taupin then quotes in a footnote from a personal letter written by Miss Moore a passage stating that she had not read Laforgue or Rimbaud when she was writing certain verses. This subject forces one into the field of personal letters and reminiscences; Mr. Taupin makes use of them, and I have done so once; I shall have to do so again. From about 1921 until sometime after she became editor of the *Dial* Miss Moore had the patience and the good nature to correspond with me rather regularly. As late as 1923 she expressed to me her ignorance of Laforgue, and a very slight knowledge of Rimbaud and Mallarmé, along with the most active distaste for Apollinaire and for certain American Laforguians (of whom Mr. Eliot was not one). If it is a matter merely of offering personal convictions, and that is all Mr. Taupin has done for Miss Moore, my own conviction is that Laforgue's moral attitude is one profoundly unsympathetic to Miss Moore, and that his style is almost as remote from hers as possible, despite her frequent use of a kind of structure, which I have elsewhere called the double mood, found commonly in Laforgue's work. What then is the proper classification of her work? It would be easy to say that she is Yankee, a spiritual descendant of the New England tradition, whose moral sense has all too frequently become a sense of etiquette, but can we show precisely what we mean by this? One might find a very crude

antecedent in the humorous verse of Holmes and Lowell, a body
of verse that may have served as some kind of background for a
few brilliant poems by that disciple of Blake and the Symbolists,
Mr. S. Foster Damon, notably for his poem *A Family Portrait.*
The sharp observation, especially of small things, animals and
the like, possessing at the same moment an aura of magnificence
and elusive implications of irony, is like nothing whatever in
Symbolist literature and is very like Emily Dickinson. Her gift
for epigrammatic moralizing recalls Miss Dickinson, Emerson,
and Mr. Robinson—the great Yankee tradition, in short. Yet
about 1923 Miss Moore wrote me asking the source of a stanza
which I had quoted without giving the author's name: she did
not know Mr. Robinson well enough to recognize one of the most
striking passages from his best-known book, *The Man Against
the Sky.* She had previously expressed to me her "respect" for
Mr. Robinson, but had expressed no great enthusiasm before the
discovery of that stanza. Now Miss Moore is widely read and an
excellent linguist: facts of this sort merely force one to recognize
that one cannot always trust to a genuinely lettered poet's having read the things that he obviously must have read. The two
modern poets for whom Miss Moore expressed to me, and has, I
believe, expressed publicly, the most profound admiration, are
Hardy and Yeats. It will take a subtle scholar to find their influence in her work. In one of her early poems (*Fear Is Hope*) she
quotes Skelton, a fact which might give us a hint; but if we pay
too much attention to Miss Moore's quotations we may find the
telephone book as an influence. Nevertheless, her earliest lyrics,
which contain the germ, apparently, of her later manner, things
like *To an Intra-Mural Rat,* show a strong resemblance to many
early Elizabethan epigrams, such as Turberville's *Advice to the
Reader* (I thee advise/ If thou be wise/ To keep thy wit/ Though
it be small/ 'Tis hard to get/ And far to fet—/ 'Twas ever yet/
Dear'st ware of all) or Queen Elizabeth's epigram on the Tran-
substantiation (Christ was the Word that spake it/ He took the
bread and brake it/ And what that Work did make it/ So I accept
and take it). The number of such poems is large (one can add to
them a few earlier pieces of similar tone, such as the different
versions of *Earth upon Earth,* and a little of Skelton); they

belong to a body of literature that everyone studies; Miss Moore probably encountered them early. But then what becomes of the Yankee hypothesis? And what of Laforgue? And a few years ago, I had still another disconcerting experience. I happened to encounter a very young writer, Miss Rowena Lockett, who later appeared in a small magazine of which I was an editor, Miss Lockett being at the time about nineteen years old. I was immediately struck, not only by a very feminine fastidiousness in Miss Lockett's work, but also by a strong resemblance to Miss Moore and Miss Dickinson. Yet Miss Lockett at that time had never read the latter and never heard of the former; nor had she ever heard of the French Symbolists. She became familiar with them, and with the Elizabethan epigrammatists, only after her style was formed. If Miss Lockett could write like Miss Moore without having heard of her, Miss Moore could have written like the Elizabethans without having heard of them.

Similarly, toward the end of his book, Mr. Taupin quotes a passage from *The Marriage of Faustus and Helen Part II*, by Hart Crane, and finds in it the style of Rimbaud. Mr. Crane, as Mr. Taupin remarks, does not read French, but he numbers among his friends such men as Allen Tate and Malcolm Cowley, who know Symbolist poetry very well, and he has studied all the available translations. He has the greatest of admiration for Rimbaud, as far as he knows him, and has beyond a doubt tried to learn from him. But how much *can* he learn from him? There have been some very good translations from Rimbaud's prose and a few very bad translations from his verse. The vocabularly of some of Mr. Crane's work suggests somewhat the vocabulary of Rimbaud's prose and of a very little of his verse, in its quality of intellectual violence, of almost perverse energy; but this quality is more Mallarméan than Rimbaldian (most of Rimbaud's lyrics, even when they are presenting a state of hallucination, or what seems such, present it in a style as limpid as the style of Shakespeare's songs or of Blake's), and the quality is not primarily Mallarméan. Mr. Taupin refers to this fragment under its original title *(The Springs of Guilty Song)*, as it appeared first in *Broom*, without Parts I and III, with which it was published later in *Secession* and finally in Mr. Crane's volume, *White*

Buildings. Now, if the style of Part II recals either Rimbaud or Mallarmé, it recalls much more strongly the style of Part I and III; which, in turn, recalls very strongly indeed the style of the passage from Jonson (whose name, incidentally, Mr. Taupin spells with an *h* every time he uses it, whatever lack of familiarity with English poetry that may indicate) which Mr. Crane sets at the head of his poem. The passage comes from *The Alchemist* and is one of the numerous passages in that play in which the central figures make nonsense speeches purporting to contain deep alchemical secrets or to express a feignedly distraught state of mind—this particular passage serves both functions at once. The nonsense is necessary to Jonson's plot: the reader recognizes the necessity and can make no objection; and the reader is forced to accept with unalloyed pleasure whatever elusive but apparently genuine poetic implications there may be in such passages, since he receives these implications absolutely gratis. Jonson would seem, then, to have been wholly aware of the theory of the "poem writing itself," a theory formulated critically by Mallarmé (though not for the first time), and usually regarded as a Mallarméan or neo-Mallarméan innovation. Jonson knew how to control the method satisfactorily when writing in his own name and how to let it run wild in the name of his cozeners. The not quite to be isolated poetic implications in these passages are of great beauty and are very frequent; it is the "oblique method" (Mr. Tate's phrase) of modern poetry in absolutely perfect form. Where, then, did Mr. Crane get the method? And the perhaps Rimbaldian, but certainly somewhat Jonsonian, diction? If my reader is sceptical about the definite consciousness of so irresponsible a method existing among mere Englishmen, let me quote the following passage from Samuel Johnson on Dryden: "Dryden delighted to tread upon the brink of meaning, where light and darkness mingle. . . . This inclination sometimes produced nonsense, which he knew; and sometimes it issued in absurdities, of which perhaps he was not conscious." To illustrate the point, Jonson quotes the following stanza from *Annus Mirabilis:*

> Then we upon our globe's last verge shall go,
> And see the ocean leaning on the sky;

From thence our rolling neighbors we shall know,
  And on the lunar world securely pry.

This might almost pass for an imitation of *Bateau Ivre*. It seems almost certain that Chapman employed the same kind of semi-obscurantism, and rather systematically, perhaps at the instigation of that "affable familiar ghost" (who nightly gulled him with intelligence), of whom he seems to have written so much. Chapman, too, of course, is a man of genius. The reader curious of esoteric theory might consider also Emerson's *Merlin*, the ten lines beginning "He shall not his brain encumber." The words with which Emerson introduces this versified definition, seem, at times, to have been prophetic.

But the matter of influence, with which these remarks began, is not so easily settled. If this method was known to English poets in the past, it was rarely used by them openly; to find it so used one will have, after leaving a few names in the sixteenth and seventeenth centuries, to come down to Poe and Emily Dickinson, in whom at times it seems fairly obvious, and to the Symbolists and those who have written later. Recent examples come to mind by the dozen. Shall we assume that the increase in the popularity of the method is due to Rimbaud? His hallucination was probably in part, at least, of another sort, but he might have moved his admirers to study hallucination of this sort as the only sort available to them. Few of his supposed followers, certainly, get very near the actual quality of his style. Or shall we lay it to Mallarmé? He used the method, but with greater circumspection than Mr. Crane or Mr. Joyce. His logic can almost always be discovered; what seems an evasion of logic into pure obliquity, often turns out to be mere periphrasis. But a careless reading of his work, especially by foreigners, might make him seem about as strange as a poet could be. Are these men the causes of the movement, then, or are they merely exemplars of it, of a tendency, rather widespread, to an increasingly great preoccupation with the fringe of consciousness, to an increasing emphasis on the concept of continuous experience, to identify, under the influence perhaps of scientific or romantic monism, subconscious stimuli and reactions with occult inspiration, and to employ in writing from such attitudes as these interests provide a language previously reserved to the religious mystics? Such a movement would involve along its course such indefinable philosophies as Bergsonism, such semimetaphorical sciences as psycho-analysis, and especially the popular myths and superstitions which they and physical science and biological science have engendered.[2] Our poets, then, whether they are to be classed as effective causes or as mere effects, or as both, of the movement (and Mallarmé and Rimbaud certainly have a considerable causative influence, at the same time that they are probably not the entire causative influence, and in spite of the fact that they both—unlike many of their disciples—held the method under fairly adequate control[3]), our poets, then, are they not writing a little too much as Jonson's alchemists spoke, with a philosophical background insusceptible of definition, but as their own dupes, not to dupe others? Mr. Crane, despite his remarkable genius, and one could say as much of Mr. Joyce as he appears in his latest work, seems to answer Jonson's scoundrels across the centuries in their own language, but like a somnambulist under their control. Is it certain that this trust in the semi-automatic responses of the edge of consciousness results in increased awareness? Or is it merely a dilution of awareness that appears strange because of its very thinness? Man would seem to be man in so far as he is not automatic or seems not to be; the ideal organic automaton is not the poet, but the parrot. Can this method be profitably extended farther than Donne and Jonson were willing to extend it without more being lost than is gained? I doubt the possibility profoundly. And finally can we blame this extension entirely on the French? It would seem to be almost inevitably the result of an era of intellectual uncertainty and charlatanism—inevitably, that is, for a certain percentage of the poets, not for all. We can hardly blame it on the French, though they first practiced the method extensively, despite Mr. Taupin's conviction that we not

---

2. See *Flux and Blur in Contemporary Art,* by John Crowe Ransom. *Sewanee Review.* July 1929.

3. Since Rimbaud did not explain his abdication, one hypothesis is as good as another. Did he perhaps see the necessary conclusion of his method, realized by a few of our contemporaries?

only can but that it is one of their chief claims to glory. For Mr. Taupin assumes that all of Mr. Pound's favorite Symbolists exert a good influence when they exert any influence, and that everything good in American poetry must be the result of French influence. He writes of Mr. Stevens: "La précision stricte des mots et des vers de Rimbaud et des parnassiens français est encore bien adaptée au vers blanc anglais." Shades of Jonson and Milton! He makes this comment, indeed, in connection with a poem with a mildly French subject, but he says nothing of the subject—he is speaking of stylistic qualities. He writes elsewhere: "Grâce à la psychologie moderne, on savait que le symbole, s'il était total, était l'expression la plus directe qui fût." Poets have "known" a great many other strange things in the last thirty years on the same authority. Grâce à la psychologie moderne indeed![4]

This brings us to the last serious objection to Mr. Taupin's treatise, which, indeed, I have already mentioned in passing, his failure to classify and evaluate influences, his basic assumption that American poetry untouched by French influence is bad or negligible and that all of the influences imported by Mr. Pound and Mr. Eliot from France are about equally good. I have said in this essay and elsewhere what I believe to be the dangers of what passes for Rimbaldianism or Mallarméism; I have spoken elsewhere of Laforguianism. When Mr. Taupin makes near the end of his book his already famous remark that American poetry to-day is speaking French, one is moved to wonder—not what Mr. Taupin means, for by this time one is willing to admit the possibility of his meaning almost anything—but what the statement might mean. Mr. Taupin in writing of Mr. Pound admits that Mr. Pound in employing the modern French as models after leaving his earlier models did not change principles but merely changed examples. The order of examples ought then to be reversible. In general, a young writer learns the principles of good

---

4. Direct expression of what? The most direct expression of anything is itself; if a poem can be a more or less direct expression, then, it is an expression of something other than itself, a kind of shorthand. But poetry, though it communicates experience indirectly and incidentally, is, in so far as it is good poetry, a new kind of experience, an expression merely of itself, and such a statement as this becomes nonsense. A correspondent of mine, Mr. J. V. Cunningham, once accused me, unjustly, I believe, of this error.

writing most easily from someone fairly near him in time, who has wrestled with something like his own materials. For a few Americans in Mr. Pound's generation and the next, the Symbolists were the best poets near them in time except for a few English and American poets too mature spiritually, too profoundly a part and masters of the English tradition or of certain aspects of it to be comprehensible to poets at a certain stage of immaturity. Many modern Americans discovered that the Elizabethans might serve as models through Mr. Eliot's attempt to fuse them with Laforgue, or through the attempt of Mr. Stevens to fuse in such a poem as *Le Monocle de Mon Oncle* certain French traits and certain late sixteenth-century traits. No poet speaks another poet's language unless he is a weak poet or the influence is a weakening influence. I believe that the Laforguian influence and the so-called Rimbaldian-Mallarméan influence are subversive and they are the only radical departures from poetic tradition in the Symbolist Movement. To that extent Mr. Taupin may be right, especially when the more easily isolated Laforguian influence is concerned. Even so remarkable a genius as Mr. Stevens was bullied out of a share of his seriousness by the Laforguian temper of one section of his generation. Mr. Taupin has shown that French free verse, influenced the beginnings of Imagist free verse, but seems unaware of the profound differences existing between the two finished products; this, however, is so difficult a subject that I shall have to reserve it for separate treatment.

One of the minor flaws in Mr. Taupin's book is his habit of providing elaborate explanations of some of the more irresponsible and inane utterances of the early Imagist movement, utterances that can be shown to mean anything and that probably meant nothing. He writes, for example, with the utmost gravity: "Ford Madox Hueffer, dans son livre: *Thus to Revisit*, nous renseigne précisément sur ce point. Il parle des trois groupes voisins qui s'appelaient: imagistes, symbolistes et vorticistes: 'Au fond il me semble que le point essentiel de leur sympathie et de leur contact est leur désir de faire sentir au monde leurs propres images, ou bien, disons que le premier point de leur doctrine est que l'artiste doit exprimer par son art sa propre personnalité' et il poursuit ainsi en rapportant une conversation qu'il eut avec Pound et au cours de laquelle celui-ci lui avait dit: 'Ce que le public veut, c'est MOI . . . parce que je ne suis pas un imbécile, comme les membres qui composent le public!' " Then follows a chapter of elaboration. This sort of thing should either be left to accumulate the dust it merits or else it should be given its proper rhythmic setting, a place, say, near the end of the 22nd Canto (Those ain't buttons, them's bobbles).

Mr. Taupin's book is large, and contains a great deal of valuable research to which I have referred only in passing. I have emphasized its weaknesses because they are common to other critics and are likely to be common in the criticism of this particular field within the next few years unless due precautions are taken. The painstaking arrangement of parallel passages in the chapters on Eliot, Pound, Fletcher, and Amy Lowell is extremely enlightening, and very few of the parallels are unconvincing. I myself am especially grateful for the praise that Mr. Taupin gives Dr. Williams, a writer who has seemed to me for ten years or so one of the principal geniuses of our time, and whose work has been stupidly neglected and ridiculed. And yet Mr. Taupin's critical faculties are inadequate to his task; his knowledge of English poetry appears superficial. Were it not for these deficiencies he might have written a final and authoritative work; as it is, he has merely provided a great deal of invaluable material for one.

POETS AND OTHERS

I

Poems 1928-31, by Allen Tate. Charles Schibner's Sons. 1932.

Poetic defects may be considered under two heads, defects of detail and defects of conception. Defects of detail do not extend their influence beyond the passage of phrase affected; defects of conception, like Mr. Jeffers' non-moral narrative procedure, Laforguian irony, the fundamental obscurity of most of Mr. Crane's themes, the graceful elegiac sprawl of the later Eliot and of Mr. MacLeish, are part of the very texture of a poem and affect it pretty evenly. Mr. Tate's defects are, except in a few poems, defects of detail. They are distressingly numerous and even elementary, but one can pick an impressive poet out from among them.

Thus in the *Ode to Fear* Mr. Tate drops two syllables from one line and one from another, relying on long syllables to fill the line. But he is not writing quantitative verse and the attempt to shift into it at will is destructive of whatever convention may previously have been established:

World over, crouched on the air's feet.

From *Hound and Horn,* V no. 4 (1931-1932), pp. 675-686.

The line is supposed to be equivalent to an iambic pentameter line.

Careless run-over lines, with run-over stops at the end of the first foot, the failure to correlate line and content, may all be observed and rather frequently. In the *Ode to the Confederate Dead* one finds this:

> Those midnight restitutions of the blood
> You know—the immitigable pines, the smoky frieze
> Of the sky.

Since one has visualized the sky at the word *frieze*, the words *of the sky* are an anti-climax and are very awkwardly placed. They help break the next line into several units; they are bad meter. The only revision necessary here was their omission.

The metrical emphasis too often receives little or no attention. One of the sonnets closes on the line:

> But gentle death, who is confusion's king.

The words *who is* are superfluous; if used at all, they should be unstressed; but they are used and stressed heavily.

There is frequently a ludicrous failure to fulfill a pretentious beginning:

> Our elder brother whom I had not seen
> These twenty years until you brought him back
> From the cyclonic West where he had been
> Stormed by the shaking furies in the track
> We know so well, which is these arteries—

After the first five and a half lines we are expecting the revelation of some dark family tragedy, something known to the family group in question and to them only, but we suddenly find ourselves standing in the public garden; nor do we get any further information about the shaking furies and the cyclonic West.

Here is another passage from the *Ode to the Confederate Dead:*

We shall say only, the leaves whispering
In the improbable mists of nightfall
That flies on multiple wing:
Night is the beginning and the end,
And in between the ends of distraction
Waits mute speculation, the patient curse
That stones the eyes, or like the jaguar leaps
For his own image in a jungle pool, his victim.

Except for the last two lines, this is one of the most moving passages I know; the last two lines seem to me hopelessly bad. To have a curse stone the eyes is a strain on the mind's eye, and to transform the curse into a jaguar and then to make the jaguar perform in a manner so impossibly unfeline is worse. The lines fail, however, not only because of the mixed figure, but because the act of stoning and the act of the jaguar are not perceived poetically—they are simply mentioned because of some vague feeling the poet has associated with them. Even Mr. Eliot's sleek Brazilian jaguar, verging on doggerel as he does, has more poetic identity.

As I have said, few of the poems display vices of conception. One might mention the *Ode to Fear*, which rests on an initial assumption of violent feeling nowhere clarified or communicated: the poem is a fog of meaningless excitement. The neo-Websterian meter of *Causerie*, similarly, establishes vagueness of feeling as its norm. I mean that the movement of the verse is of necessity slipshod, an uneasy compromise between the lyrical and the didactic that simply cannot speak with precision. This compromise is inherent in the very conception of the poem.

Nearly always the blunders are specific and are limited in their influence. This is an important fact: there are so many blunders that Mr. Tate is frequently regarded as inferior to Mr. MacLeish, let us say, or Mr. Eliot, since they commit fewer blunders of detail, and since their defects of conception correspond to the popular sentimentalities of the moment. Mr. Tate's blunders are sufficiently irritating and even bewildering, but to throw him out because of them is like throwing Shakespeare out for irregular spelling.

Mr. Tate is usually trying for something unimpeachably adult, for unqualifiedly major poetry. One may safely say that except for Mr. Stevens at a few rare moments, no poet of the generation preceding Mr. Tate, and except for Mr. Howard Baker, no poet of his own generation, has aimed at anything comparably serious. The quality of Dr. Williams is superb, but the range is limited; Mr. Pound and Mr. Crane are ambitious, but their inspiration is a trifle suspect.

Mr. Tate's range is religious, philosophical, moral, social, and personal, and in each of its aspects is mature and astute, and in its wholeness is coherent. He is the most mature poet to appear in America since Mr. Robinson, and despite his clumsiness he writes better than Mr. Robinson. Mr. Robinson is often satisfied with neat doggerel; Mr. Tate is always willing to flounder like a gentleman.

It is this deadly seriousness in most of Mr. Tate's work that often gives even his worst poems moments of greater power than nearly any other contemporary work. His *Sonnets of the Blood* are the most abominable written series of sonnets this side of Barnabe Barnes, yet out of them one can pick lines with the grandeur and perfection of the greatest tragic poetry:

> This message hastens, lest we both go down
> Scattered with no character to death. . . .

> I ask you therefore will it end tonight. . . .

> In Shenandoah and along Bull Run
> Sunk in a time inimical to date. . . .

More than any poet since Hardy, Mr. Tate has felt the country in which he lives, not only the country, but the people, whether dead or living; his poems are heavy with history:

> Unkempt the fathers waste in solitude
> Under the hills of clay. . . .

> It seemed the grandfather of his mother

In knee-breeches silver-buckled like a song
His hair long and a cocked hat on his head
A straight back and slow dignity for stride,
The road, red clay sun-cracked and baked
Led fearlessly through scrub pines on each side.

On this feeling for place and for the past, Mr. Tate can build his *Mother and Son*, dealing with the decadence of his tradition, a great tragic poem in spite of its defects; he can build his *Ode to the Confederate Dead*, which I venture to suspect is one of the greatest odes in the language. The more personal poems on wholly religious or philosophical themes, are enriched by this background. *The Last Days of Alice*, in fact, is a lyric by a man who finds himself at last torn out of his background and existing in a quantitative and humanly meaningless society, of which the political expression is Mr. Hoover or Mr. Coolidge, of which the social expression is Mr. Henry Ford, and of which the moral expression and the literary ideal are Mr. Jeffers or Mr. Cabell. Mr. Tate's essay in the symposium *I'll Take My Stand* provides a fair gloss to the poem if the reader needs one.

The Last Days of Alice (along with a few other poems by Mr. Tate) is remarkable historically in a way that needs to be mentioned: it is ironical, but the irony is not of the post-Byronic or Laforguian sort, that is, it is not directed at the author by himself for trying to define untenable values. It is directed at Alice, the symbol of modernity, and it is directed from Mr. Tate's own point of view, in which he feels himself secure. There has been no comparably adult use of irony in several generations.

Since I have objected to Mr. Tate's blank verse, I had better offer a warning in connection with his rhymed verse. All of his verse has been heavily influenced by Websterian rhythms, but in the best of his rhymed poems he succeeds in refining those rhythms and making a very firm and sensitive instrument from them. In the passage which I have quoted from the *Ode to the Confederate Dead*, the passage ending with the jaguar, the rhythm wavers toward prose, but the wavering is controlled and very expressive. *Emblems I*, as beautiful a poem in its way as Mr. Tate has ever written, illustrates the same quality.

Finally, I do not wish to leave the impression that Mr. Tate's poetry is entirely a matter of fragments to be salvaged from a general mass of wreckage. There is a reasonable number of poems in which the flaws are negligible, or from which they are absent: in his first book *The Subway* and *Ditty* at the least; in this book *The Cross, The Twelve, The Eagle, Last Days of Alice, Emblems I* and *III*, and *Records I* and *II*, if no more. These, and the imperfect but magnificent *Mother and Son* and *Ode to the Confederate Dead*, probably mark the highest level to which twentieth century poetry has attained.

II

The Poems of Wilfred Owen. A New Edition Including Many Pieces now First Published, and Notices of His Life and Work by Edmund Blunden. New York. The Viking Press, 1931.

Wilfred Owen was killed in action at the age of 25, a few days before the beginning of the armistice. He learned to write poetry in the trenches and on leave, and what he might have done in calmer times is a matter for speculation only. The war, though it probably matured him rapidly in many ways, must have made careful composition next to impossible. The present edition of his poems, for example, gives in the notes the first version of *The Unreturning*, the final version of which appears in the main body of the book. The final version is devoid of character; the first version, though rough, has force. How much good poetry was revised away under the stress and in distraction, how much may not have received the completion of which Owen was capable, there is no way of knowing. If he is judged on the work he left, he is not, I fear, as Mr. Blunden claims he is, another Keats. He is a very imperfect poet. But I have lived with his poems for more than ten years, and I venture the opinion that he is a poet of more than ordinary durability and interest.

The most successful poems are *The Show, The Send-off, Greater Love,* and *Apologia pro Poemate Meo. Strange Meeting,* often cited as his best work, is very even in texture, but, for me, rather evenly vague. Some of the best poetry is to be found scattered through the less successful poems: *S.I.W.*, *Mental Cases*, *A Terre*, and a few others. The writing, even in the best pieces, is never wholly adequate; the feeling is always a little muffled by an even distribution of slightly weak diction and insensitive rhythm; it reads like the powerful but not quite satisfactory translation of greater poetry. Yet the conviction behind the lines is intense and is in some way communicated; when all the faults have been checked over, there remains a large fund of very real power in the poetry. This is from *Mental Cases:*

> These are men whose minds the Dead have ravished.
> Memory fingers in their hair of murders,
> Multitudinous murders they once witnessed . . .
> Therefore still their eyeballs shrink tormented
> Back into their brains, because on their sense
> Sunlight seems a blood-smear; night comes blood-black;
> Dawn breaks open like a wound that bleeds afresh
> —Thus their heads wear this hilarious, hideous
> Awful falseness of set-smiling corpses.
> —Thus their hands are plucking at each other;
> Picking at the rope-knouts of their scourging. . . .

The next passage is from *A Terre:*

> O Life, Life, let me breathe,—a dug-out rat!
> Not worse than ours the existences rats lead—
> Nosing along at night down one safe rut,
> They find a shell-proof home before they rot.
> Dead men may envy living mites in cheese,
> Or good germs even. Microbes have their joys,
> And subdivide, and never come to death.

Passages like these are fragments, nothing more. Were the entire poems from which they are taken as good, they would still be fragments. Yet they have a toughness, a casual but not uncalculated violence, that reminds one of some of the better passages in the secondary and lesser Elizabethan dramatists. The rhetorical sophistication of these passages is slight beside that of men like Marston and Dekker, and there is no attempt here to imitate such writers, but there is some generic similarity in the mode of apprehension. Yet this kind of rhetoric requires a drama back of it, to sustain it and justify it: just as we tend to imagine the play that Dekker should have written when we come to a great passage, we are forced here to reconstruct the drama in which these lines were spoken, which Owen took for granted as a part of his environment, but which for us has fallen away, the War. Without the reconstruction, such passages are melodramatic and incomplete, but if we are willing to value the passages as fine fragments, the reconstruction is possible. Owen did not live long enough to objectify and write his drama; he might never have comprehended it adequately. But these declamations from the living maelstrom are probably the most impressive records of it that we have, and simply as poetry their value is considerable.

The next to the last line of *The Send-Off* is marred in this edition by an alteration. "Still village wells" has become "village wells." The adjective is necessary, and if Owen ever had it there in any of his versions, it ought to be left.

This edition contains notes on Owen by Edmund Blunden and Frank Nicholson, as well as extensive quotations from Owen's letters from the front. The letters are detailed and moving. Owen, like Sassoon and others in their group, hoped that his writings might reduce the possibility of future wars, but in all likelihood his reputation will rest wholly on his poetry as poetry. Our governing criminals and the slack mass of their victims will probably never hear of him.

III

The Signature of Pain, and Other Poems, by Alan Porter. The John Day Company. 1931.

Thrust at the Sky, and Other Poems, by MacKnight Black. Simon and Schuster. 1932.

The Dark Land, by Kathleen Tankersley Young. The Dragon Press.

Thurso's Landing, and Other Poems, by Robinson Jeffers. Liveright, Inc. 1932.

Mortal Triumph, and Other Poems, by Selden Rodman. Farrar and Rhinehart. 1932.
Now That the Hawthorne Blossoms, and Other Poems, by Althea Bass. Bruce Humphries, Inc. Boston. 1931.
The Flowering Stone, by George Dillon. The Viking Press. 1931.

Mr. Alan Porter is by far the best poet in this group. He has endeavored in much of his work to acquire something of the style of the 17th century, but has imitated it from without, with small evidence of comprehending the sensibility that produced it. To this extent he is "literary" rather than traditional. Most of his work, however, is graceful, and a good half of it is readable. The best poems in the book are *The Signature of Pain,* a tricky and shallow but amusing exercise in early 17th century blank verse, *The Shining of Peace* and *The Window,* two excellent lyrics in a discreetly 17th century idiom, and two others, probably the best in the book, which quite frankly display a post-Symbolist method and sensibility, *Museum* and *When from the Alien Multitude.* The Symbolist sensibility is not much like the Metaphysical, and is for the most part far inferior to it, but it is Mr. Porter's own sensibility; through it, he touches whatever reality he is equipped to recognize. Building upon it, he is very likely to get somewhere. The last two poems are very fine in their way:

> The day was empty. Very pale with dust,
> A chalk road set its finger at the moors.
> The drab, damp air so blanketed the town
> Never an oak swung leather leaf. The chimneys
> Pushed up their pillars at the loose-hung sky;
> And through the haze, along the ragstone houses,
> Red lichens dulled to a rotten-apple brown.
>
> .   .   .   .   .
>
> Suddenly, turning a byeway corner, a cripple,
> Bloodless with age, lumbered along the road.
> The motes of dust whirled at his iron-shod crutches
> And quickly settled. A dog whined. The old

Cripple looked round and, seeing no man, gave
A quick, small, piping chuckle, swung a pace,
And stopped to look about and laugh again.
"That," said a girl in a flat voice, "is God."
Her mother made no answer: she remembered,
"I knew an old, lame beggar who went mad."
He lumbered along the road and turned a corner;
His tapping faded and the day was death.

There is something irreducibly obscure about the intention of this passage, but the firmness and richness of the presentation are remarkable. The best work in the book is worth keeping and rereading. The book opens with an amusing barrage of commendatory verses by Mr. Porter's friends, most of them charmingly bad and hence excellent of their kind.

Miss Young's second book of verse displays exactly the same virtues and limitations as her first. The limitations are those of the entire contemporary school of writing which depends wholly upon mood—usually the dream-convention—as a principle of coherence. The logical content of words is not utilized to any great extent; their fringe of feeling becomes almost their entire source of meaning. This means that only a small fraction of their value is brought into play and that more words must be used to get anything said—the method makes for diffusion and is usually ruinous to small talents.

Miss Young's talent is a small one, but it is definitely a talent and has survived the ordeal in so far as the ordeal can be survived by any talent. She is wholly aware of the kind and measure of diffusion which her method necessitates and has adjusted her style very skillfully. Her perceptions are of tenuous, yet of indubitable, interest; her meter—a free verse that is almost a nervous prose—is exactly related to the quality of her perceptions. Her poems are always thin, but are always alive. Mr. MacLeish and Mr. Eliot are somewhere in her background, and, though she is slighter than either one of them at his best, she is definitely more skillful than either within her narrower range and she displays no trace of their sickly self-pity—her work has an admirably clean impersonality which is rare in work of its kind. She is one of the two or three writers under forty who display any knowledge whatsoever of free verse.

I might excuse myself from quoting her work on the grounds that she has frequently appeared in the *Hound and Horn;* actually there is a better reason, that to feel the quality of her work one really needs to read a book of it. She interests me, but I do not approve of what she is doing: one book of this sort is enough—there is no possibility of variety in such work, one poem melting into the next in the memory as one reads. She has a talent of about the order of Turbervile, but instead of concentrating it into a few ponderable and durable epigrams she has spun it out into a fine cobweb which is visible only when the light is right.

MacKnight Black's *Thrust at the Sky* is a narrative poem of moderate length, which he had not yet completed at his death. It deals with an architect's love for a young woman and of his giving her up to a rival in order to obtain the commission for a skyscraper which he has been longing to design. The subject is dangerous but is not uninteresting; it could very easily be sentimentalized beyond endurance, or it might possibly be given a good deal of power. Black's treatment is simply meaningless. He sees his people and they see each other only as fragmentary perceptions, planes, edges, clouds, of light and dark. There is no feeling for the plot whatever, no clue to the real thoughts or feelings of the characters. Black's free verse is too loose to be really sensitive to the kind of perception that most occupied him; it is as if one should try to translate Verlaine into Whitmanian cadences. The shorter poems in the book show the same insensitivity.

In the spring of 1930 I published in *Poetry* a review of Mr. Jeffers' *Dear Judas*, in which I summarized the chief weaknesses of his narrative poetry. The same weaknesses persist in *Thurso's Landing*, though in a milder form. The doctrinaire hysteria of the earlier narratives is seldom to be found here. There is an attempt at some sort of coherent narrative, but the result is merely dogged and soggy melodrama. Mr. Jeffers' verse continues to miss the virtues of prose and verse alike: it is capable neither of the fullness and modulation of fine prose nor of the concentration and modulation of fine verse. There is an endless, violent monotony of movement, wholly uninteresting and insensitive, that may have a hypnotic effect upon a good many readers, much as does the jolting of a railroad coach over a bad roadbed:

> After twenty miles he turned
> The carburetor-connection, slyly regarding
> His seat-mate, she fogged with misery observed nothing.
> The engine went lame. "What's the matter?" he said, turning
> The carburetor-connection. . . .

And again:

> Against the black horror of death
> All living miseries looked sweet; in a moment of aimless
> Wild anguish she was unable not to cry out. . . .

For brute clumsiness and emptiness such writing can hardly be equalled, and the second passage is a mosaic of stereotypes. Both passages are typical. The book is composed almost wholly of trash.

Mr. Rodman is gently adventurous in his technique, and has done a good deal of experimenting with a kind of shuffling accentual meter which may stem back through free verse to Hopkins. It is loose, however, and its movements never have definite significance. Mr. Rodman feels his material readily and with no particular distinction. Althea Bass is laborious and honest, but uninspired. Mr. Dillon is feeble and saccharine, and, in some way hard to define, unwholesome.

IV
A Postscript

A chronicle of this sort usually passes, I suppose, as an indication of the good verse available; a moment's reflection will show that it is really nothing of the sort. If the reader has stayed with me all the way to this postscript, it is because he has some vague curiosity about my opinion. Yet these books were sent me by Mr.

Kirstein, who, I imagine, selected rather well from what he had; and they were selected for Mr. Kirstein by a number of publishers' readers, for the most part of no enormous abilities, and of names unknown to me. Six of the books I have reviewed were not worth printing, if considered as poetry. Mr. Jeffers justifies himself to his publishers by selling; it is possible that Mr. Dillon does likewise. But most books of poetry are published in the interests of art; the publishers really try to do the right thing.

They make a bad mess of it. Mr. Grant H. Code is now in his thirties; he is one of the most distinguished poets living. Yet he has never published a book and he has published little otherwise. I quote one of his poems, obscurely published several years ago, entitled *Division*.

> Our severed thoughts crowd to accuse, despise;
> We step apart as if on tiptoe, hate
> Rapidly in great strides; yet, starlike, rise
> Even in winter when the sun has set.
>
> As multitudes of lamps that push their knives
> Into the dark become less keen at morn
> We melt our spiteful individual lives
> In one cool grey complacency of scorn.
>
> Our heavy separate spirits feed and sleep
> Indoors, until a gradual spring sets free
> New-living noisy flesh that step by step
> Draws near this wall, yet does not care to see,
>
> When acres of bright newborn land are spread
> With rapid mortal crocus lifting quickly,
> Slowly to fall disordered and afraid,
> The dark sun-shadows spread and circle quickly.

Mr. Howard Baker, younger and a less varied metrist than Mr. Code, is in some respects a sounder poet, though he has never written a finer poem than the one I have just quoted. Despite his having recently published one of the three or four most distinguished novels of the last ten or twelve years (*Orange Valley:* Coward McCann, 1931) he remains, if anything, a more obscure figure than Mr. Code. He possesses in his best moments and to a very high degree most of the virtues that I recently attributed in these pages to Robert Bridges. Though not invariably a flawless stylist, he is one of the few securely classical talents in America. His best work is unpublished, and I am not at liberty to quote it, but I offer a sonnet published some years ago as obscurely as was the poem by Mr. Code:

> When I think that sometime I'll look on you
> As I am looking now, and that those same
> Dark lids will then be darker, and the blue
> Eyes must stay hidden when I call your name;
> Your curious lips now quick to draw my flame—
> Then sealed with a change I can't construe;
> The sigh of sleep, your aura, is my fame—
> Then sightless sleep untouchéd by my rue;
> There are no terms to measure what I face:
> A clear wall infinite in height and depth,
> A level sea of cold unwordly breadth.
> What savage runes are potent in this place?
> What lover's kiss? O Death, your glassy sea
> No firmer than her image is to me.

This restraint, intellectual competence, and intense quiet are not accidents in Mr. Baker and Mr. Code. They are ideals sought and understood (a very different matter) by at least a few of the younger writers. I quote from a recent issue of *The Commonweal* a poem as complete and unimpeachable in its way as the two above, by Mr. J. V. Cunningham. It is called *Retreating Friendship:*

> Our testament had read:
> Affection is secure,
> It is not forced or led.
> No longer sure

Of hallowed certainty,
I have erased the mind:
As mendicants who see
Mimic the blind.

If these three poets could be published in some kind of bulk and given circulation, contemporary literature would be a great deal richer, and the cause of the contemporary intelligence would be notably strengthened. First-rate verse *is* being written here and there, in spite of what one sees in print.

TRADITIONAL MASTERY

The Shorter Poems of Robert Bridges. Enlarged Edition. Oxford University Press.

This latest edition of the lyrics of Dr. Bridges represents a selection, sanctioned by himself before his death, and not a complete edition. It omits *Prometheus, Demeter, Eros and Psyche,* and *The Growth of Love,* which were contained in the *Poetical Works* (Oxford, 1914) and contains a very restricted and, but for the omission of the epigram, *Who goes there,* a wholly satisfactory selection from two small volumes published subsequently to the *Poetical Works.* It contains the first fifteen only of the Later Poems (*Poetical Works*), omitting the *Odes.* The omissions represent no serious loss, I suspect, barring the epigram I have already mentioned and a few of the sonnets from *The Growth of Love,* especially number fifty-one, which described so beautifully the poetical quality that Dr. Bridges was to realize in his greatest work:

> O my uncared for songs, what are ye worth,
> That in my secret book with so much care
> I write you, this one here and that one there,
> Marking the time and order of your birth?

From *Hound and Horn*, V no. 2 (1932), pp. 321-327.

How, with a fancy so unkind to mirth,
A sense so hard, a style so worn and bare,
Look ye for any welcome anywhere
From any shelf or heart-home on the earth?

Dr. Bridges' meters have been so often and so fruitlessly discussed that I shall omit entirely to analyze them, though his importance as a subtle and learned renovator of English meters is sufficiently great. It is my belief that he has been long enough patronized as a sugar-coated pill for those who wish to brush up on their metrics, as a minor manipulator of outworn graces, and that he should be recognized once and for all as the sole English rival of Hardy in nineteenth-century poetry, as, in all likelihood, considering his formal versatility, the range of his feeling, and the purity of his diction, a diction so free from any trace of personal idiosyncrasy that a successful imitator of it could never be detected as an imitator but would appear only as that most unlikely of phenomena, a rival, that he should, I say, in all likelihood be recognized as the most valuable model of poetic style to appear since Dryden.

Since Dr. Bridges has never been popular, especially in America, I shall risk a very roughly classified list of the poems on which I base my opinion, all of them to be found in the present collection. Short lyrics, first level: *Wherefore tonight so full of care, The birds that sing on autumn eves, Love not too much, The north wind came up, Why hast thou nothing, The south wind strengthens to a gale, As our car rustled swiftly, How should I be to love unjust, Beautiful must be the mountains, Whither O splendid ship.* Short lyrics, second level: *Clear and gentle stream, The wood is bare, Poor withered rose, O bold majestic downs, Again with pleasant green, Behold! the radiant spring, Perfect little body, My bed and pillow are cold, The hill-pines were sighing, April advance in play, The sea keeps not the Sabbath day, Will love again awake.* Longer lyrics at a slow tempo, first level: *Sad sombre place, Joy, sweetest life-born joy, How well my eyes remember the dim path;* second level: *Voyaging northwards.* There are in addition two fine epigrams in this volume, *Mazing around my mind,* and *Askest thou of these graves;* there are several fine occasional sonnets, at least two of which, *Beloved of all to whom that Muse is dear,* and *Folk alien to the Muse,* would cast no discredit on Milton; there are two admirable didacic poems of some length, *Thou art a poet, Robbie Burns,* and *Je donnerais pour revivre a vingt ans,* of which the second deserves a place very nearly at its author's first level of achievement; and there is a formal ode, *Assemble all ye maidens,* no whit inferior, I suspect, to Dryden's Ode on the death of Mistress Anne Killigrew.

Dr. Bridges possessed much more curiosity about the possibilities of various forms than has been shown by most of our modern experimenters. Mr. Pound, Dr. Williams, and Miss Moore, for example, have all worked in a straight line, as if impelled by some more or less fanatical dogma, toward a certain form or tempo, and, having once perfected it, have become slaves to it. Miss Moore, indeed, seems to have exhausted the possibilities of her style and to have abandoned writing; even Mr. Stevens writes, or at least publishes, less and less; and Mr. Pound appears to have entered upon "the old age of a watery realist," indulging in looser and looser repetitions of cadences and mannerisms in Canto after Canto. In fact, some of his recent Cantos are scarcely more coherent than his correspondence. Dr. Bridges seems to have been fully aware that a change of tempo involves a complete or nearly complete change in the range of feeling perceived, that it opens up, in other words, a fresh field of subject matter; if one follows his career step by step one finds him taking up one tempo after another, exhausting its possibilities (for himself) and dropping each, once he has thoroughly mastered it and before it has mastered him.

The longer and slower lyrics should be approached only after the shorter have been studied, since in the shorter pieces the diction is more concentrated, less consciously toned down, and the quality of the style is more immediately apparent. I quote three stanzas from a fairly early poem entitled *Dejection:*

> Wherefore tonight so full of care,
> My soul, revolving hopeless strife,

> Pointing at hindrance, and the bare
> Painful escapes of fitful life?
>
> Shaping the doom that may befall
> By precedent of terror past:
> By love dishonoured, and the call
> Of friendship slighted at the last?
>
> By treasured names, the little store
> That memory out of wreck could save
> Of loving hearts that gone before
> Call their old comrade to the grave?

Compare the above lines to the following, from one of the latest lyrics, *Low Barometer:*

> The south-wind strengthens to a gale,
> Across the moon the clouds fly fast,
> The house is smitten as with a flail,
> The chimney shudders to the blast.
>
> On such a night, when air has loosed
> Its guardian grasp on blood and brain,
> Old terrors then of god or ghost
> Creep from their caves to life again. . . .
>
> Unbodied presences, the packed
> Pollution and remorse of Time,
> Slipp'd from oblivion, reenact
> The horrors of unhoused crime.

The quality of language over the gap of time is constant. In restraint, economy, richness of feeling, in what I should call an extreme generality or universality of import accomplished with no loss in the specification of the perception, these poems and a few others in the volume will stand the most scrutinizing comparison, I believe, with any of Shakespeare's sonnets. No living poet is capable of such masterly writing, and the number of poets dead is very small.

In his longer and more meditative lyrics, Dr. Bridges achieved a poetry, the norm of which is scarcely more intense than the norm of distinguished prose, but which, thanks to the quality of its diction, syntax and cadence, never falls short of extreme distinction, and which rises at need and without shock from distinction to extraordinary beauty. Poetry of this sort is not inferior to poetry of the shorter and more lyrical sort, though it may be harder to appreciate and is certainly less popular at the present time. It can handle material impossible in the more specialized lyric: what it loses in concentration, it can regain in subtlety of detail, completeness of description, range of material, and structural elaboration. In *The Summer House on the Mound (How well my eyes remember)* Dr. Bridges employed the heroic couplet, the form that traditionally seems to lend itself most readily to discursive writing and wide ranges of feeling within a given composition. The poem describes in retrospect the summer house from which the writer as a child was accustomed to watch passing ships at a distance, through a telescope. The house, the mound, and the distant sea are described quietly and precisely; then comes the close-up view of the docks through the telescope:

> There many an hour I have sat to watch; nay, now
> The brazen disk is cold against my brow,
> And in my sight a circle of the sea
> Enlarged to swiftness, where the salt waves flee,
> And ships in stately motion pass so near
> That what I see is speaking to my ear:
> I hear the waves dash and the tackle strain,
> The canvas flap, the rattle of the chain
> That runs out through the hawse, the clank of the winch
> Winding the rusty cable inch by inch,
> Till half I wonder if they have no care,
> Those sailors, that my glass is brought to bear
> On all their doings, if I vex them not
> On every petty task of their rough lot
> Prying and spying, searching every craft
> From painted truck to gunnel, fore and aft,—

> Thro' idle Sundays as I have watched them lean
> Long hours upon the rail, or neath its screen
> Prone on the deck to lie outstretched at length,
> Sunk in renewal of their wearied strength.

There follows a description of sailing ships, then a description of the first steam dreadnoughts, one of the most magnificent descriptive passages with which I am acquainted and a passage which, despite its grandeur, does not detach itself from its context:

> One noon in March upon that anchoring ground
> Came Napier's fleet unto the Baltic bound:
> Cloudless the sky and calm and blue the sea,
> As round Saint Margaret's cliff mysteriously,
> Those murderous queens walking in Sabbath sleep
> Glided in line upon the windless deep.

Then came an enumeration of some of the ships, a few intimate details of the poet's family and the old age of the Duke of Wellington, and the half-literary, half colloquial, and superbly handled conclusion:

> But now 'tis other wars and other men;—
> The year the Napier sail'd, my years were ten—
> Yea, and new homes and loves my heart hath found:
> A priest has there usurped the ivied mound,
> The bell that called to horse calls now to prayers,
> And silent nuns tread the familiar stairs,
> Within the peach-clad walls that old outlaw,
> The Roman wolf, scratches with privy paw.

The poem, despite its discursiveness, is flawless in detail and in structure; despite its hovering near the verge of prose, it is never prosy; and despite the wide range of feeling treated, there are no rhetorical gaps. It is a vision of the rising Victorian empire, all the more moving for its immediate familiarity, for its being a vision from a summer house within sight of the Duke of Wellington's castle. This poem alone was sufficient justification of Dr. Bridge's Laureateship.

In *Elegy among the Tombs (Sad sombre place)* and *Joy, sweetest life-born joy* a longer stanza is employed at a comparably slow tempo, the material being dictated by a somewhat more logical intention. To quote from these poems is even more unfair than to quote from the preceding one; so much depends on the structure, musical and logical, of the entire piece. Lines that may seem insignificant in a quoted fragment, take on significance in relation to the whole, take on a significance of a sort that can be established only by the greatest stylists, in fact, since it depends upon the subtlest and most minutely controlled of stylistic relationships. These poems, like so many others by their author, may even appear insignificant when read complete for the first or even the fifth time, only to become profoundly moving on the fifteenth or twentieth. Most readers, unfortunately, are nearly always ready to judge as dull that which surpasses them in technical knowledge or in human wisdom to any very great extent; what is not understood seems bad. And Dr. Bridges so far surpasses nearly any of his readers in these respects, is so utterly free of any impure attraction, any undisciplined "personality," that his genius has been ignored more unjustly than that of any other writer since Landor.

In the last two poems mentioned, in *Dejection*, and in a good many others, one encounters an attitude that may seem at first glance mere Victorian optimism, and which in a very few pieces *(Fortunatus Nimium*, for example) comes near to verging on Victorian optimism, but which is, in reality, something far more sombre and intelligent, a more or less classical resignation, with frequently, as in the professedly optimistic close of *Dejection* and *Elegy among the Tombs*, an undercurrent of calm and carefully restrained bitterness.

Dr. Bridges has been so often and so angrily compared to his friend Gerard Hopkins that I may perhaps be pardoned for a word on this subject. Hopkins seems to me to have been a truly great poet, though I cannot carry my enthusiasm as far as do his most violent admirers. The qualities that have won Hopkins almost immediate recognition during the past few years are, I fear, the very reasons for his limitations and his definite inferiority to Bridges. The mere fact that a man is a radical technical innovator does not render him a greater poet than the man who is less an innovator; extreme originality of method almost always involves extreme departure from the norm of experience, involves specialization and limitation of feeling. The greatest technical experimenter in English literature is, I suppose, Milton, and he is muscle-bound by his magnificence and the intricacy of his syntax. When he is not grand, he is grandiloquent; there is no transition between the two in Miltonic blank verse; and he killed English blank verse for two centuries. So with Hopkins: he can express with his violent rhythms an extremely special kind of excitement arising from religious experience, but he can express little else, and even the religious experience is incomplete, for if he does not deal wholly with the resultant excitement, he certainly throws his emphasis very heavily upon it. We are told, for instance, in superbly impassioned verses that the mind has mountains, but the nature of those mountains is never wholly clear. In Bridges the nature of the mountains is absolutely clear —that is, the experience is rendered whole—and the terror of the mountains is not isolated from all other experience but is seen in firm proportion. There is in the metrical experimentation in the present volume of Bridges quite as much originality of thought as in the experiments of Hopkins, coupled with a much more thorough knowledge of English meters and the complexities of feeling involved in their history. Bridges' technique, if the less obviously original of the two, is the more sensitive and the more widely applicable instrument of perception. In saying this, I do not wish it to be thought, let me repeat, that I am blind to the sensitivity or the power of Hopkins, a poet, who moves me very deeply.

This limiting effect of the elaborately original may be one reason for the extreme shortness of so many of the most brilliant of contemporary careers: a narrow vein of feeling only can be explored, and once it is finished, the author has got himself so far from a fresh starting point that he lacks either the courage or the vigor to do anything about it; he has systematically deadened himself through specialization. If there is any truth in this supposition, extreme originality of style would appear to be one of the shortest cuts to that condition of atrophy, from which its most fanatical devotees seek, by its means, to escape. On the other hand, traditionalism is not equivalent to dullness; the diction of Dr. Bridges is as fresh and living as that of Dr. Williams; his meters allow him greater freedom, or rather greater range; he is in general a more civilized man. It is to be hoped for the sake of twentieth-century poetry, that he will receive the study which his own poetry merits.

THE OBJECTIVISTS

An "Objectivists" Anthology. Edited by Louis Zukofsky. To (Le Beausset, Var, France and New York).

This anthology is of clinical rather than of literary interest. Its chief literary virtue resides in its reprinting from obscure sources several of the best poems of Dr. W. C. Williams, though one of his best poems (*Full Moon,* from the *Dial*) is ruined by being cut in half. It contains also Mr. Eliot's *Marina,* a loosely written affair with several charming lines, and some facile twaddle by Mr. Pound. The other contributors are Basil Bunting, Mary Butts, Frances Fletcher, Robert McAlmon, George Oppen, Carl Rakosi, Kenneth Rexroth, Charles Reznikoff, R. B. N. Warriston, and Louis Zukofsky.

Mr. Zukofsky's preface is so badly written that it is next to impossible to disentangle more than a few intelligible remarks. I offer two isolated examples of the style: "A poet finds the continuously present analysis of his work preferable to criticism so-called." And: "Tho perhaps gratifying to the poet whose poem is under observation—this prose, with all its poetic direction and impetus, should, to the critic himself with his merely poetically charged mentality, seem secondary even tertiary and less, i.e. compared with that act which is a poem, not, of course, compared

From *Hound and Horn,* VI no. 1 (1932-1933), pp. 158-160.

with 'critical' backsidebeforeness." Let these sentences be my apology if I misrepresent their author. They are selected at random. The context throws no light on them.

There seem to be in the preface two principles that can stand as principles, independent of personal taste. Both are quoted from Mr. Pound, and they contradict each other: (1) "Emotion is the organizer of poetic form." And (2) "Words . . . are organic, they interpenetrate and tangle with life, you cannot detach them as pieces of an anatomical figure." The objection to these two statements is that the contributors to this volume interpret the second in terms of the first: they are unaware that the rational intelligence should (and in this modern age of chaos, etc., still can) play as great a part as emotion in the organization of poetic form, that it plays, or should play, a greater part than emotion in human life. This unawareness results in a narrow limitation of subject matter in the work of so fine a stylist as Dr. Williams: half or more of an intelligent man's experience is unintelligible to him and is ruled out of his poetry, and when he meets it in the poetry of other writers he regards it as affectation, as a literary hangover. In Mr. Pound's best work the same unawareness leads to the aimless progression, the endless expansion, of a shifting mood. In most of Mr. Eliot it leads to a kind of psychic impressionism. Mr. Eliot, unlike the other contributors to this collection, has one of the finest minds extant, but the intellect practically never provides any part of the structure of his poems—he moves from the feeling attendant upon one thought to the feeling attendant upon another as the feeling alone demands, and he achieves no more coherence than Mr. Pound achieves while wandering through history in some of his second-best *Cantos*. Mr. Eliot, despite his critical writing, remains as typical a poet of his own generation as Mr. Pound or Miss Moore.

The younger contributors to the anthology display the weakness of their elders, without their virtues of style. Mr. Rexroth, the best of a bad lot, employs a method of construction similar to that which I have just described in connection with Mr. Eliot, but his thought is less original and appears ill-digested. The others are sensory impressionists of the usual sort, and know nothing of writing.

The rest of Mr. Zukofsky's preface appears to be an awkward struggle to define the principles of good taste. As far as I can follow him, I agree with him, but that does not mean that I shall like the same poems. Mr. Zukofsky does not say what he means by "particulars," nor does it occur to him that every poet writes with an "objective," that any critic finds the attainment of an objective in any poem he admires. This kind of chatter is mere childishness. It is even less coherent than the criticism of Mr. Pound or Dr. Williams. One is left merely with the possibility that Zukofsky may have good taste. I have quoted from his prose. Let me quote a few lines from his poetry:

> The reason we're not further along (But this is a swell sun,
>   brother comrade,)
> Ask Faust aquaplaning, Go-ethe, his spiritual (whew)!
>   MacFadden,
> (Hu!) he-er vent Hel-ee-na squat from our Sidewalks . . .

The passage illustrates the quality of Mr Zukofsky's irony, rhythm, and carefully modulated phrasing, in short, of his general objectivism. It exemplifies the taste which has brought the present collection together.

It is curious commentary on recent editing that Mr. Zukofsky has filled more space in the four or five leading British and American literary journals than almost any other writer of his generation. It is symptomatic of the intellectual bankruptcy of the middle generation that Mr. Pound will actively back such a man, that Mr. Eliot, Dr. Williams and Miss Moore have been willing to put up with him. The book, however, is encouraging in one respect: none of the talented writers of Mr. Zukofsky's generation are included, and the theories that Mr. Zukofsky struggles hopelessly to express, the methods of composition that he and his friends have debauched till they no longer deserve even ridicule, seem to be sinking rapidly to lower and lower literary levels; they should be in a few more years no serious cause of consternation.

T. STURGE MOORE

The Poems of T. Sturge Moore, Volumes I and II. MacMillan Co.

These two volumes contain little more than half the poetry of their author; a third volume has been announced, and I imagine that a fourth will be necessary. Yet since Mr. Moore appears to have taken great pains to destroy all traces of the order of composition, these volumes present a fair cross-section of his work and provide a good basis for an estimate of his importance. These two volumes contain poetry, I believe, that has been equalled by not more than two or three living writers, and more great poetry than any living writer has composed.

In my opinion Mr. Moore is a greater poet than Mr. Yeats. He has lived obscurely, and has not displayed Mr. Yeats's talent for self-dramatization; for these reasons and others he has never become a public figure or a popular writer. Mr. Yeats began as a rather bad poet of a kind exactly suited to the popular taste of his decade, and through some miracle of destiny retained his following when he became serious, whereas Mr. Moore has been a master, of a kind, from the outset. Mr. Yeats, as a dramatist of his own personality, writes with an histrionic tone seldom entirely justified by his ideas and perceptions but which beguiles many

From *Hound and Horn*, VI no. 3 (1933), pp. 534-545.

readers: it is a similar tone (but superimposed on extremely bad poetry) which accounts for the popularity of Mr. Jeffers. Mr. Moore, on the other hand, is never his own dupe, and has received the neglect that is commonly the lot of a perfectly lucid mind.

Most interesting of all the reasons for this difference in reputation, however, are the relationships in which the two poets stand to the generation of poets which succeeded them, the generation of Pound, Eliot, Stevens, Williams, Miss Moore, and Miss Loy, and of which Hart Crane, a much younger writer, was probably the last important disciple and, so far as the crucial defects of the generation are concerned, perhaps the most illuminating example. The generation bore the same relationship to the Romantic poets which the French Symbolists bore: that is, they endeavored to correct the stylistic defects of looseness and turgidity tolerated by the Romantics, without understanding the conceptual confusion which had debauched Romantic style and Romantic character alike. The result has been a poetry superior to most Romantic poetry, but, by virtue of is superiority, rendering the Romantic deficiencies even more plain than they appeared in the Romantics. That is, the looseness of Whitman's form is more clearly demonstrated in Pound's *Cantos* than in Whitman; the confusion of Whitman's ideas is more clearly demonstrated in *The Bridge*, by Hart Crane, than in Whitman; because Pound and Crane write precisely enough in detail to point directly to those issues with which they cannot deal precisely. All cats are gray in the dark, and everything is gray in Whitman.

The fundamental post-Romantic defect is the abandonment of logic, either in favor of an undisguised form of what Mr. Kenneth Burke calls "qualitative progression" (that is, progression governed wholly by mood), as in the *Cantos*, or as in *Anna Livia Plurabelle*, or in favor of a pseudo-logic, such as one finds discreetly distributed (amid much real logic) throughout Mr. Eliots' *Gerontion*, in most of Crane, and frequently at crucial moments in poems by Mr. Yeats. The abandonment of logic is a defect for two reasons: it eliminates a half of human experience, and so limits the poet's range and often falsifies his feeling; and it is an uneconomical use of words, half only of the power of the words being brought into play. These types of non-logical writing represent the ultimate boundary of the uncritical emotionalism of the Romantics: they represent the stylistic *definition* of that emotionalism, its ultimate formal equivalent, to which the Romantics seldom attained, an emotionalism which is frequently merely sensationalism, and which is largely unmotivated (that is, unformulable.)[1]

This will be clearer if we consider a few individual poets for a moment. Mr. Pound, in his *Cantos*, can treat of an unlimited variety of subjects, but is forced to deal with them all at the same level, the level of fragmentary and wandering (though highly stylized) gossip: his poetic instrument simply does not admit of a searching examination of his material; he reminds one inescapably of an old woman hanging (in a very extraordinary manner) on the back fence. Mr. Yeats, in *The Gift of Harun al Rashid*, amid the superb rhetoric of the close, allows his aged scholar to praise his young wife in moral and aesthetic terms for her effectiveness as a kind of supernatural telephone instrument, and the confusion cannot be glossed over, I believe, in spite of Mr. Yeats's desperate efforts to make such glossing appear possible. Mr. Pound abandons the appearance of coherence; Mr. Yeats achieves a factitious coherence. The danger inherent in Mr. Yeats's poem is more evident in *The Dance*, by Hart Crane, where the language and feeling traditionally associated with love and the conviction of immortality appear to be applied to the experience of personal annihilation, so that the logical meaning of nearly every

1. Mallarmé, writing in the forward to René Ghil's *Traité du Verbé* as if his generation had discovered for the first time the fact that words have a feeling content as well as a rational, could speak of the necessity of separating "le double état de la parole, brut ou immédiate ici, la essentiel." The strange thing about this phrase, of course, is the last word, which is unexplained, a bit of arbitrary sentimentalism, with funest consequences. If feeling content is essential in relation to rational content, the latter is inessential and should be eliminated. Thus Dr. W. C. Williams (in *The Symposium* for Jan. 1933, pp. 115-16) writes of Messrs. Zukofsky, Rexroth, and Rakosi: "There is nothing here that *seductively* takes us up—as a man might carry a child. Nor is reason used to *cudgel the mind into unwilling submission*." The italics are mine. If reason in poetry is corruption, then the abandonment of it is salvation; post-Romantic talents approximate the state of beatitude in various measures. If, however, the denotative value of a word is impaired, the connotative value is dependent largely upon denotations in previous contexts; the composition becomes proportionately parasitic and "literary." And if the denotative value could be wholly destroyed, the connotative would go with it. This is one of the many obvious facts that our greatest minds display a devastating ability to ignore.

term at the crux of the poem is wholly at odds with the feelings implied. This seems to me a serious matter and probably has some relationship, at least, to the manner of Crane's end.

In this poetic pseudo-logic the forms of logic (that is a definite and fairly elaborate syntactic structure) may be employed with nonsense deliberately in view. This appears to be true of Crane's *Faustus and Helen I and III*, the style of which was probably modeled on the style of the nonsense passages in *The Alchemists*. It is curious that a man of Crane's talents should have set out to model his poetic character, not on Jonson, but on two scoundrels and obscurantists whom Jonson satirizes. As a matter of fact, however, it is almost equally curious, that Mr. Eliot and subsequent neo-Websterians should have allowed themselves to be so profoundly influenced by that ambiguous and unconvinced villain, Bosola, who, of all Webster's characters, is the most inflated and evasive in his metrics and his feelings alike, the most profoundly "Websterian" of them, in what appears to be the recent sense of the term. Such attempts to create for oneself a poetic character after models given by older masters, not of The Poetic Character, but of dishonesty and villainy, are bound to result in confusion: the modern experimenters have been neither dishonest nor villains, and their tortuous efforts to raise the conventions adopted to the level of universal morality, have been an interesting but also a distressing spectacle. A poetic convention has a life of its own, and limits of its own: the election of a poetic convention involves perils of no mean order.

Romantic and post-Romantic irony, from Byron, through Gautier, Laforgue, Eliot, Stevens, and others, to Kenneth Burke, represents an awareness that something is wrong, along with an inability to adjust feeling to motive. The Romantic ironist endeavors to save his face socially by ridiculing his irresponsible feelings, but he seldom makes an effort to understand and control his feelings. Mr. Burke[2] defends the practice in the interests of skepticism: really it is an instance of blind faith of at least two kinds, for Mr. Burke believes his own inability to perceive accu-

---

2. *Counterstatement,* a volume of criticism by Kenneth Burke. Harcourt Brace and Co. 1931.

rately to be universal in our period, and he places his faith in an automatic counterpoise. His entire doctrine of balanced excesses is an extension of the ironic formula, and it has all of the perfection, the triviality, the futility of canned food or machine-sliced bread. It eliminates the need of judgment: the hero of Mr. Burke's novel, *Toward a Better Life,* goes mad for the reason that, the need of judgment having been removed by his (and Mr. Burke's) theories, the power of judgment atrophies; and Mr. Burke continues to preach the doctrine which brought him to this end. Few post-Romantics have proceeded beyond this criticism of Romantic feeling, a feeling which falls considerably short of comprehension.[3]

The defect which gives rise to Romantic irony, the intellectual confusion which causes a greater or less measure of meaningless

---

3. These criticisms are greatly generalized and do not apply equally to every member of the Middle, or Experimental, Generation of American writers. Eliot's early work, and Pound's *Mauberly,* illustrate both defects, that of Romantic irony most plainly; Pound writes a lugubrious lament for the passing of Pre-Raphaelitism, yet deliberately makes Pre-Raphaelitism (and himself) appear ludicrous. The result is a kind of slipslop elegance: the firmness of the secure ironist (see Churchill's *Dedication to Warburton*) is impossible. Stevens displays neither vice in some poems, and has written great poetry: his tendency to self-parody, which cheapens *The Comedian as the Letter C* and many lesser poems is a form of Romantic irony. The basis for Stevens' self-distrust is not evident in his best work, and the feeling is probably inherited from earlier poets who had better reason for it; one feels justified in suggesting that it may at least have contributed to his present sterility. Miss Moore makes a great show of rationality when her rational content is relatively small: She says "the future of time is determined by the power of volition" when she means "volition determines the future." Bosola and his followers are guilty of a similar inflation of syntax. In Miss Moore, this style is often ironic, but it defeats its purposes in a measure, since the instrument of irony (the poetry) is weakened in the interests of irony; except in this respect, Miss Moore's irony is traditional, and not post-Romantic as she satirizes not herself, but her neighbors from a secure point of view. She is crippled by the narrowness of her point of view, however, being a satirist not of morals, but of manners, and in a very narrow sense. Williams limits his matter to that which can be treated by direct sensory perception and treated fully thus; he so preserves texture where Pound and Miss Moore sacrifice it, but limits his range. His best work has remarkable power in spite of these limitations: *On the road to the contagious Hospital, Love in a Truck* (the sea elephant), *The Widow's Lament,* and *The Bull* show him at his best. Mina Loy displays both defects and sometimes avoids both, as in the *Apology of Genius* and *The Widow's Jazz,* which displays both vices at their most obvious and most tawdry. The entire generation is so shot through with one or the other of these defects, and appears to be so thoroughly contented with them, that one cannot but feel that the moments of freedom are accidental.

feeling, Mr. Yeats shares with the entire generation subsequent to him. His irreducible obscurities, his moments of inexplicable excitement, have appeared to be kinds of profundity. The lucidity of Mr. Moore, on the other hand, is unappreciated by writers laboring in confusion: much of what he says is beyond the range of his readers, and so appears to confuse or dilute his poems; his wisdom, which is traditional, appears banal to those nourished on the unformulable; and the precision with which he renders his feelings appears mild to those nourished on over-statement. When, in the *Criterion* for July 1930, he revised and greatly improved two of the most confused poems of Gerard M. Hopkins, he aroused a great rumbling of indignation among the younger intellectual leaders. The occurrence is symptomatic of the entire condition of contemporary taste.

Mr. J. V. Cunningham, in the *Commonweal* for July 27, 1932, describes Mr. Moore's favorite theme as that "spiritual pride which would over-reach natural limits . . . the effort to violate human relationships by imposing one's identity on others," together with the criticism of such spiritual pride. Mr. Cunningham cites the excellent poem *On Four Poplars* as an instance of the subject-matter, and many other poems could be cited. The theme, however, is not limited to the ethical sphere in Mr. Moore, but has its religious counterpart, in a mysticism related to that of such diverse poets as Hart Crane and Robinson Jeffers, which leads to the attempt to violate our relationship with God, or with whatever myth we put in his place, even with Nothingness,[4] and which leads concurrently to the minimizing of moral distinctions, that is, of the careful perception of strictly human experience. Mr. Moore differs from the Romantic mystics in defining this temptation without succumbing; in defining not only the temptation, but its legitimate uses, and its dangers. His repeated poems on the subject of Silence, and his repeated references to Semele, are indications of his interest in the subject. His great lyric *To Silence* (not included in the first two volumes of the new edition) may be taken as an allegorical summary of this theme

4. For further elucidation of contemporary ideas (or attitudes) of mysticism and inspiration, see Mr. H. B. Parkes on Emerson, the *Hound and Horn* for the Summer of 1932.

and of his own relationship to Romantic tradition, the tradition of rejuvenation through immersion in sensation, the mystical communion of the Romantic, or, as Mr. Tate puts it, in pure quality. Mr. Moore's immersion has actually led to rejuvenation, to an inexhaustibly fascinating freshness of perception: the immersion of other poets has too often led to disintegration.

I shall endeavor to illustrate Mr. Moore's style by quotation, with no immediate reference to the subject matter which I have been describing. In the poem entitled *From Titan's Bacchanal*, his blank verse appears at its best, together with an astonishing command of the resources of reiteration (a command more subtle, more controlled, though less immediately obvious, than that of Mr. Pound in his *Cantos*) and with a sensuous richness and a profundity of feeling scarcely if any inferior to those of Keats's *Ode on a Grecian Urn:*

> Beside her foot three shadowed blue flowers glow,
> Speedwell, or gentian, or some now lost gem
> That then was found in Crete; some gem now lost,
> Some precious flower, that then endeared the isles
> To hearts of traveling gods and sailor princes.
> Though friends of such an one here revel now,
> And laugh, carouse, and dance, she hears them not;
> Brown satyrs, maenads, men, these sing; and hark!
> Birds sing, the sea is sighing, and the woods
> Do sound as lovers love to hear them:—Sleep,
> Sleep, oh! and wake no more; Bacchus has kissed
> Thy lips, thine eyes, thy brow; thy joy and his
> But lately were as one, therefore sleep on:
> Be all past woes forgotten in thy dream!
> This noisy crew still haunts thee;—but unheard
> They sing, and birds are singing! thou dost sleep . . .

Perhaps the greatest single poem in which he describes the magnificence of inanimate Nature and approximates the attitude of the Romantic pantheist is the double sonnet, *Apuleius Meditates*. I quote the first half:

An old tale tells of Gorgo's gaze distilled
Horror to petrify men's mobile limbs:
Endymion's moonlit beauty never dims,
Hard-frozen as the fond chaste goddess willed:
Niobe, by her ceaseless weeping chilled,
Drips, a white rock: and when stone Memnon hymns
The dawn, camped travelers whom the desert rims
Rises from the sand they slept on and are thrilled.
I, having wandered through the pines alone,
And felt their hush up from dark ages roll
Like last faint echoes of a lion's roar,
Or storm that ripples out on a smooth shore,
Quaffing their vivid silence with my soul
Have longed to change me then and there to stone.

The attitude, however, is not that of the Romantic pantheist, for
Mr. Moore merely defines a splendor which appears greater than
his own, and does not confuse two irreconcilable states of being.
The poem is marred by the crowded consonants in the first four
lines, and the awkward run-over from six to seven, but in spite
of these defects is very powerful. In the double sonnet, *Silence*,
the same theme is skirted by way of more human material; the
poem, though disclaiming morality, displays, with precise and
lucid wit, careful moral perception:

No word, no lie, can cross a carven lip;
No thought is quick behind a chiseled brow;
Speech is the cruel flaw in comradeship,
Whose self-bemusing ease daunts like a blow
Though unintended, irrevocable!
For wound, a mere quip dealt, no salve is found
Though poet be bled dry of words to tell
Why it was pointed! how it captured sound!
Charmed by mere phrases, we first glean their sense
When we behold our Helen streaming tears.
Give me dry eyes whose gaze but looks intense!
The dimpled lobes of unreceptive ears!
A statue not a heart! Silence so kind,

It answers love with beauty cleansed of mind.

Each line in the poem is a masterpiece in itself; the poem is a perfectly coherent commentary. The fifth line, in which the sentence runs over into the new quatrain and stops, with the momentary illusion of an unrhymed line and the attendant feeling of bemused regret, is illustrative of the sensitivity with which the medium is handled. I shall beg indulgence for one more quotation from the lyrics, to exhibit Mr. Moore's command of another theme and of a song movement. I quote the second stanza from *Love's First Communion:*

> '——Listen, ponder, understand!
> Love lies ambushed in each bud
> Like a lady's maiden hand
> Stowed in warm and scented glove;
> And as through her veins the blood
> Circling sweetens, so flows love
> Like ripe syrup through a fruit,
> Secret tingling rich and mute,—
> Like, ah! like on midnight hush
> Tears that under eyelids gush.'

These quotations do not exhaust Mr. Moore's range, either of material or of technique. He is never trivial, or an actively bad poet, and he is seldom uninteresting. A list of his poems which move me unmistakably would include, I imagine, three-fourths of his titles. I shall therefore call particular attention to a few poems only, in addition to those already mentioned, and shall then pass on from the lyrics. I should like to mention the following poems: *To Slow Music, The Vigil, Reason Enough, An Aged Beauty's Prayer, The Deeper Desire*, the sonnets on Sappho and perhaps the sequence entitled *The Deed*.

As a dramatist, Mr. Moore is one of the most important figures in an extremely important dramatic period. Synge is widely popular, and the dramas of Mr. Yeats are widely read. Synge is largely disappointing, however, for the reason that, like most prose-poets and some other poets, he dilutes his perception with a vast excess of mannerism: the verse and prose of writers so varied in talents and aims as Carl Sandburg, Ezra Pound, Marianne Moore, and Elizabeth Madox Roberts, suffer rather seriously from the same vice. Only one of Mr. Yeats's plays, *The Only Jealousy of Emer*, rises far above sentimentality of conception and triviality of execution, but that one play is a great work of its kind. The dramas of Mr. Moore and of Robert Bridges have never to my knowledge been taken very seriously, yet it seems to me beyond all question that Bridges' two plays on *Nero* are the greatest tragedy since *The Cenci* and (if we except that furious and appalling composition, *Samson Agonistes*, which, though a tragedy, is no play) are quite possibly superior to any English tragedy outside of Shakespeare, that his *Christian Captives* is nearly as fine, and that his *Achilles in Scyros* is a performance nearly as lovely as Comus, though doubtless less profound. The nearest rival to Bridges since Shelley, I believe, is Mr. Moore.

Bridges was probably he most finished and original master of blank verse since Milton: the principles of his blank verse are available in his study of Milton's prosody. Mr. Moore's blank verse is sometimes as brilliant, but is less consistent—it appears the product of inspiration rather than mastery—and Mr. Moore has in a smaller measure than Bridges the gift which Bridges possesses in a greater measure than almost any dramatic poet since Shakespeare, and which Mr. Yeats possesses scarcely at all, the gift of utilizing every movement in his blank verse, even in the most casual remark, as a means of exposing the full character of his speaker and the full import of the situation.

Bridges possesses, in fact, a grasp of character, even in its minor aspects, unusual even among the English dramatists, whose leisurely procedure and extended and widely varied scenes have always tended to encourage such a grasp of character in a way in which the more rigidly classical forms have never ecouraged it. Mr. Moore's greatest and only truly dramatic play, *Diamonassa* (not reprinted in these two volumes) is unlike Bridges in that it is a one-act tragedy, which observes the unities rigidly, and which is concerned less with the full perception of character than with the rapid simplification and generalization of a situation: it is Racinian rather than Shakespearean. It is one of the greatest plays of its kind that I know.

The Only Jealously of Emer aims at the same kind of excellence as *Daimonassa*, but achieves it in a more fragmentary way: the variety of meters indulged in by Mr. Yeats does not permit of the careful variations and graduations of feeling possible within a single meter, and the effort to maintain a lyrical intensity throughout the play results in some pretty thin lyricism, especially in the opening, that portion of a drama which is normally informative and at a relatively low level of feeling. Further, in a short play, at least, the use of a chorus probably detracts from dramatic effectiveness for this reason: poetic drama, given a good plot and a great stylist (and *Emer* has both), deals essentially with the awareness on the part of the tragic character of the universality of his plight, an awareness becoming more intense as the plight becomes more evident, and which may become explicit but which is more frequently implicit in the quality of the feeling. Now if the statement is taken from the mouth of the actor and turned into a subsidiary lyric, the actor himself (and he embodies whatever is dramatic in the drama) is rendered less self-conscious, and the awareness that might lead to further action is given, not to an actor, but to an observer. Mr. Moore's *Aphrodite against Artemis* suffers from the same defect, the struggle between Phaedra and Hippolytus being largely transmuted into allegorical and lyrical argument between the goddesses.

Most of Mr. Moore's plays are less dramatic than spectacular: they are pageants with appropriate chorals. The action does not develop continuously through the lines: rather, the lines are more or less lyrical commentary on isolated scenes which illustrate a progress. Such a structure, though it is legitimate, is less powerful than the truly dramatic, for the poetry tends to be casual rather than cumulative. There are few strikingly poetic lines in the dialogue of *Emer*, but each has the entire weight of the past action behind it, the entire weight of the future action implicit within it. Such also is the power of *Daimonassa;* such is the power of Racine. Much of the best poetry of *Aphrodite against Artemis*, however, might be as relevant to a good many actions

as to the action in which it finds itself. This tendency is sometimes strong in Mr. Moore's plays and sometimes very week. Except in *Daimonassa* it is usually discernable. The most striking
of these half-dramatic pageants is *Absalom*, a very great poem of
its kind, at times one of the most powerful of Mr. Moore's compositions. The following passage is typical of the poetry with
which the piece abounds. It is spoken by David when he despairs
of overcoming his son, and is without desire to overcome him:

> O Policy, O Cunning,
> Have I then treated with thee for thy love
> As with a little child, e'en smiled on Cunning?
> Took I a step beyond these times in hope?
> Have I learned from my poor ill-builded past
> As from a tower-top, and leaned too far,
> Fain of the arms of angels passing on
> Winged for a later time and better men? . . .

This, I believe, is great writing. In its half-eerie feeling, which it
inherits perhaps in part from the Symbolist movement, its feeling
of the unreality of reality, and in the precision of its meaning in
its own context, which Symbolist poetry too often lacks, and in
its profound moral vision, its sense of the seriousness of reality,
it is typical of Mr. Moore's genius.

It is worth observing before leaving the plays that Mr. Moore
has usually chosen Greek or Hebrew themes, which have weath-
ered much narration and have acquired strong outlines and definite implications, which are a part of the main current of occi-
dental tradition, whereas Mr. Yeats, in pursuit of the elusive
ghost, national feeling, has chosen most of his subjects from the
formless and sentimental myths of Celtic tradition, myths very
few of which can be altered from their original condition of irrele-
vance and obscurity.

Mr. Moore's naratives are less successful than his plays. In
Judas he succumbs to the stream-of-consciousnes procedure: his
immersion in sensation results in temporary disintegration. There
is no sequence of events; there are few ideas. There is much excellent writing, and some beautiful writing (as in the last forty-five

lines), but there is no structure. The thoughts of Judas merely wander for one hundred and twenty pages. Every new thought, every new incident, is a new beginning; the poem does not accumulate meaning as does a well-constructed narrative, but is merely an intolerably long and confused lyric dealing with a disordered mood, and is essentially meaningless. *Danae*, though it contains much that is lovely, is too deliberately naive, a bit pseudo-Keatsian, and Mr. Moore writes heroic couplets as if he were ashamed of them and wished they were anything else: his line is crowded, both with sound and with imagery, and neither the couplet nor the line is sufficiently defined by the syntax for the essential powers of the couplet to be brought into full play. Some of the shorter and less ambitious narratives have extraordinary polish and charm, however, among the loveliest being *Isaac and Rebekah* and *Two of the Lord's Anointed*.

In the background of the American and British poetry of the last two decades—the poetry of the Modern Movement—there are four great figures, exerting little influence, but offering us a better means of evaluating our immediate past than is to be found in the immediate past itself, could our criticism catch up with them and elucidate them: Thomas Hardy, a colossally great folk-poet, confused as to philosophy, but guided by a folk-wisdom so profound that his philosophy does no harm to most of his lyrics; Robert Bridges, a scholar and a classical master, immune to the disintegrating influence of Romanticism; W. B. Yeats, an unregenerate Romantic; and T. S. Moore, a regenerate Romantic. Mr. Yeats is widely admired but little understood; Mr. Hardy is slowly gathering a following. The other two are little read and are understood scarcely at all. It is time that we became acquainted with them. Mr. Moore, placed as I have said, between two Post-Romantic periods, that of French Symbolism and the English-Irish decadent school on the one hand, and, on the other hand, the American Experimental School of the two decades past, has been misunderstood in the latter period in proportion as he has transcended the limitations of the former, since the principles governing the two periods are for the most part similar. The handicap under which he has suffered is the measure of his immediate value to us: he has more to teach us of our present literary difficulties than has any other writer of our century.

AGNES LEE

Agnes Lee Freer died on July 23rd of this year, in Chicago. She had been a lifelong friend of Harriet Monroe, and most of her poems, since 1912, had appeared in *Poetry*. She had published five volumes, not counting translations, of which the last two, *Faces and Open Doors*, and *New Lyrics and a Few Old Ones*, both published by R .F. Seymour in 1922 and 1930, contain, I imagine, everything of any great value. She had translated *The Gates of Childhood*, by Fernand Gregh, and a large portion of the verse of Théophile Gautier.

The translation from Gregh I have not seen. The Gautier is not successful, but the task of translating Gautier must resemble that which a foreigner would encounter in rendering Herrick: it is really hopeless. The translations, however, are symptomatic of a life-long immersion in French literature, especially Parnassian and Symbolist, which began, I should judge, in her childhood, when she was being educated abroad. One of her finest poems, *A Statue in a Garden*, is purely Parnassian; it is the best piece of Parnassian poetry in English and is equaled by only a few specimens of the school in French. There is an unyielding grandeur in the poem, which is not in Heredia even at his best, much less in Verlaine or Samain. This quality is characteristic of all her best work, and sets her off sharply from all the women

From *Poetry,* LIV no. 7 (1939), pp. 335-338.

poets of our time whether good or bad. It is not that her work was unfeminine, but that it was impersonal and absolute. She was a great lady, and would have been at home in the court of Louis XIV. Among women poets, she reminds me most nearly of Mme. Deshoulieres, who was, however, the lesser poet; among American writers, regardless of medium, her spiritual quality seems to me closest to that of Mrs. Wharton.

She was not in the usual sense an intellectual poet, and I believe had small critical understanding of philosophy or of history. Her critical understanding of poetry, including her own, seems to me to have been weakened by this limitation. She belonged to a literary period and society of which she did not wholly approve, and which she did not understand well enough wholly to escape, and she often tried, it would seem as a matter of duty, to experiment with subjects and methods which were foreign to her. Her power was a power of personal character united to an extraordinary grasp of certain poetic conventions. When the character, the convention, and the subject were happily met, the result was magnificent; when unhappily, the result was a loss of control almost complete. As a result, one need know nothing of her unsuccessful work, which is experimental and almost casual, in order to understand her best. She is the author of a handful of separate but beautiful poems, an anthology poet, essentially, but one of the finest. No American poet of her generation except Robinson is comparable to her.

Her three finest poems, so far as I am concerned, are *A Statue in a Garden, Her Going,* and *Black Flowers and White.* Equally perfect, but smaller in subject, are *The Sweeper, The Ilex Tree,* and *Convention.* There are a few other poems, a trifle less successful in execution, but none the less very beautiful, which should be included in any final selection of her work: *Brief Return, At Dawn, In an Old Homestead,* and *A Meditation.* And such a selection should include a few of her poems of modern life, which, though slightly melodramatic, are hard and clear: *On the Jail Steps, Hospital Doors, In the Morgue,* and especially *Mrs. Malooly.*

My own admiration of Mrs. Freer's poetry is of more than twenty years duration. For nearly as long, she has been a regular correspondent with myself and my wife, and by that means one of our best friends. I saw her only twice, on my last two visits to Chicago, a good many years ago: at that time she appeared past middle age, but one of the most beautiful women I had ever seen. The loss of her friendship I shall feel deeply, the more so as it was first offered me when I was young, with no literary friends beyond two or three of my own age and state of ignorance, and when I was forced by ill-health and various other circumstances to live in a desert country, remote from books and much of the time from anything approaching civilized society.

POETRY OF FEELING

The Complete Collected Poems of William Carlos Williams, 1906-1938. New Directions.

W. C. Williams, in his view of life and of poetry, is an uncompromising romantic. He believes in the surrender to feeling and to instinct as the only way to wisdom and to art: *The Trees* is one of his many explicit statements of this notion. He believes that art is the product of a character which is "automatically first-rate" (*Blues* for May, 1929). Such a character would have, of course, no need for ideas and no awareness of them; indeed, one may ask whether he would display any consciousness whatever. In any event, Dr. Williams distrusts all ideas and seeks value as far as may be in the concrete: in the poem called *Paterson* he reiterates the phrase "no ideas but in things." And he distrusts the entire range of feeling which is immediately motivated by ideas, for he is in no position to distinguish good ideas from bad, and hence, in this realm, sound feelings from false. In *A Poem for Norman McLeod*, he writes: "The revolution/ is accomplished/ noble has been/ changed to no bull." Any feeling arising from the contemplation of an idea, whether moral, metaphysical, or religious, appears to him merely sentimental: this is a defect, but he at least displays the virtue of his defect and

From *Kenyon Review,* I no 1 (1939), pp. 104-107.

almost wholly eschews the realm of experience which he does not understand, so that his poetry, though in certain ways limited, is at its best not confused or sentimental. He distrusts traditional form, as a kind of restraint or inhibition: since he fails to grasp its significance, it appears to him another mechanical sentimentalism; and he desires that the theme create its own form. But in this desire he has in part fallen short of his ambition, for his own excellent ear has made of free verse a complex accentual meter, very difficult to control, and creating very binding conventions of feeling.

His poetry therefore concentrates on the concrete; the only ideas which it occasionally expresses are those which I have outlined, and since the ideas are bad, the poetry is best when Dr. Williams follows his favorite formula and eschews ideas altogether. At its simplest, it resembles nearly all of his prose: that is, it offers merely sharp impressions of objects observed, either in isolation, or in accidental sequence, or forced by a purely rhetorical violence, as in *Romance Moderne*, into a formal and emotional unit. In such a case as this last—and there are many such —the form, or emotion, which enacts the violence is unmotivated, and the whole effect, in spite of much brilliant detail, is one of excited overstatement. Some of the simplest, and purely isolated, descriptive notes are among the best; as for example, many of those in the sequence called *January Morning*; and occasionally, as in *Complaint*, by virtue, perhaps, of some metrical or otherwise rhetorical miracle, one will take on inexplicable power. Dr. Williams' belief in this kind of thing no doubt accounts for his own high opinion of the poem about the red wheelbarrow in the rain, as compared to his other and often more valuable poems. Often his confidence in the intrinsic value of the physical object results in a poem composed of perfectly unrelated items, a passage of crystalline chaos, amusing but empty, as in the sixth poem of *Descent of Winter*. He has not been without doubts in this connection, however; in *This Florida: 1924*, he writes: "And we thought to escape rime/ by imitation of the senseless/ unarrangement of wild things—/ the stupidest rime of all."

His theory, however seems to permit his dealing with certain richer material; that is, with some of the simpler events of human relationship, chiefly love, seen primarily as something deeply desired but which passes. The best of these poems is probably *The Widow's Lament in Springtime*, a poem both rich and somber, and one of the most moving compositions of our time. There are many others, nearly as fine, among them *The Bull, A Coronal, Arrival, Portrait of a Lady, The Hunter, The Lonely Street, To Mark Anthony in Heaven, To Waken an Old Lady,* and *Waiting.* In spite of the simplicity of theme, when the poems are viewed in bare outline, the sensuous and emotional awareness is extremely rich and is perfectly controlled; in style, the poems are masterly.

Here and there something else occurs that is even more impressive. His romantic view of nature and of art results in his experimenting with symbols of elemental forces and instincts. When, as in *The Trees*, he passes an explicit judgment on these symbols in relationship to the intellectual values which he misapprehends and derides, the result is sentimental and essentially unsatisfactory. When, however, he represents the force in isolation, defining merely the power and the terror, he is perfectly sound and defensible; on at least three occasions, he has succeeded brilliantly with such symbols: in *Spring and All*, No. I ("By the road to the contagious hospital") and No. XXVI ("The crowd at the ball game"), and in *The Sea-Elephant*. In these poems the violence of the theme supports even his most rapid and muscular rhetoric, and he raises the metrics of free verse and poetry in free verse to the highest level at which they may be found. No other poet using free verse is even comparable to him on these occasions.

The romantic principles which have governed Dr. Williams' work have limited his scope in the ways which I have mentioned. The combination of purity and of richly human feeling to be found in his language at times reminds one of Hardy or of Bridges, and in beauty of execution he is their equal, though in so different a mode; but his understanding is narrower than theirs, and his best poems are less great. On the other hand, when poems are so nearly unexceptionable in their execution, one regards the question of scope regretfully: Herrick is less great than Shakespeare, but he is probably as fine, and, God willing, should last as long. If I may venture, like Arnold, to make a prediction, it is this: that Williams will prove as nearly inde-structible as Herrick; that the end of the present century will see him securely established, along with Stevens, as one of the two best poets of his generation. He is handicapped at present by the fact that the critical appreciation of free verse has not got beyond the long and somewhat obvious rhythms of Pound and of the less expert Eliot, so that Williams' artistry goes all but un-perceived with most readers.

The present collection contains 313 pages and nearly all of Williams' poems. There are no regrettable omissions that I can discover; there are few omissions of any kind. There are no poems butchered by hasty revision at the last minute, and a few that were so butchered in previous volumes have been repaired. The book is essentially complete and definitive, and it brings the author's work down to date. It is thus indispensable to anyone seriously concerned with American poetry. In regard to physical appearance, the book is beautifully and durably made, without being in any way pretentious; it is a luxury to handle it after having dealt for twenty years or so with the other volumes in which many of these poems have appeared.

IN POSTSCRIPT (1965)

The preceding essay was written more than twenty-five years ago. My general remarks may stand, but by this time, I would restrict my choice of successful poems much more narrowly. *The Sea-Elephant* and *The crowd at the ball game* display Williams' foolish and sentimental ideas much too nakedly and can hardly be called successful. *The Widow's Lament* and others like it now strike me as soft, although charming in a gentle way; they are perhaps too obviously influenced by Pound's *Cathay*. The best poems, I feel sure, are these three from *Sour Grapes* (1921): *To Waken An Old Lady*, *Complaint*, and *The Great Figure*; and these two from *Spring and All* (1923): "By the road to the con-

From J. Hillis Miller, ed. *William Carlos Williams*, Twentieth Century Views, 1966, p. 69. Prentice-Hall.

tagious hospital," and "Pink confused with white" (*"The Pot of Flowers"*). These are all minor poems, most of them very minor indeed, but they come close to perfection in execution. If I were to name another, it would be *The Hunter* from *Sour Grapes*, but it is a trifle florid as compared to those I have mentioned. To say that Williams was anti-intellectual would be almost an exaggeration: he did not know what the intellect was. He was a foolish and ignorant man, but at moments a fine stylist.

THE POEMS OF
THEODORE ROETHKE

Open House, by Theodore Roethke. Knopf.

These is much in this book for which I care little, but every poet, I suppose, has a right to his own kind of failure; at least most poets find them. At the lowest level there are semi-ironical and almost mechanically melancholy poems written in the meter of nursery jingles, more or less, and employing too often a kind of easy phychological jargon that has very little of precision:

> Delicate the syllables that release the repression;
> Hysteria masks in the studied inane.
> Horace the hiker on a dubious mission
> Pretends his dead bunion gives exquisite pain.

This is the first stanza of the best poem of its kind in the book; the rest of the poem is better than this, but it is not, I think, good enough. Horace hardly merits the attention paid him, and the sad irony is stereotyped. There is a little of the anatomical imagery which became familiar about fifteen years ago, with the first attempts to emulate the Metaphysical School. "I'm naked to the bone," says the author in the first poem, and he repeats the notion and others similar. And in a few poems there seems

From *Kenyon Review,* III no. 4 (1941), pp. 514-516.

to be evidence that the author has absorbed with incomplete success a good deal of imagery from at least one of the best poems of Robert Bridges, *Low Barometer*. An example is *Feud*, a poem which would nearly succeed, except for the word "blubber" in the third line (a word which no context could save), did one not remember the older and a very great poem in the background.

This influence, however, if I may be pardoned for suggesting the idea, is a very good one; and it may, with other and similar influences, be in part responsible for Roethke's style at its best. "The Adamant," which is short enough to quote complete, is one of the best things in the book and in recent poetry:

> Thought does not crush to stone.
> The great sledge drops in vain.
> Truth never is undone;
> Its shafts remain.
>
> The teeth of knitted gears
> Turn slowly through the night,
> But the true substance bears
> The hammer's weight.
>
> Compression cannot break
> A center so congealed:
> The tool can chip no flake;
> The core lies sealed.

It requires courage to deal with Platonic abstractions in a season of nominalists triumphant and untrammeled—and, were they not so learned, one would add uneducated. Roethke has no desire, it would seem, to write poetry which, in the language of a distinguished contemporary, is sufficiently ambiguous to be self-explanatory. His thought is clear, and he feels it to be of sufficient importance to be left clear; the feeling of the poem is his personal realization of that importance. This kind of poem, if written by a weak hand, could be wholly inane; no more inane, perhaps, than many of the poems widely praised by our lovers of ambiguity, but inane in a manner that would be immediately obvious. The hand is not weak, however, and the poem is in its way a masterpiece.

Roethke is occasionally brilliant in a simpler form of poetry, pure description. His heron, who "jerks a frog across his bony lip," is a veritable heron, standing in perceptibly cold water; and *Night Journey* has extraordinary power:

> Full on my neck I feel
> The straining of a curve;
> My muscles move with steel,
> I wake in every nerve. . . .
> Beyond the mountain pass
> Mist deepens on the pane;
> We rush into a rain
> That rattles double glass.
> Wheels shake the roadbed stone,
> The pistons jerk and shove,
> I stay up half the night
> To see the land I love.

A few other poems that ought to be mentioned are *Reply to Censure, Long Live the Weeds, The Reckoning,* and *Highway: Michigan*. There is in all of these a comparable seriousness both in the selection of the subject and in the desire to render the subject honestly and for what it is worth. Roethke is ashamed neither of having subject matter nor of the kind of subject matter he has, and he writes in a style that is good in this period and would be good in any other.

IN PLATO'S GARDEN

In Plato's Garden: Poems 1928-39, by Lincoln Fitzell. Alan Swallow, 1940.

The poems in this book are the product of about a dozen years; they are the work of a man who had reached his full growth in the earliest of them, and who has not perceptibly altered. The poems are short, and they are limited in theme: they are largely elegiac, and elegiac without much complication: even the Platonism of the title poem affects that poem alone—it is not a philosophy permeating the book as a whole. The scope of the poems is limited, and I suppose they are what we must call minor; but such poems may have extraordinary power and permanency (as we use that term) if the style be that of a master.

The style is sometimes masterly, though too often it is mannered, and frequently it is merely careless. My own favorite poem is an early one, entitled *Erosion*. I quote it in full:

> Between the antlers tossed and wide
> The crag is marked, the mountain tried,
> Flint-high, the fired hoof is clear
> To lift on rock the head of fear.

From *New Mexico Quarterly*, IV no. 7 (1944), pp. 110-111.

Oak root is shrunken from the rock,
Earth-tendril and the breast unlock,
And, tremor, where the foot had edge
Dirt runs upon the infirm ledge.

Through the snow red berries press,
As blood of these will fall on grass,
Rodents, that famish at the bone,
Unknit the stern career of stone.

In arid sleep the summits nod,
The gopher falls away in sod,
But dark on crevice rock is worn
Wreath of the granite splintered horn.

The poem is precise and moving throughout, but the writing in
the second and fourth couplets and in the last three lines is
especially fine. In the third line of the poem there is an unusually
beautiful employment of elliptical statement, of a kind which the
author frequently abuses, as in the last stanza of *Spring Bar-
riers:*

Grass runs beneath the hare's wild feet,
Hedge rodents grit in bramble hole:
Wind-fire tracked through pathless wheat,
Earth burns the crevice-gusty mole.

The image of the first line above has a good deal of beauty, but
the accents and the consonants, there and throughout the stanza
and often elsewhere, are impossibly awkward; and the grammar
of the last two lines is so foreshortened as to be merely bad and
as to render the lines all but incomprehensible. This mannered
harshness and confusion damage a large part of the book, and
when they are applied, as in the poem just quoted, to extremely
simple matter, one cannot help feeling that the resultant statement expresses more of insecurity than of anything else.

I have known *Erosion*, however, for about ten years, and have
remembered it and often reread it; it is, for me, one of the most

truly living poems of my generation. My opinion of *Conflict*, a poem which I have known nearly as long is nearly as high, and I should not be surprised if *Gravestone*, which is new to me, would wear as well. Among the other poems which I like best are *Fragment, In Plato's Garden, Church Picnic, A Day of Earth, A Village Dial, Earth Marriage*, and *Through a Gate*. The author of these poems seems to me surely one of the memorable poets of our time.

The printer and publisher, Mr. Alan Swallow, is to be congratulated on his selecting a poet of fine quality with whom to inaugurate his publishing business, and on the excellent appearance of the book as well.

THREE POETS

Losses, by Randall Jarrell. Harcourt, Brace.
The Dispossessed, by John Berryman. William Sloane Associates.
The Judge Is Fury, by J. V. Cunningham. The Swallow Press
and William Morrow.

The two marks by which we most readily recognize a poet, I
presume, are first an ability to grasp and objectify a particular
subject so that it is rendered comprehensible both as an individual thing and as a symbol of general experience, and second
a command of the potentialities of language, phrase by phrase,
including the rhythmic potentialities. Neither of these abilities
will ever develop very far by itself: the subject cannot be defined
satisfactorily in general unless it is defined well in detail, and
the language, phrase by phrase, cannot be made to say much
unless the poet knows what he is trying to say. Nevertheless, the
gift of language can sometimes carry a poet a fair distance without much support from thought: the poetry so achieved will
always be in a large measure unsatisfactory, but it may be memorable at least in part. Swinburne is an example, and so in
somewhat different ways are Collins and Mallarmé. When Valéry
writes "Massse de calme et visible réserve," when Stevens writes
"Than mute bare splendors of the sun and moon," when Tate

From *Hudson Review,* I no. 1 (1948), pp. 402-406.

writes, "So blind, in so severe a place," we know that we are in the presence of living language and that if we master the whole statement we may conceivably find ourselves in the presence of great poetry. But without the gift of language, the best subject in the world will fall absolutely dead from the hand.

What I wish to point out, and I do it regretfully, is this: that Randall Jarrell is wholly without the gift of language. With the best of intentions and some reasonably good topics, he displays, line by line, from beginning to end of his book, an utter incapacity to state anything memorably; and he frequently displays a distressing capacity to make serious topics appear ludicrous. There is not much one can do in a case like this except to illustrate the defect. This is from *Pilots, Man Your Planes:*

> The carrier meshed in its white whirling wake,
> The gray ship sparkling from the blue-black sea,
> The little carrier—erupts in flak,
> One hammering, hysterical, tremendous fire.
> Flickering through lashes, the stained rolling clouds,
> The air jarred like water tilted in a bowl,
> The red wriggling tracers—colonies
> Whose instant life annexes the whole sky—
> Hunt out the one end they have being for,
> Are metamorphosed into one pure smear
> Of flame, and die
> In the maniacal convulsive spin
> Of the raider with a wing snapped off, the plane
> Trailing its flaming kite's-tail to the wave.

If I had received this description, written out as prose, from a student in freshman composition at Stanford, there is scarcely phrase in it which I should not have underlined as either trite or clumsily obvious; furthermore, I think that there is scarcely a teacher of freshman composition at Stanford (I should hesitate to speak for the teachers in the great universities of the east) who would not mark it similarly. The passage is dead; furthermore, one will find nothing appreciably better in Jarrell. Occasionally, however, as he approaches the ludicrous, one may find something worse. This is the last stanza of *The Breath of Night:*

> Here too, though death is hushed, though joy
> Obscures, like night, their wars,
> The beings of this world are swept
> By the Strife that moves the stars.

This is the first stanza of another poem:

> When I was home last Christmas
> I called on your family,
> Your aunts and your mother, your sister;
> They were as kind as ever to me.

These two stanzas (and there are many more like them) are the sort of thing that one would expect to see published by a female genius in a country newspaper.

I realize, and in fairness should confess, that the world is against me in this judgment. Among the eminent critics who praise Jarrell in very high terms on the jacket are Joseph Warren Beach, Arthur Mizener, Dudley Fitts, Delmore Schwartz, Alan Swallow, John Crowe Ransom, and Theodore Spencer. The praises are similar in tenor; so I shall quote only one, and the shortest, which is Ransom's: "He has an angel's velocity and range with language."

If one were inclined to use the critical technique which Jarrell himself habitually employs, the technique of explosive epigram and Menckenesque ridicule, I believe that one could, between the poems and the comments on the jacket, write a fairly entertaining essay. But it seems to me more profitable to drop the subject.

John Berryman has at least in a limited degree the gift for language which Jarrell lacks, but it is frustrated by his inability to define his theme and his disinclination to understand and discipline his emotions. Most of his poems appear to deal with a single all-inclusive topic: the desperate chaos, social, religious, philosophical, and psychological, of modern life, and the corresponding chaos and desperation of John Berryman. No matter what the ostensible subject, this is commonly what emerges, and most of the poems are merely random assortments of half-realized images illustrating this theme. It is hard to tell one poem from another; the poems blur together in memory; and much of the time the passages from different poems could be interchanged with no great change of effect. The loose monotony is increased by the fact that most of the poems are in the same meter, a somewhat loose iambic pentameter, which displays no real organization of lines into carying rhythmic and rhetorical units, but moves heavily line by line in a manner which comes to seem interminable. The rhythm is not quite the same as that employed by MacLeish, but the effect of disorganization and monotony reminds one of MacLeish:

> The Irish and the Italians own the place.
> Anyone owns it, if you like, who has
> A dollar minimum; but it is theirs by noise.
> Let them possess it until one o'clock,
> The balconies' tiers, huddled tables, shrouded baleful music,
>   and the widening crack
> Across the far wall watching a doomed crowd,
> The fat girl simpering carnations to the boys.

This sort of thing if continued very long is both dull and benumbing; and it benumbs the poet, for moving in this undefined rhythmic fog, and feeling impelled to enumerate all the horrors of the cosmos, he realizes few of his details and does not know where to stop.

Berryman's most notable attempt at organization is perhaps the piece entitled *Chinese Checkers;* but so far as I can understand the poem, the organization is largely factitious. The game is perhaps symbolic of an intellectual or professional pursuit which fails to engage most of the author's interests and faculties; or perhaps it is symbolic of something else; or perhaps it is not symbolic. The game, however, provides the frailest possible continuity. The poem starts with it, refers to it a few times, and returns to it (though I find the figure of the game in the last stanza very difficult to grasp); but for the rest the poet lets his mind wander as freely over his past experience as it wanders in any of the other poems, and most of the experience in question is quite irrelevant to the game.

One finds passages in a few poems which indicate a sharper talent: lines in *Cloud and Flame* for example, and the third stanza of *Letter to His Brother*, although both of these poems are pretty heavily influenced by Yeats. I will quote one short poem entire; it is called *Parting as Descent*:

> The sun rushed up the sky; the taxi flew;
> There was a kind of fever on the clock
> That morning. We arrived at Waterloo
> With time to spare and couldn't find my track.
>
> The bitter coffee in a small café
> Gave us our conversation. When the train
> Began to move, I saw you turn away
> And vanish, and the vessels in my brain
>
> Burst, the train roared, the other travellers
> In flames leapt, burning on the tilted air
> Che si cruccia, I heard the devils curse
> And shriek with joy in that place beyond prayer.

The first two stanzas of this poem are sharp, self-contained, and admirable; in the third stanza, where Berryman endeavors to rise to a climax of emotion, he loses control of his style, and indulges in stereotypes as bad as anything in Jarrell. If Berryman could learn to think more and feel less, and to mitigate, in some fashion, his infinite compassion for himself and for the universe, he might bring to some kind of real fruition the talent which one can discern in his better lines; but until he does so, he will not be a poet of any real importance.

J. V. Cunningham is a man who began as a Catholic and who in the process of losing his faith acquired a good deal of philosophical erudition and a restless yet uncompromising mind. Of his original faith he retained, as nearly as I can discover, only a few metaphysical convictions, and those of a type which offer more certitude than consolation. I do not share all of his convictions, and I hold a few convictions which he does not share; yet it seems to me certain that his mind is more lucid, more sure of its own contents, and more profoundly "modern" (if we must have such a mind) than that of anyone else writing poetry today, and it seems to me equally certain that he is more surely a master of his craft, within the forms which he has used, than is any other poet writing today. I quote a poem entitled *Meditation on Statistical Method:*

> Plato, despair!
> We prove by norms
> How numbers bear
> Empiric forms,
>
> How random wrong
> Will average right
> If time be long
> And error slight,
>
> But in our hearts
> Hyperbole
> Curves and departs
> To infinity.
>
> Error is boundless.
> Nor hope nor doubt,
> Though both be groundless,
> Will average out.

This is not, as I have known occasional readers to think it, a piece of neat light verse. It is a serious comment on a major topic; intellectually, it is absolutely lucid; and it exhibits that combination of passion and irony which is supposed in our time to be essential. In my opinion (and I believe in Cunningham's) passion can get along without irony quite as well as with it, though not without intelligence. However, passion, irony, and intelligence are all present in this poem, and are beautifully

related to each other. My second quotation is an epigram entitled
On the Calculus:

> From almost naught to almost all I flee,
> And *almost* has almost confounded me,
> Zero my limit, and infinity.

And my third and final quotation is an untitled epigram, the last
piece in the book:

> In whose will is our peace? Thou happiness,
> Thou ghostly promise, to thee I confess
> Neither in thine nor love's nor in that form
> Disquiet hints at have I yet been warm;
> And if I rest not till I rest in thee
> Cold as grace, whose hand shall comfort me?

These three poems, and fifteen or eighteen equally fine in Cunningham's two books, will not appeal to those who consider
poetry to be a "revery over remembered sensory impressions."
Neither will they appeal to those who share what is popularly
regarded as the modern temperament and who have little
experience with the modern (or any other) mind. These are not
the work of an unhappy adolescent; they are the work of a
mature scholar, thinker, and craftsman. And I believe that they
will stand the most rigorous comparison with the finest short
poems in English.

A DISCOVERY

The Cricket, by Frederick Goddard Tuckerman. Cummington Press.

The past twenty years of editing and criticism have made one thing (at any rate) clear to myself, in spite of the normal confusion of the period. The history of American literature, especially with reference to the nineteenth century, will have to be drastically revised. The discovery of Edward Taylor, of the colonial period; the gradual emergence of Emily Dickinson and Herman Melville (neither of them too well understood even yet by most of their admirers); Witter Bynner's recovery of F. G. Tuckerman from obscurity (a recovery as yet but scantly appreciated); my own recovery of Jones Very; and such major figures as J. L. Motley, as the Henry Adams of the *History,* as the Bryant of *Thanatopsis,* who are even yet awaiting some approximation of just evaluation—these writers, and the facts which I have indicated, cast a somewhat different light upon our literary history than that which we saw or thought we saw a generation ago. Longfellow, Lowell, and most of Holmes, to say nothing of others comparable, are now regarded as negligible, or so I suppose. Whitman and Poe will shortly disappear into the twilight of queer historical phenomena and bad influences; and Emerson

From *Hudson Review,* III no. 1 (1950), pp. 453-458.

will disappear into it to emerge only fragmentarily, or perhaps as the most shining example of a hopeless cause. What is emerging now is a group of writers who were obscured in their day (and in most of ours) because of a provincial audience, but who themselves were not provincial, or, if provincial, only superficially so, writers all of whom were profound and most of whom were (at least part of the time) finished masters of their respective arts.

But I am concerned at present with Tuckerman.

Frederick Goddard Tuckerman was born in 1821 and died in 1873. His wife died in childbirth in 1857, and her death is the explicit source of much of the melancholy in the poems written after this date. However, some of the earlier poems are equally melancholy, and the source of the melancholy in many poems, both before and after her death, is obscure: Tuckerman seems in some measure to have cultivated the prevailing Romantic mood, and even to have let it gain a kind of neurotic domination over him. He appears frequently to be a decadent poet, almost as Verlaine is a decadent poet (though frequently, if one is to be fair to him, with little if any less distinction in perception and execution).

Tuckerman's poems were first published in 1860 and were reissued in 1864 and 1869. There was an English edition in 1863. He must have had a fair number of readers to justify these editions, and he was not without his distinguished admirers, Tennyson having been one of them. In 1909 Walter Pritchard Eaton published an article on Tuckerman in *The Forum*. This seems to have come to the attention of Witter Bynner, who in 1931 issued through Alfred A. Knopf a selection entitled *The Sonnets of Frederick Goddard Tuckerman* (unless I am mistaken, this volume is still in print). Bynner had access to the published work and to the notebooks. A short time before these remarks were written, the Cummington Press issued *The Cricket*, a single ode, previously unpublished from the notebooks. *The Cricket* is the occasion of my present comments. My knowledge of Tuckerman is confined to *The Cricket*, to a few unpublished poems which I have seen by the courtesy of the Cummington Press, and to the *Sonnets*. The gentlemen of the Cummington Press inform me that Jones Very was at one time Tuckerman's tutor. For the rest, my biographical and bibliographical information are derived from Bynner.

The sonnets are in the main, though not entirely, elegiac and descriptive. The two most beautiful, I believe, are numbers XVI and XVII of Part II (Bynner's edition). The first of these describes a deserted house which had once been inhabited by the two beautiful sisters who haunt so many of the sonnets. It concludes:

> The house stands vacant in its green recess,
> Absent of beauty as a broken heart.
> The wild rain enters; and the sunset wind
> Sighs in the chambers of their loveliness
> Or shakes the pane—and in the silent noons
> The glass falls from the window, part by part,
> And ringeth faintly in the grassy stones.

The second of these sonnets contrasts the civilized scene of the present with the savage scene of a few years before:

> Here but a lifetime back—where falls tonight
> Behind the curtained pane a sheltered light
> On buds of rose or vase of violet
> Aloft upon the marble mantel set—
> Here in the forest heart hung blackening
> The wolf-bait on the bush beside the spring.

And there are occasionally lines of "pure poetry," faint and derivative, I suppose, but curiously haunting, like this from XX of the same group (the line refers to the two dead sisters, Gertrude and Gulielma):

> They have their tears, nor turn to us their eyes.

Such passages, like the sonnets from which they come, have great beauty, marred occasionally by facile phrasing. The melancholy in these sonnets is comprehensibly motivated; in others it is less so, in spite of the fact that brilliant details, for the most part descriptive, may emerge. The poetry is decadent, sophisticated with respect to the qualities which it actually possesses, sensuously rich, and too often somewhat careless; on the whole, however, it is so lovely as to deserve a high place in our poetic literature of the nineteenth century.

The Cricket is an irregular ode, containing five sections of various lengths. The meter is iambic, and the lines are predominantly pentameter, but there is much variation in the length of the lines, and the rhyming is irregular. The rhetorical formulae are those of the Romantic ode, especially of the Keatsian ode. The formulae themselves are beautifully managed, but it is in the substance and in the details of perception that the poem surpasses its models.

The poem moves into its subject slowly and quietly. The first section, a matter of eleven lines, is a kind of invocation to the cricket as the subject of the poem, but superficially is devoted to the setting in which the cricket is found. It is gentle and bucolic, but perfectly executed. The second section continues and enlarges upon the theme of the first: the poet here appears in a superficial aspect as the descendant of Milton's shepherd and Gray's youth; if one wished to speak of him unkindly, one might say that he languishes amid the landscape. But the languishing and the landscape equally are handled very well in themselves, and both become gradually more important in relation to the central theme; they are not merely sentimental decorations. As the section proceeds, we are made aware not only of the scene and of the cricket, but of the infinite multitude of crickets within the scene—"acres of cricks"—and their sound is compared to that of the sea, the traditional symbol of nature (the impersonal source and conclusion of life), the symbol of that aspect of the universe which is distinct from human personality and intelligence.

In the third section, the cricket reappears in his familiar aspect, "dear to the child," and so on, but presently becomes the night-lover, "bringer of all things dark" (a notion not too remote from the affections of the child), and the sea-image is picked up and developed; and following the sea-image, the cricket is related explicitly, as he had not been before, with death, in some of the greatest lines in the poem:

> Thou bringest, too, dim accents from the grave
> To him who walketh when the day is dim,
> Dreaming of those who dream no more of him—
> With edged remembrances of joy and pain:
> And heyday looks and laughter come again;
> Forms that in happy sunshine lie and leap,
> With faces where but now a gap must be—
> Renunciations, and partitions deep,
> And final tears, and crowning vacancy!
> And to thy poet in the twilight's hush
> No chirping touch of lips and tittering blush,
> But wringing arms, hearts wild with love and woe,
> Closed eyes, and kisses that would not let go.[1]

The fourth section is a relatively gentle and conventional one. The cricket, like Keats's nightingale, is placed in antiquity; but whereas the antiquity of the nightingale is largely a decorative and sentimental adjunct to the poem, the antiquity of the cricket has begun to seem and later quite obviously becomes an aspect of his prehuman and subhuman nature, of his symbolic embodiment of the archaic and of death; so that this section is not merely Romantic decoration, but contributes definitely and beautifully, though slowly, to the growth of the theme.

In the fifth section, which is the final one, and the longest, the aspects of the theme which have been broached are stated fully and are brought together. The section opens with an explicit admission of the evil, which, along with the fascination and beauty, is inherent in the theme. The poet compares himself, in his desire to understand the cricket more fully, to an enchanter who employed poison for the purpose of understanding the speech of the beasts:

So that articulate voices now he hears

---

1. In a later version of the poem, discovered since the publication of *The Cricket,* the unfortunate phrase "and tittering blush" appears "with laugh and blush."

In cry of beast or bird or insect's hum—
Might I but find thy knowledge in thy song!
   That twittering tongue
Ancient as light, returning like the years.

Yet this knowledge, he is fully aware, is not the mystical knowledge assumed by Emerson and his disciples; it is the knowledge of death, or of the increasingly close approach to death:

   So might I be
Unwise to sting, thy true interpreter
Thro denser stillness and in sounder dark
Than ere thy notes have pierced to harrow me.

But the fascination of this approach, even as he sees its evil and terror, remains with him; this fascination is carried over in part from the third section, in which he laments a death which has occurred earlier, presumably that of his wife, although she is not explicitly identified in this poem, as she is in some of the sonnets. And in this vision of the desirability of extinction, he rises to a vision of the impersonal universe lying in sunlight as magnificent as any of the similar passages in *Le Cimetiere Marin*, and in this passage he recalls by suggestion his comparison of the sound of crickets to the sound of the sea:

   For larger would be less indeed, and like
The ceaseless simmer in the summer grass
To him who toileth in the windy field,
   Or where the sunbeams strike
Naught in innumerable numerousness.
   So might I much possess,
   So much must yield.

Gently, almost casually, but in magnificent language, he leaves his topic as impracticable (for he must live now and die eventually); and he returns to a kind of melancholy common sense:

Then cricket sing thy song, or answer mine:

> Thine whispers blame, but mine has naught but praises.
> It matters not.—Behold, the autumn goes,
>   The Shadow grows,
> The moments take hold of eternity;
> Even while we stop to wrangle or repine
>   Our lives are gone
>   Like thinnest mist,
> Like yon escaping color in the tree:—
> Rejoice! Rejoice! whilst yet the hours exist;
> Rejoice or mourn, and let the world swing on
> Unmoved by Cricket song of thee or me.

The poem may seem on a careless reading to be loosely organized, to be merely a series of notations on death and on landscape, but such an impression, if one receives it, is unjustified. To establish the cricket as a symbol, and temporarily almost as a deity, of nature and of death is no simple feat. Had the attempt been made more simply and directly, it would certainly have failed; to succeed, the poet was forced to place the cricket in its natural setting, to examine the setting in as many as possible of its implications, and to involve slowly and carefully in this his own relationship with death. It is a poem in which are related little by little the poet and his personal longing for death, his realization of the terror of death, his love for the natural landscape, his realization of the natural landscape as an impersonal thing and hence a symbol of death, his love of the cricket as a small but charming creature, and his realization of the cricket as a timeless part of the non-human landscape and hence as a symbol of the whole theme. It is a complex affair, but it is all of a piece, and the subject is fully and beautifully explored. The cricket, who is introduced with affection and left, with melancholy regret, is made in the course of the poem a symbol of the darkness of nature and of its severance from the human, of "renunciations and partitions deep," and he becomes, like Melville's whale, ubiquitous in time and place.

Americans since the 1840's have been obsessed with the significance of death conceived as union with nature. Emerson speaks of such a union as good, though he cannot define it; he preaches his doctrine with something close to a Calvinistic intensity, and thus gives it a quality of religious feeling which it never achieved in England or in Europe. It is this religious fervor among the American pantheists which in turn makes possible so serious an investigation and rejection of the doctrine as Tuckerman's poem, or, on a smaller scale, as Emily Dickinson's *Further in summer than the birds*. In so far as Tuckerman is concerned with speculation upon the pantheistic mystical theme, he is representative of this American tradition, or rather obsession. But the poem is greater than that: it is one of the great meditations on death to be written since the seventeenth century, along with *Le Cimetière Marin, Sunday Morning,* and *Thanatopsis*. It is probably the greatest single American poem of the nineteenth century; and the British poems of the same period which can be compared with it are few indeed.

THE POETRY OF EDGAR BOWERS

The Form of Loss, by Edgar Bowers. Alan Swallow.

Edgar Bowers is about thirty-three years old, and this is his first book. The book contains twenty-nine titles and thirty-three actual poems. Six or seven of these poems could probably be dispensed with; the rest seem to me among the best American poems of this century, and nine or ten of them among the very great poems.

Bowers is a Southerner, born and raised in Georgia, and raised as a Presbyterian. He served three years or more with the Army during World War II, the last year and a half or so with the occupation forces in Germany, in counter-intelligence, and he later spent a year in France on a Fulbright fellowship. He took his Ph.D. in English at Stanford, and is now an assistant professor of English at Harper College, in Endicott, New York. His German, I believe, is passably good; his Latin is good; and his French is better. His knowledge of the history of poetry and of critical theory in both French and English is detailed and profound. These facts may seem trivial, perhaps merely academic; but they have a real bearing on his poetry.

Although raised a Presbyterian, Bowers appears to be no longer a Christian. But he has a Calvinistic tendency toward

From *Sewanee Review,* LXIV no. 4 (1956), pp. 657-662.

mysticism, combined with an inability, both temperamental and intellectual, to delude himself: this is one of the important facts to be remembered if one is trying to understand his poetry. The words *guilt* and *deceit* recur several times as indicative of attitudes which turn one from one's real beliefs toward something that one would like to believe, and hence toward spiritual corruption. In the opening lines of the poem *From William Tyndale to John Firth,* a letter supposedly written shortly before both men were burned for heresy, one gets the theme, without these particular words:

> The letters I, your lone friend, write in sorrow
> Will not contain my sorrow: it is mine,
> Not yours who stand for burning in my place.
> Be certain of your fate. Though some, benign,
> Will urge by their sweet threats malicious love
> And counsel dangerous fear of violence,
> Theirs is illusion's goodness proving fair—
> Against your wisdom—worldly innocence.
> And just persuasions' old hyprocrisy.
> Making their choice, reflect what you become:
> Horror and misery bringing ruin where
> The saintly mind has treacherously gone numb. . . .

Bowers has a somewhat un-Calvinistic sympathy for Catholic doctrine and civilization, but he examines them from a non-Christian position: nostalgically, at times, if you wish, but unmistakably from the outside. *The Virgin Mary* is one of the earliest poems in this collection, but will illustrate my point, and will exhibit Bowers' style at its most magnificent:

> The hovering and huge, dark, formless sway
> That nature moves by laws we contemplate
> We name for lack of name as order, fate,
> God, principle, or primum mobile.
> But in that graven image, word made wood
> By skillful faith of him to whom she was
> Eternal nature, first and final cause,

The form of knowledge knowledge understood
Bound human thought against the dark we find.
And body took the image of the mind
To shape in chaos, a congruent form
Of will and matter, equal, side by side,
Upon the act of faith, within the norm
Of carnal being, blind and glorified.

Bowers is involved intellectually and emotionally—and quite
consciously—in the history of western religion and philosophy,
and at the same time, for better or worse, is in the predicament
of the post-Christian intellectual. But as a post-Christian intellectual, he is not a modern provincial: quite the contrary.

Along with this feeling for western intellectual history, goes a
deep feeling for the antiquity and grandeur of western history
generally and for the evidence of decay and destruction within
that civilization in our time. *The Prince,* one of the two or three
latest poems of the volume, may be used to illustrate a part of
this theme. The poem is a monologue spoken by an old German
prince to a counter-intelligence officer. The prince had been an
anti-Nazi, in spite of his profoundly German feelings; his son had
shared his anti-Nazi principles and had refused to serve the government, only to have his German patriotism overcome him, with
the result that he served as a spy and was shot by the Americans. The theme is complex and rich—psychologically, morally,
socially. I quote two excerpts, one from the middle, the other
from the end, to exhibit the beauty of the style:

You know despair's authority, the rite
And exaltation by which we are governed,
A state absurd with wrath that we are human,
Nothing to which our nature would submit.

Such was the German State. Yet, like a fool,
I hated it, my image, and was glad
When he refused its service; now I know
That even his imprisonment was mine,
A gesture by the will to break the will . . . .

By what persuasion he saw fit to change
Allegiance, none need wonder. Let there be,
However, no mistake: those who deny
What they believe is true, desire shall mock
And crime's uncertain promise shall deceive.
Alas, that he was not a German soldier
In his apostasy, but would put on
The parody of what caprice put off,
Enemy in disguise, the uniform
And speech of what the sceptic heart requires—
Ruthless the irony that is its thought.
The soldier's death should find him unaware,
The breathless air close round him as sleep falls,
Sudden with ripeness, heavy with release.
Thereby the guileless tranquilly are strong:
The man is overwhelmed, the deed remains.
Flesh of my flesh, bewildered to despair
And fallen outside the limits of my name,
Forever lies apart and meaningless.
I who remain perceive the dear, familiar
Unblemished face of possibility
Drenched by a waste profound with accident,
His childhood face concealed behind my face.
Where is the guile enough to comfort me?

Bowers' style is at once as modern and as rooted in history as
his subject matter. *The Virgin*, which I have quoted, might so
far as style is concerned have been written between 1595 and
1620: it offers a justification for the publisher's reference to
Greville on the slipcover. But a large part of the poetry—probably the greater part—belong to a relatively modern tradition.
In the seventeenth century, the rational structure of poetry,
which had characterized the work of the Renaissance and which
had had its origins in medieval writing, began to disintegrate;
and the ethical formulations of Shaftesbury, aided by the critical
formulations of Addison and subsequent associationists, has-
tened the disintegration. From here onward there is less and less
command of "abstract" language, that is, of precise ethical and

metaphysical thought, and more and more concentration on sensory detail and on progression governed by revery. In the *Ode to Evening* things have gone so far that syntax itself has almost disappeared from about half of the poem. In the best work of the eighteenth and nineteenth centuries—for examples, in some of Blake, Mallarmé, and Rimbaud—this concentration results in a sharper and more fascinating sensory perception than on can easily find in the earlier poetry, but the gain is an insufficient compensation for the loss. However, in the nineteenth and twentieth centuries a few poets, at least a part of the time, endeavor to recover the older intellectual integrity and at the same time to retain something of the newer sensory acuteness: among the more obvious examples—and these are probably the main influences on Bowers—are Baudelaire, Leconte de Lisle, Valéry, Sturge Moore, and Stevens. The result is sensory perception not for its own sake and not in the form of the traditional metaphor or simile, but sensory perception offered as sensory perception, yet charged with perfectly explicit meaning by the total context. Bowers' poem *The Stoic,* too long to quote in full, is a clear example of the method: the protagonist, a German woman, listens to distant cannonading and bombing, regards the German Alps (the symbol of geographical antiquity and grandeur) and the rural scenes closer at hand, reflects upon "Eternal Venice sinking by degrees Into the very water that she lights" (the symbol of the antiquity and slow decay of civilization), upon the brightness and neatness of recent civilization in pre-war Berlin, upon the lion released from his cage in Berlin by a random bomb, and upon the man killed by the lion, and then retreats into the stoicism approaching but not really reaching mysticism which is so characteristic of Bowers. The details are quiet but precise; each carries its own meaning unmistakably; the rhythmically slow release of the lion and his savage action give us one of the most effective images with which I am acquainted of the emergence of chaos from the semblance of civilization:

> Remembered in Berlin the parks, the neat

Footpaths and lawns, the clean spring foliage,
Where just short weeks before, a bomb unaimed
Had freed a raging lion from its cage,
Which in the mottled dark that trees enflamed

Killed one who hurried homeward from the raid.
And by yourself there standing in the chill

You must, with so much known, have been afraid
And chosen such a mind of constant will,

Which, though all time corrode with constant hurt,
Remains, until it occupies no space
That which it is; and passionless, inert,
Becomes at last no meaning and no place.

Or one may consider this passage from an elegiac song, written
in three-beat accentual verse:

Flesh old and summer waxing,
Quick eye in the sunny lime,
Sweet apricots in silence
Falling—precious in time,

All radiant as a voice, deep
As their oblivion. Only as I may,
I come, remember, wait,
Ignorant in grief, yet stay.

What you are will outlast
The warm variety of risk,
Caught in the wide, implacable,
Clear gaze of the basilisk.

These are the poems of a man between the ages of twenty-five
and thirty-two, approximately. They are not perfect, at any rate
not all of them. A native clumsiness sometimes shows itself, on
occasions resulting in obscurity. But this does not happen often.

The mind and the matter—the two are inseparable—are complex and profound, and it is small wonder that the technique occasionally falters. But it falters very seldom. The aim is mastery, not eccentricity or obscurity. And the aim is sometimes achieved.

ESSAYS

NOTES

The painter invents relationships between form and form and form and color; the musician between sound and sound; but the poet invents relationship between form (often including color) and sound, between idea and idea and sound, or between form and idea and sound, between form and form and sound, between idea and sound.

A fallacy that invalidates a certain amount of the work of Verlaine is that he often attempted to subordinate sense to sound, apparently believing verbal sound to have much the same properties as musical sound, which it has not in any comparable degree. Moreover, the very nature of words involves both sound and at least the shadow of meaning, and if one be subordinated to the other, that one becomes an excess and unreasoned weight, and the other suffers from lack of its natural support.

The poetic image is capable of actual motion, which the painting is not; and it is capable of taking the reader, as the painting is not, through a progression of vanishing images, thus achieving a complex series of superimposed moods. Moreover, in a painting a form is presented, not by its identification at any given point, with another form, but entirely by its method of juxtaposition to another form; whereas the reverse may be true in a poem; and in a poem a relationship of the entire form com-

From *Modern Review*, II no. 3 (1924), pp. 86-88.

bination to the sound is involved. This makes it possible (especially, sometimes, by the aid of motion) for the poem to present a panorama entirely devoid of the painter's "significant form," but in itself and in its sweep beautiful and impressive; to present a landscape composed of minute and beautiful details, uncorrelated as regards the painter's forms; things which on the canvas could be nothing save banal. Furthermore, the literary landscape may contain the discoveries of all the senses, while the pictorial is limited to one. And lastly, the symbolic value of the parts of the landscape, although present to a greater or a lesser extent upon the canvas, are enhanced in the poem—or can be enhanced—by the symbolic values of sound. These are the differences between pictorial and literary landscape or imagery; although one landscape may be treated in both ways with equally great, if diverse success.

A common modern fallacy which is due largely to the work of certain Americans is the misinterpretation of the truism that form and matter must be related. That is, they tell us, that since America is a large, loose, uncorrelated country, our verse must be large and loose and uncorrelated in order to express that land. But verse which is loose and uncorrelated is weak, and can obviously express very little of anything. A sense, a perception, of largeness and looseness can be contained in a very concise image or anti-image, and must be so contained if it is to have any impact. A loose poem about America is in no wise more praiseworthy than a loose poem about a Flemish garden. Nor is a chaotic poem about New York any more praiseworthy than a chaotic poem about Helen of Troy. The poem will be inaccurate and lacking in cumulative power in either case. This is the fallacy of Whitman and his decadent followers, Sandburg and Anderson. And living poets, William Carlos Williams, notably in his prose *Improvisations*. For the most part however, Dr. Williams is the foremost example that I know of the possibility of attaining method in one's madness, and the first poet I would quote to prove my point.

An artistic tradition is the accumulation of man's discoveries with regard to any art over any given period of time, in literature, in any given language or languages; and criticism is an analytical history of those discoveries, and a comparative analysis of various traditions and of the relationship of individuals to a given tradition or traditions. Criticism is after the fact, and can hope to do no more than define what has already passed, select, and recommend. It will never be able to control the future, although it may possibly forecast it to some extent, and, if acute, make the arrival of the inevitable more rapid and more efficient. This is its only utilitarian function, so far as the artist is concerned.

Those who say that American tradition has not yet appeared are mistaken. They should rather say that they have not yet discovered it. It commenced to appear when the first English sentence was written in America, and has continued more or less steadily since that event. It remains to determine what American work has possessed the greatest intensity and efficiency—decidedly not to determine that which fits into any personally preconceived notion of what the American attitude ought to be—and to find out what that work has in common, if anything, and wherein, if anywhere, it differs from foreign work. Such differences are likely to be slight. Metrical and stylistic devices diffuse themselves rapidly throughout the modern world. The only differences are likely to be shades of emotional tone resulting from the effect of slightly differing environments upon normal or typically abnormal Caucasians. The vigor of any national literature depends less upon the "originality" of any group emotions or feelings than upon the perceptive vigor of individual artists. "O Erd! O Sonne! O Gluck! O Lust!" is sufficiently typical of a race, but as poetry it is negligible.

The relation of the mental process of a normal man to those of the protagonist of a novel, is about the same as the relation of the movements of a walking man to those of the walking man in Gautier's poem.

The various poetic images and anti-images appear in prose as well, but at lower tension, owing to the slower rhythm of the medium.

THE TESTAMENT OF A STONE

Being Notes on the Mechanics of the Poetic Image

FOREWORD

These notes presuppose a knowledge of Fenollosa's *The Chinese Written Character*, a large part of T. S. Eliot's *The Sacred Wood*, and scattered paragraphs from Pound, Lewis, Croce, and the Hindus.

I reserve the right to add to or alter these notes later in case of any second publication. It is possible that they are not complete (the last section is obviously incomplete, as my interest in it is temporarily secondary), but they are an attempt to incite the beginnings of a scientific criticism of poetry, which up to date we do not have, except in a few scattered fragments.

The poet himself will be more sensitive to, or more moved by, some material than other material, will perceive it more completely, and so will write his best poems when dealing with it. Speculation upon the sensitivity of the individual poet and its possible modification by his environment is of some psychological interest and perhaps more "human interest," but it has little to do with the art of poetry. The degree of fusion of the parts of

From *Secession,* VIII (April 1924), pp. 1-21.

194

a poem will depend upon the degree of fusion of the poet with his material, and that, to be sure, is the result of the nature of his sensitivity and his environment. But one is usually—and theoretically—forced by circumstances to approach the poet and his environment—if one so desires—through his poems, and not the other way round. Supposing one to be possessed of some intelligence, it is possible, after a reasonable amount of study, to decide whether a poem represents a perfect fusion of perceptions or not, and supposing one to have some education, it is possible, after similar study, to decide whether the poem be original or merely a restatement of the perceptions of others. As different poets are moved equally by different types of material, finished poems, composed of different types of material, may be equally intense; thus indicating that the material is of no importance to the critic, who is dealing with poems; but only to the poet, who is dealing with material, and that is his own affair. The cause of a perfectly fused poem is the fusion of the poet's consciousness with an object or a group of objects of whatever nature. The means by which this fusion is achieved is the poet's "technique." In the mature poet, the technique is the medium of fusion; and the ratio of what the poet sees or feels to what he gets down is in direct proportion to the perfection of his technique. Why one poet is moved by this and another by that, it is impossible to say. It is possible only to remark the fact. But technique can be analysed, and analysed minutely; and this analysis may be of value to other poets in perfecting and extending the range of their perceptions, and it may be of value to critics, private and public, insofar as it may make them more acutely aware of their poets' achievements.

A poem is a state of perfection at which a poet has arrived by whatever means. It is a stasis in a world of flux and indecision, a permanent gateway to waking oblivion, which is the only infinity and the only rest. It has no responsibilities except to itself and its own perfection—neither to the man who may come to it with imperfect understanding nor to the mood from which it may originally have sprung. It is not a means to any end, but is in itself an end, and it, or one of the other embodiments of beauty, is the only end possible to the man of intellect.

The artist whose deity is art, has a religion as valid and as capable of producing great art as any religion of the past or as the recently defined religion of money. As a conscious and intelligent being, no other religion will be possible for him, and he cannot, because of his religion, be called a decadent, a heretic.

Driven into a corner of which we are unaware, we pursue our ends. For in infinity, those who withdraw in terror are those who drive us off with bitterness, and at the same instant, in the same thought and gesture. Yet equanimity is all we seek.

A poem is the result of a poet moving in a milieu. A poet is born into a certain intellectual and physical milieu, and this milieu may, to some extent, form the poet. But the poet will also be born with certain peculiar and unchangeable qualities, and these will, in the course of time, modify the milieu with respect to the particular poet. If the poet be of a very plastic nature, he may be greatly changed by his milieu. If he be of a more or less immobile nature, he will absorb into his own mind, and, in the process of absorption, change as becomes necessary, such part of his milieu as is to some extent forced upon him.

A poet's technique is a portion of the milieu into which he is born (tradition) modified by his peculiar qualities to serve their needs.

The milieu of any place and time is a relatively constant factor. The peculiar qualities of individual poets are infinitely variable. The resulting milieu of the individual poet is therefore infinitely variable. So it is infantile to say that a poet "does not interpret his time," to demand that he write in any specified manner. It is infantile to say that he can do this or that only with this or that technique. The individual can only say truly, "I can do this or that only with this or that technique." And even then he cannot be too sure.

So that the poem can be judged, not in relation to any time or place, nor to any mode of thought, but to itself alone, and as a part of literature; for it is not a means, but an end. The mind that can judge a poem accurately is very rare—even more rare than the mind that can create a poem. For this act of weighing requires a mind infinitely balanced, infinitely sensitive, and infinitely familiar with all the technical phases of the medium. Such a mind is, with one exception in a thousand, the mind of the master poet.

The intellectual poet is often accused of obscurity, merely because his reader is unfamiliar with the milieu in which his moves. If we imagine a poet writing in our own language but on a remote planet, whose vegetation and population, whose entire physical aspect, are different from anything we know, and expressing himself largely in terms of the physical, we cannot imagine ourselves receiving from his poems more than a very blurred impression. So is the poet moving in a world that is largely composed of thought and otherwise greatly modified by thought, to the reader unacquainted with the philosophies.

The poet moving in a world that is largely thought, so long as he regard it curiously and as a world, perceives certain specific things, as a walker in a field perceives a grassblade. These specific things are the material of the image, of art. When he loses his sense of the infinite nature of his world and organizes it into a knowable and applicable principle, he loses sight of the particulars themselves and sees their relationships to each other and his newly-created whole; and so becomes a philosopher; for it is only in the finite that the particular can be detected as a complete and uncoordinated whole; but he may still have occasional perceptions, and at times revert to the poet. When he becomes more interested in the application of his principle, in its possible effects, than in the principle itself, he becomes a preacher in perceptions, but he attempts to save a humanity that he cannot possibly understand by fitting it into a mutilated fragment of an infinity whose nature he once felt, but could never understand, and has now forgotten.

The poet, in creating, must lose himself in his object. If he becomes more interested in himself observing than in his object, and still continues to write about his object rather than himself observing, he will create a mannerism but no image. It is from this weakness that the various familiar pretty and paternal mannerisms arise. Such a mannerism may be held down to the point of producing poetry of whatever degree of impurity, or it may not.

The poet who is preoccupied with his object desires a speech without idiom and a style without mannerism, that the clarity of his perception may not be clouded by inessentials. In any absolute sense, both are impossible, but both can be closely approximated.

Perhaps it is true that the poet, moving through his world, reaches, for chemical or other reasons, a point of spiritual intensity, and that those objects that fall under his eye or his mind's eye at this point are transformed into something simpler and greater than actuality, with or without his consciousness of any sequence save the actual sequence of their appearance; that the reproduction of this simplification in words will reproduce in the reader the original emotion or point of intensity. Perhaps it is true that the poet, moving through his world, becomes aware of beautiful existences, and being moved by them to a sufficient point of intensity, is able to reproduce them in words with sufficient accuracy to create in his reader the emotion which they created in him. Or perhaps, and this is probably nearer to the truth, he is sufficiently moved by certain beautiful existences, to be able to create other beautiful existences; and this approaches T. S. Eliot's analogy of the catalyst, and his "significant emotion," which is probably the only sound statement of the creative process that we have.

All functions of man save the creation of art and pure thought tend to complicate his physical life without simplifying his mental life. The sciences, as abstractions, might have the same value as art. Indiscriminately applied, they have wrecked the world.

SECTION I

Definition of Observation, Perception, Image, and Anti-Image

It has been said that art is an elimination of the superfluous, but this statement is capable of several interpretations. It is certain, however, that the poetic image is an elimination of the superfluous in a definite and fundamental sense. Everyone of whatever degree of intelligence, walking about the world, sees certain things: trees growing, their leaves and branches moving in the wind; bees flying across fields; men and women working in the fields or walking in the streets or moved by various passions and emotions. These sights and others of a similar nature may be called *observation*. If I say: "I saw a man walking," or: "I saw night come," it will convey no sharp or lasting impression to the brain of the listener. It is a general statement, which is a vague statement, like a mist without form, a block of unhewn granite, a chaos.

But there are persons who see those things which differentiate one observation from another: they see the outline in the mist. The vision of this outline may be called *perception*. And there are yet other persons, fewer in number and of finer vision, who can take the outline from the mist and make it stand alone. This is done, in poetry, by seeing and placing in juxtaposition two or more observations that have one quality in common: that is each of these observations will be differentiated from other observations of its class by the same perception; and when these observations are placed together they will fuse at the point where they are the same, or, to be more exact, *they will be the same at one point*. These two perceptions, coming together with an almost infinite speed across the mental distances that naturally lie between two separate observations (such as a man walking and the coming of night) cause a kind of mental vibration that is known as aesthetic emotion. Or, to state it in another fashion, this fusion, or sameness at one point in two observations, reinforces that point, and makes it stand out as clearly above the vaguenesses of the two observations as those two observations stand out above a state of no-observation or unconsciousness. And perhaps these two statements of the phenomenon are not incompatible. This phenomenon may be called an *image*. The image, in the case of the two observations used as examples, is:

At one stride comes the dark.

The quotation may help to clear the ground.

The image, so defined, being a fusion of sense-perceptions, *presents* the emotion: that is, the emotion is seen in the concrete and acts directly, without the aid of thought, just as the sight of a tree registers directly, without the aid of thought. But it is possible in *thinking* of observations, to find intellectual *correlations* that are not evident to the simple senses, but that may transmit an aesthetic emotion, not directly, as in the case of sense perceptions, but through the intellect. Here the emotion is transmitted by intercomment, rather than by fusion. This phenomenon may be called the *anti-image*, as the sense-impressions of the observations do not here fuse at any point. It will be noted that the anti-image, where a physical fusion is not intended, is different from an attempted image, or fusion of sense-perceptions that is not successful.

As the image and anti-image make a sharp and lasting impression on the brain, and as the simple observation does not, the image and anti-image stay, and the observations disappear; and this is the process of elimination that was alluded to above. It is that quality in an observation of the approach of night that is different from any other observation of the approach of night, that gives such an observation a life of its own. And it is this differentiating, or unique, quality in any observation, that, when presented permanently, by means of an image or anti-image, is known as beauty.

The terms, *observation, perception,* and *image,* may have been used at various times with meanings slightly different from those I have given them; but I have applied them to certain phenomena, defined as clearly as I can define them, for lack of better terms. The phenomena seem to me sufficiently distinguishable from one another. It may be argued that a perception, as I have defined it, does not really exist until it becomes an image; but this possibility can be taken into consideration without disturbing the trend of my discussion. The anti-image is the only pure logopeia; but as the term *logopeia* has been applied in ways that do not seem to me accurate, I shall not here use it.

SECTION II

Types of Perception

Perceptions may be divided into two general types: those perceptions which are expressed in the *sound* of words, and those perceptions which are expressed in the *meaning* of words.

The first of these types will be referred to in this essay as *sound-perceptions*. Sound perceptions possess two qualities: tone and rhythm. The first of these is the quality of individual vowel or consonant or syllabic sounds. The second is the rate and variation of movement from tone to tone. It will be seen that tone and rhythm are inseparable, but occasionally one or the other seems to predominate. This results from a perfect or nearly perfect fusion of the predominant sound quality with the meaning of the words, and an imperfect fusion of the other sound quality. Insofar as this is true of any poem, that poem will be imperfect.

Perceptions which are expressed in the meaning of words may be called *meaning-perceptions*. They fall roughly into two classes: perceptions of concrete facts of which one becomes aware through the simple senses, and which may be called *sense-perceptions;* and perceptions of abstract facts or qualities — that is, of facts or qualities which are imperceptible to the unaided senses—of which one becomes aware through thinking about a concrete or abstract fact, and which may be called *thought-perceptions*.

SECTION III

Types of Image and Anti-Image

1

There is the simple physical movement, not "caught" in any fusion of the meaning of words, but rather in a fusion of the sound of words and a simple statement of the movement—in the fusion of the sound perception and a simple meaning perception. The movement has no necessary connotations as a movement: that is, it is not a movement one thinks of as having any relationship to sorrow, joy, or ecstasy. But any unemotional physical movement, stated cleanly and in psychological order, in a rhythm that fuses with that movement, may become a profound image. By fusing with the movement, I do not mean that the rhythm should imitate with its own movement the physical movement that it contains, but rather that it should purify that movement as it appears in actual physical life, giving it a regularity or at least organized variation of beat, and usually greatly acclerating it; so that the movement takes on something of the nature of a dance movement, but again is much purer and swifter than even a dance movement, by nature of its limitations, can be. From this last it may be seen that a movement that has been purified and formalized to a certain extent in actual life, such as a dance or religious procession and which has, therefore, a certain emotional connotation in itself, can be further formalized, purified, in a poem, so that it takes on a new significance—even if that new significance be only a variation upon the purification already effected in the dance or religious procession. There are also movements in actual life that are expressions or semi-expressions of emotion, such as joy, sorrow, etc., and these may, as well as other movements, be given form simply by a rhythm; but the danger here lies in the temptation offered to the weak, at least, to be content with a lax rhythm and to trust to the connotations of the movement to "put over" the emotion; which is akin to the use of an inherited symbolism or any other sentimentality. The pure form of this

type of image, that is, the physical movement without connotations, animated merely by a rhythm, is apt to produce the
cleanest beauty. The last-named form of the image seems to
me the least desirable, as it cannot possibly be freed from at
least a taint of sentimentality, though this taint, in certain
cases and if handled by a master, may have a value.

We may, for lack of a shorter name, call the type of image
discussed in the last paragraph, the *simple physical movement
fused with a rhythm*. This image seems to occur most often in
rhymed poems that move to a fixed metre. There seems to be a
cumulative effect, sometimes, in the still-echoing rhythm of
several preceding stanzas. The same cumulative effect may
come in poems whose metre varies as much as or less than, say,
that of the *Ancient Mariner*. It would, I should think, be difficult to produce this cumulative effect in a meter not having a
large amount of repetition; and certainly the reinforcement of
rhyme is an aid; but the use of the *simple physical movement
fused with a rhythm* does not depend upon cumulative rhythm.
Cumulative rhythm is merely a possible modification, or, sometimes, intensification.

Two of the finest examples of this image that I know—
examples of the physical movement without, in itself, any emotional connotations—are in the opening of T. Gautier's *Les
Affres de la Mort*:

> O toi qui passes par ce cloitre,
> Songe a la mort!—Tu n' est pas sur
> De voir s'allonger et dêcroitre,
> Une autre fois, ton ombre au mur.
>
> Frère, peut-être cette dalle
> Qu aujourd'hui, sans songer aux morts,
> Tu soufflettes de ta sandale,
> Dèmain pèsera sur ton corps!

The physical movement here is in the first, third, and fourth
lines of the first stanza, and in the third line of the second
stanza. These lines are slightly modified from without by the

"Songe a la mort!", but the modification is slight and not such as to cloud their value as examples. Another example of this type of image in one of its less pure forms is to be found in the latter half of Gerard Hopkins' *The Habit of Perfection.*

> O feel-of-primrose hands, O feet
> That want the yield of plushy sward,
> But you shall walk the golden street,
> And you unhouse and house the Lord.

The last two lines show the purification in verse of a movement that has already been purified in life as a religious symbol. H. D. has achieved in free verse animations of physical movements that have no emotional connotations:

> I saw the first pear
> as it fell—
> the honey-seeking, golden-banded,
> the yellow swarm
> was not more fleet than I.
> (spare us from loveliness)
>   and I fell prostrate
>   crying . . .

The movement of the first two lines has in itself no emotional connotation whatever, the movement of the next three lines has infinitely little, and the movement of the seventh and eighth lines have a very definite one. All three are handled successfully and have their place in the poem.

The simple physical movement fused with a rhythm is the commonest variation of the *simple physical fact fused with a rhythm,* which may or may not have movement. This image need not be visual.

1a

The statement of simple thought, or the statement of a simple physical fact, punctuated, or commented upon by a rhythm, is the simplest form of what Pound has roughly classed as logopeia, and of what I have called the anti-image. A rhythm that has traditional associations, or innate (i. e., more remote or not immediately obviously traditional) associations, or one that has acquired associations in the given poem, by previous fusion, may comment upon its meaning-content either by contrast or augmentation. It will be seen that each type of image has its converse, or anti-image, and this first type of anti-image is the converse of the simple physical fact fused with a rhythm. Laforgue achieves this anti-image by putting a ridiculous fact into a traditionally plaintive metre, or by putting a sentimental or tragic fact into a ridiculous metre, or by various shadings between these two extremes. The result is one phase of his rather mournful satire:

> Alléz, steriles ritournelles,
> La vie est vraie et criminelle.

To discussion of symbol. The function of sound in the anti-image ("a rhythm that has traditional associations," etc.) is a symbol-function and may exist simultaneously with an image-function.

2

The second type of image is the *complex physical fact fused with a rhythm*. This is the same as the first type of image, except that here the fusion is between two or more sense-perceptions and one sound-perception. The line quoted in *Section I* of these notes belonged to this type of image, and also the third, fourth, and fifth lines of the quotation from H. D. (if taken as a unit). There are various devices for constructing an image of this sort, some of which I shall describe, that the image, when come upon, may be the more easily recognized.

First: The direct comparison of sense-perceptions, as in the so-called metaphor and simile. The line quoted in *Section I* is of this nature.

Second: The putting of two sense-perceptions in sequence, so that while they have no direct or grammatically indicated connection with each other, each reflects upon the other because of the quality they have in common:

> So wore night; the East was gray;
> White the broadfaced hemlock flowers. . . .

Movements may be similarly put into sequence:

> And Neptune made for thee a spumy tent,
> And Pan made sing for thee his forest hive,

Here the first line is a fusion of two sense-perceptions with one sound-perception, and the movement of the sound-perception, carrying with it an echo of the "spumy tent," holds over and dies into the movement of the humming bees.

Third: An adjective, being a generalization taken from a series of more or less related observations, may, if applied to a more or less remote observation, effect a fusion. This is the "transferred epithet" of rhetoric:

> the parakeet—
> trivial and humdrum on examination. . . .

Fourth: It is perhaps not amiss to mention a certain fallacy fairly common to a large number of second-rate but occasionally good poets when they attempt to use this image. That fallacy is an attempt to give existence in that which we perceive as space to a perception that has no such existence, and to fuse this perception with that side of a second perception which actually exists in space. Or, to speak more concretely, to fuse, in the meaning of words, a perception of sound and some visual perception, usually color. Now it seems that certain persons do sense a relationship between colors and sounds, but it is also certain that many of the persons who do so, disagree among themselves as to the details of this relationship. And even if it were possible to find an absolute relation, mathematical or perceptive, between sound waves, which move slowly through the air, and the hypothetical (and doubtful) light waves which move with terrific rapidity through an imponderable substance known as ether, it would not necessarily follow that related emotions would be produced by related waves, for these waves are perceived through entirely different organs, and the organs of perception are obviously factors of the emotion. Further-more, as I have already inferred, sound *as we perceive it*, has no existence in space, but only in time, or what we perceive as time; for it is only that which is *seen* that can be said to fill space, which is a purely visual concept. But the visual, if it have existence in space, has also existence in time, and this existence is more evident if the visual perception have motion, which is a relation between space and time, and still more evident if that motion have rhythm, which is time consciously broken up and organized with respect to those existences and their intervals that it contains. Now sound, having existence in time, can also have rhythm. So it follows that whereas the auditory and the visual will have no common ground in that which we know as space, they will have a common ground in that which we know as time, and that common ground is rhythm—the actual rhythm of the thing perceived, and not the rhythm of the words containing the thing. Now if an auditory and a visual rhythm be stated in the meaning of words, a fusion may be possible:

And like a giant harp that hums
On always, and is always blending
The coming of what never comes
With what has past and had an ending,
The City trembles, throbs, and pounds
Outside, and through a thousand sounds
The small intolerable drums
Of Time are like slow drops descending.

Here the rhythm of the sound of the "drums of Time" and the rhythm of the motion of the drops fuse.

It must be recollected that in speaking of the rhythm of a

sound, or rather of sounds, in this connection, I do not refer to the rhythm of sound waves, which belong to science and not to unaided human perception; but I refer to the rhythm or rate of movement from sound to sound, as those sounds actually strike, or may be imagined to strike, the ear. And similarly, I refer to actual visual perception of rhythm and not to the rhythm of light waves, which is imperceptible, as such, to the eye.

2a

The anti-image corresponding to the complex physical fact fused with a rhythm is of four possible sorts. In the first sort, that of two thought-perceptions and one sound perception, a fusion of the thought-perceptions is possible, as they are of the same substance. But these thought perceptions, having no physical existence, and the sound perception having only physical existence cannot fuse with the sound perception, but can only comment through the mind. The only example of this variation upon the second anti-image that I can find at present is in a poem of my own:

> We perish, we
> Who die in art,
> With that surprise
> Of one who speaks
> To us, and knows
> Wherein he lies.

The second variation upon this anti-image is composed of one sense-perception, one thought-perception, and one sound-perception intercommenting:

> Streets that follow like a tedious argument
> Of insidious intent,
> To lead you to an overwhelming question.

The third variation is of two sense-perceptions which may or may not fuse, and one sound-perception that comments. The fourth variation is composed of two remotely separate facts, at least one of which must be physical and which fuses with the rhythm and takes on an image existence of its own, as in the case of the simple physical fact fused with a rhythm. The unfused fact comments. This is sometimes known as the *conceit*. An example of the conceit is Donne's comparison of two souls to a pair of compasses, toward the end of the *Valediction Forbidding Mourning*.

3

There is a third type of image that seems to fall about halfway between the first and second types that I have defined. This image is composed of two physical facts, each fused with the sound, and, while neither fused with each other nor commenting upon each other, altering and defining each other's value quite definitely, simply by the juxtaposition of their physical qualities or by the action of the one upon the other:

> The maidens taste
> And stray impassioned in the littering leaves.

The straying maidens and the littering leaves are here the physical facts. They have no point in common, as had the walking man and the approaching night of the first example, but they do fuse into a single movement, a single image, of which the sound of the whole is a part. And by that fusion, each is sharply limited, separated from the general.

If the sound of each element of an image possibly of this group or possibly of the first fuses with each element respectively, it belongs to this group (quotation in 3, 1st two lines of Hopkins quotation). If the sound of both elements fuse with one element, it belongs to the first group. In the Gautier "cloitre" and "mur" contribute solely to the movements of the man and the shadow respectively. Hair-line for sake of convenience.

3a

The corresponding anti-image is of two thought-perceptions placed together, and the one acting upon the other, to such an extent as to effect the defining of both, without any attempt at fusion or intercomment at one point:

the future of time is determined by the power of volition.

4

A perception—almost invariably a sense-perception—that has acquired, by long association or by personal association for whatever period of time, an emotional overtone or symbolic value, may be used in a poem, so long as it be given in the poem a new existence as image or anti-image. If the fusion or inter-comment necessary to this existence be not achieved, the symbolic value of the perception is useless as the perception is without life. If, however, the perception be given this existence, the symbolism may augment the emotion of the image considerably, and the emotion resulting from the symbolism can scarcely be separated in the mind from the emotion resulting from the image. The symbolical overtone is more or less analagous to what is known in painting as "literary" beauty.

There are symbols in literature whose symbolic value is evident, and there are those whose symbolic value is only in part evident, and still others the mere existence of whose symbolic value is only implied. Glenway Wescott once wrote in a letter: "the legitimate field of movement clearly seen, intention unknown."

Symbolism is commonly thought of as something vaguely metaphysical, but it need not be. Any fact or object which sums up or evokes any set of conditions or emotions, whatever their nature, is to some extent a symbol. Thus T. S. Eliot's Sweeny is symbolic of a certain type of ugliness, Rachel nee Rabinovitch and the rest are symbolic of certain smaller divisions of that ugliness. Mr. Eliot gives movements to these figures that are very often of a quite impersonal nature—that is, they are movements that are in no wise connected with their ugliness or are presented with a curious detachment from their ugliness; and these movements are usually of supreme sinuosity and beauty. So that, by placing these symbols of ugliness in contrast to the impersonal beauty of the movements of their flesh, he achieves at a single stroke the functions of the image and the anti-image—something that hovers between satire and agony.

The symbol must not be confused with the physical movement having emotional connotations, or expressing emotion; for the latter is concerned with specific instances only, while the former is expressive of a concept or whole field of emotion, such as ugliness, decay, or whatnot. And yet the symbol expresses this emotion not by stating the concept, but by evoking it or reminding one of it, through some quality of its own (the symbol's) limited and specific nature.

SECTION IV

Upon the Nature of Words and Their Use

It was assumed in the second section of these notes that words had two qualities: sound and meaning; and insofar as we are able to trust our sense, this assumption is justified. That a few words (such as articles) partake, in their meaning, more of the nature of a gesture or an indication than of a fact, does not alter the general truth of the assumption. In some words one will find that the sound of the word, and the thing for which that word stands, are perfectly fused, and constitute an image in themselves. Such words are the nouns, *leaves, dresses, dust, breath.* The word, *drum,* if not quite so perfect a fusion, is very nearly so; and after noting the sound and meaning qualities of this word, consider the word, *dumb,* the sound of which is nearly identical with that of *drum,* and the meaning of which, insofar as it is a word of silence, is the opposite. Here the sound and meaning are definitely not fused, and a problem is presented to the writer. Then there are words that represent abstractions, whose meanings have no relationship to anything physical, and so can have no aesthetic necessity—that is, if the sound of any word can be proven to be other than accidental. Such a word is, for instance, *hypocritic*. Now consider these lines:

> Daughters of Time, the hypocritic days,
> Muffled and dumb like barefoot dervishes,
> And marching single in an endless file,
> Bring diadems and fagots in their hands.

Dumb, whose meaning is opposed to its sound, fuses its sound with the two sense-perceptions, *muffled* and *barefoot*, and extends and intensifies these perceptions. The sound of *hypocritic*, an abstract word, presents the short, bony, half-dance steps of the muffled dervishes. *Diadems*, a heavy-sounding word that stands for a bright object, fuses its sound with the muffled movement; and *fagots*, fairly well fused in itself, also contributes to the movement.

SECTION V

Upon the Construction of the Poem, with Relation to the Image

It is assumed that the parts of any poem have some reason for being placed in sequence. Otherwise they had better be left as separate poems.

In some poems, especially in narrative poems, one sometimes finds passages that, without great emotional value in themselves, serve to carry the action or thought from one image to another, and in this function may be necessary:

> And a good south wind sprung up behind;
> The Albatross did follow,
> And every day, for food or play.
> Came to the mariners' hollo.

The sound here does not fuse with the physical facts, nor is there any fusion between physical facts, nor can there be said to be any intercomment of perceptions. But this purely narrative passage has been made as concise as possible, and, being short, the rhythm, being the rhythm of the preceding stanzas which are successful images, carries something of an echo over into what would be an otherwise flat stanza. Often the first type of image will carry a narrative passage or one of the types of anti-image, a thought passage. Sometimes one of these purely narrative passages will come very close to being an image or anti-image.

Often a poem or a passage of a poem is made up of images that are closely related, or are sub-parts of a larger image, so that the poem or passage closely resembles an extended example of the second variation upon the second type of image.

Sometimes a definite emotion is produced by a sudden change of direction (in images of motion) from one image to the next. Note the last line of the first chorus in Swinburne's *Atalanta*. The departing image produces an effect of a somewhat centripetal nature.

Images of contrasting symbolic values may be so placed together that intercomment is achieved. T. S. Eliot has done this in *Sweeney among the Nightingales* and elsewhere.

One image of any type may act upon and limit another image, as one part of the third type of image acts upon and limits the other part.

Many poets have entirely omitted any intellectual sequence from one image to the next, depending upon an emotional unity, and there is nothing to be said against this. Other poets have attempted to carry the method even further, omitting all intellectual (syntactical) sequence within the image, or trying to, attempting to create aesthetic relationships from broken words and phrases. This is interesting, and may some day succeed. The difficulty with most of these experimenters up to date, however, is that, having cast out all other thought from their

minds, they cannot cast out the clichés, the very old sentimentalities, which seem to be so deeply rooted as to be almost
mental reflexes. Their poems become, then, desperate efforts to
conceal these clichés under a broken exterior, which is evading
the question.

Poetry of this nature is often compared to abstract painting
or sculpture, and praised for this reason and for few others. And
yet, if we reduce literature to complete abstraction—that is,
sound without meaning—we no longer have literature, but
music, and we must either adopt the notation of music or else
adopt a new system of notation to provide for intonation as well
as vowel and consonant sounds. And if we do not so reduce
literature we inevitably retain an element of representation,
however broken up and distorted. That is, if we imagine a potential sculptor, let us say, living in some strange realm where
he is able to experience no sense-impressions—even impressions
of his own body or any part of it—except impressions of that
which he may be able to create out of some imponderable substance that will take form as soon as definitely imagined, he will
be able to imagine nothing, for he will have no concept of form,
solidity. Indeed, he is very likely to be entirely unconscious.
But give him a pebble—which will bring him to consciousness—
and he will be able to imagine another pebble, and variations
upon pebbles, and further variations upon those variations until he creates a world and an art. And having created a world of
variations that no longer resemble each other closely, he may
be able to resynthesize various forms into new forms that do not
as a whole resemble anything in his world, but they will inevitably be representative in some degree, of whatever number
of things. And the steps between this type of art and the type
that will in some definitely recognizable degree resemble a
definite one of his variations upon the original pebble will be
infinite in number and the differences between them infinitely
slight. So that one can only say that piece of sculpture is good
which *depends* upon its form and not upon its resemblance to
something else; and one can not say truly that is best which
resembles no natural form, for there is no such thing. Similarly,
that poetry is good which is a perfect fusion of perceptions, and

that which is an imperfect fusion of perceptions or depends mainly upon symbolic or other connotations is, to that extent, weak.

The poet wishing to write "abstract" poetry of this type, must not dispense with all thought, then, and write without consideration, for this will only lead him into the clichés mentioned above; but he must choose carefully the material which he wishes to break up and recombine, and work with at least as definite an intention and consciousness as any sculptor or painter.

STATEMENT OF PURPOSE
(The Gyroscope)

"Les grandes poetes . . . sont de étres qui, par le par et libre exer-cice de le volonté, parviennent a un état ou ils sont a la fois cause et effét, sujet et objet, magnétiseur et somnambule."

Baudelaire

The Gyroscope will be a mimeographed quarterly journal pub-lishing prose and verse and attempting to fix in literary terms some approximation of a classical state of mind. *The Gyroscope* will be opposed to all forms of spiritual extroversion: (1) to all doctrines of liberation and emotional expansionism, since they deprecate and tend to eliminate the intellect, the core of con-scious existence; (2) to all doctrines of religious expansionism, whether the Nature-worship of Wordsworth or the more ortho-dox forms of mysticism, if such can be said to exist since these attitudes cultivate a parasitic relationship to a deity, real or imagined, and minimize the moral and intellectual responsi-bilities of man as man; (3) to all doctrines of humanitarianism or "service" since these doctrines are in the main the mask of sentimentalized vices, and, where they are sincere, teach the individual to "help" his fellows before civilizing himself, and so lead to chaos; (4) to all doctrines which advocate that the poet "express" his country (Whitmanian Rousseauism) or his time

From *Gyroscope,* I no. 1 (1929).

216

(Dadaism and allied heresies), since these are merely extensions of Nature-Worship and involve the same fallacy—that of emotional escape from the inner discipline into a parasitic relationship to something ill-defined or non-human or both; (5) to the delirium of data of the realists as well as to the delirium in vacuo of the super-realists, since both negate all principles of judgment, discrimination, and organization and are the product of a passive and receptive state of mind; (6) to the contemporary ideal of the submergence of the individual character in the non-human data of busines and science; (7) to the emotional receptivism of Mr. Eliot and Mr. MacLeish, who employ despair as a drug and a luxury, and who, therefore, may be justly suspected of never having actually experienced it; (8) to all forms of stylistic looseness and grand carelessness, since these are the romantic Word (if there is one) made flesh.

The Gyroscope believes, on the other hand, that not only in drama, but in lyric poetry, in prose, and in life, the expression of inadequately motivated emotion constitutes melodrama and is contemptible; that the misfortunes of fools are not tragedy; that the forms of art are the only finally satisfactory means of evaluating the phenomena of life and of establishing a communicable attitude which may permit of such specific evaluations from a comprehensive and stable point of view; that stylistic precision is merely the ultimate manifestation of spiritual precision and strength; and that spiritual precision and strength can be developed in a satisfactory degree only through the serious and protracted study of the masters of art and thought, as well as of self and of living human relations.

NOTES ON CONTEMPORARY CRITICISM

I

I believe that the arguments supporting some sort of dualistic universe are more plausible than those supporting a monistic one, but they do not appear to me absolutely conclusive. Granting, however, the concept of a dualistic universe, it does not follow necessarily that the non-material principle is a deity in the theological nor even in the Aristotelian sense. Nor, granting the Aristotelian concept, does it follow necessarily that God is Providence. Nor granting that God is Providence, does it follow that man has an immortal soul. Nor, granting that man has an immortal soul, does it follow that immortality is any less terrifying to contemplate than mortality—which, in turn, is no less terrifying for the comparison.

To connect these ideas into a necessary sequence, one can have recourse to but a single authority and divine revelation. But because of difficulties that are mainly philological, historical, anthropological, and moral, it is impossible to accept at the present time any of the existing doctrines that are offered as divine revelations. If either of the two preceding statements can be logically and conclusively disproved, the following propositions are without value. If they cannot be disproved the most

From *Gyroscope*, VI no. 3 (1929).

recent essays by Allen Tate (the *Criterion*, July 1929) and by
T. S. Eliot (*For Launcelot Andrews*) are without value except
in so far as they point to the errors and loose writing of specific
critics. It is precisely here that Mr. Tate and Mr. Eliot must
elucidate their beliefs, and elucidate them openly, completely,
and precisely. Both Mr. Eliot and Mr. Tate assert that there is
no adequate rational basis for ethics and seem to imply that if
there were one, man would be of insufficient character to profit
by it without divine aid. Mr. Eliot has turned Anglo-Catholic;
Mr. Tate contents himself with stating his thesis. . . . One is,
however, naturally moved to wonder, of Mr. Eliot how he did
it, and of Mr. Tate what he is going to do next.

II

So long as it remains even possible that man is mortal and
that God is not Providence, God ceases to be more than a
metaphysical abstraction: He has no real meaning for man. In
constructing an ethic, one is forced to choose between two possible foundations and only two: an absolutely unshakeable
religious belief on the one hand, and, if that is not possible, the
least comforting of the various possibilities on the other. An
ethic built on any other foundation will be subject to collapse
at any critical moment and will so be without value.

We have ruled out the possibility of a firm religious belief, and
so are forced to define the least comforting possibility; namely,
that God, if he exists at all, having no practical connection with
man, ceases to exist for man, and, so far as actual human experience is concerned, the visible universe is the beginning,
middle, and end of human life. Man comes from the earth and
returns to the earth and makes of the interim what he can, of
his own unaided powers. This does not imply of necessity a
belief in a mechanistic universe nor in any system of deter-
minism. I, personally, hold no such beliefs. It is simply a bare
statement of the inescapable necessities, and nothing more, of a
belief in existence. Anything beyond this basis is inferential

and subject to revision and hence unsafe as a foundation for a rule of living.

III

A rule of living is based on some fundamental concept of Good and Evil. The belief that such a concept can rest only on divine revelation seems to me unfounded. If the Catholic Church offers an idea of Good and Evil based upon revelation, that idea can be defined rationally. If it can be defined rationally as it was, in the main, by the Greeks, before the Church took it over—it can subsist in the minds of rational beings without the aid of revelation. I do not deny that revelation, as an aditional support, is desirable. But I simply maintain that, such support being impossible, the rational being, if he devotes himself to the problem honestly and seriously, has at least a chance of maintaining himself, however precariously, without it. His position, so maintained or even lost but yet visible as a possibility, slight though it value may be as compared to the position of the believer, is nevertheless infinitely valuable so long as the position of the believer remains chimeric.

That such an ethic is not parasitic upon religion is sufficiently demonstrated by the dependence of the Christian ethic upon Greek systems, or at least by the unanimity of the Church, Aristotle, and in a measure the Stoics, upon most essential points. If it be objected that Stoicism was a religion, my answer is that theologically it was simply a form of pantheism with no romantic connotations; it involved the eventual submersion of individuality in deity, and involved no divine revelation, and so fulfilled the conditions that I have postulated for the present time. The system of Aristotle was more acute and complete but offered no practical solution of this difficulty. If this be Naturalism, a term that is coming to be used by certain critics as something of a bogey, so bet it; but in this event everything that is not Catholicism is Naturalism, and there are hence many varieties of Naturalism, and as we have nothing else to choose from it behooves us to choose carefully.

IV

The basis of Evil is in emotion; Good rests in the power of rational selection in action, as a preliminary to which the emotion in any situation must be as far as possible eliminated, and, in so far as it cannot be eliminated, understood. I say "as far as possible" advisedly, for such an elimination can never be complete; and the irreducible emotion, if properly evaluated, may even function on the side of Good. If the subsisting emotion in any situation is genuinely irreducible, there is at least the possibility of a sound moral evaluation of its character on the part of the person experiencing it; and if such an evaluation is made, right action becomes highly probable even though the emotion be definitely aligned with the forces of Evil. This personal decision, dangerous though it may be, is nevertheless not eliminated by religion. No dogma can be so complete as to fit exactly every situation.

V

If it be objected that I propose no end for which a man should reduce his emotion to a minimum and then, if need be, thwart that minimum, I answer with the Stoics that the end is a controlled and harmonious life. Any man who gratifies an unjust desire, who indulges knowlingly in a violation of equity, weakens his self-control by that much and opens the way to complete loss of it, to disintegration into pure emotionalism, which is pure mechanism: such a man is in danger of losing his humanity, or ceasing really to exist as a man. By a violation of equity, I mean an act that seems unjust to the actor after he has put himself as best and as honestly as he is able in the position of a disinterested observer. This is a dangerous standard, but it is the only one available without religion or even, on the naked edge of the act, with religion. It is emphatically not to be confused with a doctrine of self-indulgence and emotional expansionism. The standard is doubly dangerous with our present debauched educational system, but it is all we have. The danger can be reduced by discipline, constant self-criticism, and subjection to the criticism of philosophy. One should avoid not only violations of equity and the formation of bad habits, but even the formation of useless habits; for even those that do no immediate harm to others, may tend in themselves to weaken the will. The habit of easy habit-formation is in itself an insidious vice. To maintain a reasonable degree of self-control ones habits should be selected with a definite end in view for each.

Felix Ravaisson, in the second volume (published in 1846) of his more than competent work *Le Metaphysique d'Aristote*, refers to the moral collapse, the submersion in despair, of the later Stoics, such as Marcus Aurelius and Epictetus, in terms almost identical with those which we are accustomed to see applied today to the naturalistic collapse of the last and the present centuries. What he apparently fails to note is, that because the Stoics denied the emotions completely, in favor of the intellect, they failed to make any provision for them and so became easily their victims, as of an insidious consumption; the resultant spiritual enervation being very similar to that at which the modern naturalists have arrived by way of an orgy of emotionalism (over a century long) at the expense of the intellect. Aristotle, on the other hand, states specifically in the *Magna Moralia* that, "speaking generally, it is not the case, as the rest of the world thinks that reason is the principle of and guide to virtue, but rather the feelings." He provides the feelings, however, with a very powerful intellectual substructure and a profoundly difficult emotional descipline, of which the arts are an important part. These notes, then, are basically Aristotelian.

VI

I should differ from such writers as Mssrs Babbitt, More, and Foerster, in preferring, if forced to the choice, to judge a man's ethics by his poetry, rather than his poetry by his ethics. In this I should be in agreement, I believe, with Mr. Tate. I should differ from Mr. Tate, however, in this: that, in his aver-

sion to what he calls the "mechanism of moral ideas" constituting the minds of such men as Mr. More and Mr. Foerster, he
seems to accept, or at any rate fails to deny, whether adver-
tently or inadvertently, the opposite mechanism, that of Nature. He specifically states that contemporary writers *are not
responsible* for their education and attitudes. From a genuinely
Aristotelian point of view, from any indeed save a deterministic
or Calvinistic point of view, this is only in part correct; they are
not responsible for the molding they receive from their environment during their immature years, but, given a little enlighten-
ment and a modicum of will, they could modify their condition
in a fair measure by persistent effort during maturity. The
poetic equivalent of Mr. Tate's thesis is the poetry of Mr.
Eliot and Mr. MacLeish. The poetic equivalent of my thesis, to
go no farther than Mr. Tate's generation and mine, is the poetry
of Mr. Tate, of Louise Bogan, of Mr. Howard Baker—and at
certain moments of Mr. Hart Crane and of Mr. Grant H. Code.

VII

If it be objected that there should be an end to a controlled
and harmonious life, I answer that, if life is all we are given, a
controlled and harmonious life is the only available end and its
value should be self-evident. The believer removes his end one
step, finding it in salvation and life with or in God, a life which
he cannot understand and is forced to accept on faith. One
cannot, as Aristotle remarks, seek ends for ends indefinitely;
one has to face one somewhere or other in all its naked simplicity and make the best of it: the series must rest at some
point on a self-evident fact. If we are given a brief span of consciousness only, it is self-evident that the highest possible good
is the greatest possible degree of consciousness during the span
allotted; nor is consciousness synonymous with the romantic
notion of "experience" (usually at the expense of another), for
unethical action is commonly due in a large measure to blindness, as ethical to awareness (or to complete experiencing) of
the whole of any situation. The ability to labor toward this
condition in view of the ultimate annihilation of the fruits of

one's labors is a moral quality that is or may be extremely difficult of achievement. Nevertheless, if one take Aristotle, Thomas
Hardy, Emily Dickinson, or Baudelaire as examples, it is evident that the quality can be achieved. Mr. Eliot's failure to
achieve it accounts for (as it can be seen in) his verse, and,
unless he can justify logically every step of his conversion, it
accounts in all likelihood for his conversion as well. His failure
to achieve it accounts also for his apparently firm belief that no
one can achieve it and that everyone is faced with the choice
between conversion or collapse. Without conversion, collapse
is imminent; but it would appear that, with adequate strength
of intention, it can be avoided. Such strength of intention may
be the result of innate strength of character or of habit-formation or of both. Mr. Eliot's early habits of feeling, at any rate,
were formed on Laforgue; and one is inclined to wonder if his
present vision of Original Sin (a valuable doctrine in itself) is not
in some measure an apotheosis of Laforguian helplessness.

VIII

The technique for dealing with the irreducible emotion, for
that which cannot be formulated, is not dogma but art; and the
technique of literary art, with this end in view, I have analyzed
in detail in my essay entitled The Extension and Reintegration
of the Human Spirit, through the Poetry, Mainly French and
American, Since Poe and Baudelaire. Dogma, or logic, may
provide a means of *approach* to any situation, and perhaps from
many sides, but can never cover any. It thus may provide the
logical or meaning-content of a poem; but the *poetic* content
inheres in the feeling, the style, the untranslatable, and can be
reduced to no formula save itself. It may even, in fact, constitute a complete negation of the logical content; and the moral
quality of a poem lies in its poetic content. The failure of Mr.
Babbitt and his associates as critics lies in their failure to make
this distinction, or at any rate to profit by it. The contents of the
present notes are elementary, but in the light of the major
evasions of our leading critics it seemed necessary to summar-
ize them in self-defense.

THE EXTENSION AND REINTEGRATION OF THE HUMAN SPIRIT

*Through the Poetry Mainly French and American
Since Poe and Baudelaire*

FOREWORD: BAUDELAIRE MY APOLOGIST

To excuse myself for approaching the poetic problem from what is proverbially the "sterile" side, that is from the purely formal, I choose to refer to the example and to some of the comments of one of the great masters of the lyric. It is the terrific discipline, spiritual and literary, of Baudelaire that so saturates his line with meaning. He wrote of the acting of Rouvière: "Et bien que l'intensité du jeu et la projection redoubtable de la volonté tiennent la plus grande part dans cette séduction, tout ce miracle s'accomplit sans effort." That is, if the intensity of the work of art, be it ever so much greater—as it must be—than of the simple experience, is increased evenly and proportionately throughout, there will be no sense of effort so long as the mind is moving within the boundaries of the form—provided, of course, that one has taken pains to familiarize oneself with the method and materials involved, that is, really to get oneself within the boundaries of the form. Baudelaire can write quite simply, 'C'est affreux, ô mon âme!'" and it is. There are few poets of whom one can say as much—it is a faculty of the very small number of

From *The New American Caravan*, III (1929), pp. 361-402. [This essay, extensively revised and with a different emphasis, served as the basis for Mr. Winters' later essay, "The Experimental School in American Poetry," *Primitivism and Decadence* (1937), reprinted in *In Defense of Reason* (Denver, Alan Swallow, 1947). *Ed.*]

absolute masters. One finds a comparable power in the sonnets of Shakespeare, the lyrics of Thomas Hardy and of Emily Dickinson, in the tragedies of Racine. It is something over and beyond the explosive grandeur of *Bâteau Ivre* or even of Marlowe. It is not what is said that weighs so heavily; but one feels behind the line, in all that is *omitted*, a lifetime of monstrous discipline, from which is born the power of absolute wisdom without evident additional effort. Racine claimed that the entire labor of writing his tragedies consisted in plotting the action: the rest was mere routine. This is probably a great exaggeration, but it suggests an important truth.

The only godhead possible for man, *as man* (in this world, or, if you like, in the next) is not a mystical but a moral godhead. The mystic achieves godhead only through self-annihilation, which is logically inconceivable. The man who, through a dynamic and unified grasp on life, lives fully and to the point of being able to renounce life with dignity, having known it, achieves something vastly more difficult and more noble than the immediate evasion and denial of the mystic or the whimper of the nihilist. It is in the consideration of this fact that we find the true function of the poet: not to present something enheartening, cheerful, and simple to the simple-minded, nor a sentimental or decorative view of extinction and the approach thereto to the emotionalist, but to extend as far as possible the human consciousness and to organize the facts of life into a new and more dynamic synthesis. The facts of life at best are disheartening; the vision of life which man has little by little constructed (or perhaps one should say stripped bare) is all but crushing. To evade the facts and attempt bluff vigor, as Browning often seems to do, is not convincing to the man who has experienced the imaginative facts. The artist who is actually ignorant of the metaphysical horror of modern thought or who cannot feel it imaginatively— and there are many such—is of only a limited, a more or less decorative, value. But the artist who can feel the full horror, organize it into a dynamic attitude or state of mind, asserting by that very act his own life and the strength and value of his own life, and who can leave that state of mind completed behind him for others to enter, has performed the greatest spiritual service that can be performed. For it is only the superior man, the man capable of experiencing art, who finds himself in any dilemma; but the emotional tone, whether of vigor or of decadance, felt by the superior man, will eventually, by whatever devious and subtle means, filter down infecting in one degree or another the entire structure of society. The increasing popularity of several species of second hand nihilism in our own day is probably responsible in a large degree for the decreasing functioning of the will among all of the educated classes; an obvious symptom of which is the depressing but steady increase of sexual perversion, not only in our "art centers," but in nearly all of our universities, large and small, with the ultimate spiritual dishonesty and sterility that it seems in nearly all cases to entail.

Baudelaire wrote of Balzac: "J'ai mainte fois été étonné que la grande gloire de Balzac fût de passer pour un observateur; il m'avait toujours semblé que son principale mérite était d'être visionnaire, et visionnaire passionné. . . . Bref, chacun chez Balzac, même les portiers, a du génie. Toutes les âmes sont des armes chargées de volonté jusqu'a la gueule." T. S. Eliot writes: "If you compare several representative passages of the greatest poetry you see how great is the variety of types of combination, and also how completely any semi-ethical criterion of 'sublimity' misses the mark. For it is not the 'greatness,' the intensity, of the emotions, the components, but the intensity of the artistic process, the pressure, so to speak, under which the fusion takes place, that counts." But is not this very "pressure" which Mr. Eliot emphasizes the ultimate ethical criterion? It is the "will" which Baudelaire found in Balzac's doorkeepers—that is, their will to live as intensely as possible as doorkeepers fixed in the rigid vision that constituted the mentality of Balzac, a vision stretched to the utmost intensity of its sort. Art is the most intense moment of consciousness: the intensity of the moment of fusion is the final moral assertion of the artist, who by that act *makes an integral part of his own dynamic existence* the fact that he has met [life], no matter how terrible it may be. It is the final proof that he, as a self-directed integer, is morally superior to the facts of life. A successful poem, then, may even be, as an experience and a moral evaluation, a negation of the ideational

material that it contains. This fact alone can explain the spiritual
security to be found in the most terrible of the tragic poets. This
faculty I almost never find in the purely derivative poetry of
T. S. Eliot, which, so far as it presents any original attitude,
offers one that is purely negative and nihilistic. Mr. Eliot seems
to have been crushed by his vision—his sense of time in an incomprehensible universe leaves him gasping. He cannot face it except from behind the screen of the classics—he offers quotations
from the best poets, along with a few footnotes and commen-
taries of his own to prove that it is not worth while to face the
vision, to live fully. Unless one has the strength to desire to live
to the end, in full view of the horror, the tragic emotion becomes
impossible. There is no tragedy in losing that which is not
valued, nor gain in possessing it: the world will end for Mr. Eliot
"not with a bang but a whimper." Baudelaire's vision is not
essentially different from that of Mr. Eliot—much that is most
interesting in the latter's verse comes almost directly from Baudelaire, as well as from Laforgue, Gautier, and the Elizabethans
—but Baudelaire maintained himself intact and grew. It is this
growth under pressure that gives his poems their experiential
density. He was too engrossed with what he knew first hand to
borrow very often. His life was a difficult struggle to master his
own experience—not to endow with a semblance of exterior mastery a private collection of favorite quotations and references.

With regard to the influence temporarily exerted by Mr. Eliot
on the younger men, as well as to the bad start to which Mr.
Eliot himself got off in following Laforgue, I sometimes wonder
if the formula of discovery-via-technique, which I shall discuss
more at length a little later, may not apply to movements as well
as poems. The horrible in the early stages of romanticism, in
writers of the Radcliffe-Lewis type, is purely, I think one is safe
in saying, an affectation. It is probably an affectation the
greater part of the time in Poe—that is, a mechanical formula—
and occasionally at least in Baudelaire. But by means of this sort
of technical induction, Poe and Baudelaire beyond any doubt
discovered the emotional horror, the experience of horror, that
resides in the modern concept of life. One thinks of Baudelaire's
account of the actor Rouvière, who, when he wished to under-

stand the emotions, the character, of another person, cast his face in the expression worn by that person *and then knew what he thought*.[1] There is now no further escape from the thing they found and fixed. It would have existed, a vague and terrible background anyway. And it is better to have it defined and incorporated into a dynamic attitude than wandering about like an unlaid ghost. Writing of Guys, Baudelaire said: "Mais si, par hasard, quelqu'un malavisé cherchait dans ces compositions de M. G., disséminés un peu partout, l'occasion de satisfaire une malsaine curiosité, je le préviens charitablement qu'il n'y trouvera rien de ce qui peut exciter une imagination malade. Il ne recontrera *que le vice inévitable*, c'est-a-dire le regard du démon embusqué dans les ténèbres...." Baudelaire, having himself felt those same eyes in the dark, was strong enough and skillful enough to stare till he could find them and face them.

The late Jacques Rivière wrote of Baudelaire's "vers si parfaits, si mesurés, que d'abord on hésite a leur donner tout leur sens; un espoir veille quelques instants, un doute sur leur profondeur." He quote among several examples the line:

Le printemps adorable a perdu son odeur.

And yet the weight that one feels in this line when one reads it in the poem—*Le Goût du Néant*—is in a considerable part lost in isolation; and this fact reveals at least one very important part of the secret of Baudelaire's art. No less, I believe, than Mallarmé, was he a master in relating rhymes to meaning, in relating syllable lengths, tonalities, phrase-stresses, pauses, word-order, to meaning. We are told that the poet's art consists in the choice of words. But beyond the masters of rhetoric—and there are many such who are very great, men like Marlowe, Keats, Rimbaud, there are a few supreme men who seem to succeed in the most difficult realm of experience, almost without apparent effort. Mallarmé, in his later work especially, tended more and more to isolate the arcana of expression (consider, for instance, the sonnet beginning *Surgi de la croupe et du bond*, the very first line of which, with nothing to follow, no meaning no subject attached,

1. Some similar notion occurs somewhere in Poe.

is dynamic) through the logical obscurity of his style, and, frequently, through the choice of subjects that in themselves are trivial or bizarre or both. The name of Mallarmé, as a result of his concentration on this problem, has been almost synonymous with the quality; and we are likely to overlook the fact that a few poets, more obvious (and more profound) as regards the subject-content of their poems, have been at least as subtle and indubitably more profound as regards the actual aesthetic experience. But to quote the poem with which this train of thought began:

> Morne esprit autrefois amoreux de la lutte,
> L'Espoir, dont l'éperon attisait ton ardeur,
> Ne veut plus t'enfourcher! Couche-toi sans pudeur,
> Vieux cheval dont le pied à chaque obstacle butte.
>
> Résigne-toi, mon cœur; dors ton sommeil de brute.
>
> Esprit vaincu, fourbu! Pour toi, vieux maraudeur,
> l'amour n'a plus de goût, non plus que la dispute;
> Adieu donc, chants du cuivre et soupirs de la flute!
> Plaisirs, ne tentez plus un coer sombre et boudeur!
>
> Le Printemps adorable a perdu son odeur!
>
> Et le Temps m'engloutit minute par minute,
> Comme la neige immense un corps pris de roideur;
> Je contemple d'en haut le globe en sa rondeur,
> Et je n'y cherche plus l'abri d'une cahute!
>
> Avalanche veux-tu m'emporter dans ta chute?

One can point out satisfactorily, I suspect, only the more obvious stylistic elements that contribute to the massive density of the poem. There is the monotony of the two rhymes throughout, intensified by the couplet effect produced by the fifth, tenth, and fifteenth lines. There is also the preponderance of rhymes in— *utte*, the effect of which, especially in the fifth line, is to produce a feeling of tragic indifference, of sullen abruptness. Every line in the poem bears not only its own weight, but the weight of all that has gone before. It is almost never that one finds a poem so powerfully, so inseparably, a unit. One may say that this is "nothing but technique," and that the poet should say what he means in plain words. But acuteness of intelligence cannot be renounced by the possessor; and to the reader who is aware of these values they are plain enough and render the words much plainer— whereas additional words would only obscure the issue. To find a parallel in logic, such a poem is as superior to the tirades of Hugo or Byron, as is a definition by St. Thomas Aquinas to the ecstatic didacticism of Diderot or of Rousseau. It defines the experience in full, and refrains from obscuring it. These technical means are as definitely instruments of expression as are the contents of the dictionary. It is by such means that the poet produces his full effect, while having the air of understating his emotion—I believe that this accounts for the statement of Rivière, as for the failure to react highly on the part of readers conscious only of the meaning content of separate words to poems by Hardy, Baudelaire, and a few others. Between the words we are aware of the sound of the voice, the expression of the face. And it must be continually and rigidly born in mind that such expression is impossible unless something is perceived. It *is* the perception, or an integral part of it—*these technical nuances are a part of what is said, a subtle and powerful manifestation of the spirit.* One can point them out by means of rough classifications, but they are not, basically, classifiable—each one is a phenomenon, its own definition, a manifestation of the intelligence of the master.

Here is a similar quality in English from number CXVI of the sonnets of Shakespeare:

> Love's not Time's fool, though rosy lips and cheeks
> Within his bending sickle's compass come;
> Love alters not with his brief hours and weeks,
> But bears it out even to the edge of doom.

Or again, to quote Thomas Hardy:

> I say, "I'll seek her side
>   Ere hindrance interposes;"
>   But eve in midnight closes,
> And here I still abide.

When darkness wears I see
Her sad eyes in a vision;
They ask, "What indecision
Detains you, Love, from me?—

"The creaking hinge is oiled
I have unbarred the backway,
But you tread not the trackway;
And shall the thing be spoiled?

"Far cockcrows echo shrill,
The shadows are abating,
And I am waiting, waiting;
But O, you tarry still!"

The meaning-value of such a word as *spoiled* in this particular place, the sound-value of such a rhyme as *backway* and *trackway*, come closer to the effect produced by Baudelaire in *Le Gout du Néant*, than does almost anything else I can think of. This type of thing recurs constantly in Hardy, in Baudelaire, and in Shakespeare's sonnets: it is a species of slight, but precise, drop into a mastered colloquialism or semblance of awkwardness. Its spiritual implications are frequently incalculable. In Emily Dickinson and Donne, two poets about as great, or very nearly as great, the norm of expression is a shade too violent and bizarre commonly to permit of this particular means of definition.

THE MECHANICS OF THE MOOD

I. *The Scattered Method*—This is the simplest, as well as the most primitive method of attack on the subject, and remains the mosts common even today. It might well be illustrated diagrammatically by a focal point upon which equidistant lines converge —searchlights, as it were, illuminating a given idea or feeling from different angles. These various rays of light—the images and anti-images of a poem—have no intellectual connection with one another save that they all converge upon a common center, and are, or should be, in some degree related emotionally. We find this procedure, for instance, in Nashe's poem beginning:

> Adieu, farewell, earth's bliss,
> This world uncertain is.

The opening lines strike the note of the poem, and this is reverted to in the refrain at the end of each stanza. Every stanza develops this emotion or idea in a slightly different way, and there is no connection from stanza to stanza, save in so far as each deals with the same theme. In this particular poem one finds a similar method employed within the stanza, and this is common elsewhere. The description of a scene or object, as it involves no definitely logical order of details, will usually be classifiable under this heading. Very frequently, in fact, the details of such a description will not only constitute a scattered approach to a visual whole, but to a mood or emotion, as well, as in the case of Remy Belleau's *Avril.*

This method of composition, as I have said, occurs very early in literary history—is perhaps the earliest method used in lyrical writing that is in any degree sustained. Toward the latter part of the nineteenth century we find an acceleration of sequence beginning to take place. Nashe's poem moves much more rapidly than do most of the songs of his period or for some time thereafter; but in many of Emily Dickinson's poems a somewhat greater acceleration can be discerned, and this change is still more noticeable in the work of such definitely "modern" poets as Laforgue and Dr. Williams. Into much of the work of these two, however, especially of the former, there enters another element, the alternation of mood, which I shall discuss later. The method seems to me fully as valid today as ever for most purposes, and is too generally applicable to raise any of the particular philosophical problems involved in certain more narrowly limited ways of writing. It embraces what one might call the song-tradition, beginning with the *Sea-Farer*, including such thirteenth century pieces as *Alisoun* and others of the same group, Campion, Blake, Hardy, and reaching even to W. C. Williams.

II. *The Logical Method*—This method is a late and sophisticated procedure that in Europe was most widespread in the sixteenth and seventeenth centuries, though it appears earlier among the Provençaux and among such writers as Guido Cavalcanti. It is most strikingly exemplified possibly, certainly so far as English is concerned, in the work of Donne and his followers —we may with fair safety say that it is one of the chief characteristics of the Metaphysical School, perhaps the chief characteristic, though it is not invariably employed by them. *The Weeper*, by Crashaw, for example, follows a scattered interstanzaic relationship and a more or less logical intra-stanzaic one. This poem is, however, rather in the later Italian than in the English mode. The important fact about the logical method is that, as its name implies, each statement follows clearly out of the last through an apparently inevitable logical sequence. Mr. Eliot gives an excellent analysis of Marvell's poem *To His Coy Mistress*, with this trait, among others in mind. The logical development gives to the poem that quality of "tough reasonableness" which Mr. Eliot praises. Whether or not this quality is a concomitant part of "aesthetic form", which should then be weakened by its absence as in such a poem as Rimbaud's *Larme*, or whether it is an additional and more or less objective binding, not necessary to the achievement of artistic form in general but only to the achievement of form in dealing with a certain type of emotion, I should find it difficult to say. It seems to me dangerous to exclude as non-aesthetic a legitimate function of the spirit which can be demonstrated by literary examples to be at least harmless and probably beneficial in certain cases. The thing should be determined ultimately on the basis of the extent of the experience dynamized by the form, and, so far as contemporary writing is concerned, on the basis of availability. I shall therefore beg leave to postpone this question for a few more pages.

In Vaughan's poem called *The Lamp*, we have a more or less elaborate comparison of the poet's life to his reading-lamp, resulting in a frankly didactic poem of great beauty; although the method often led the English poets of the same century into elaborate absurdities—certain figures at times got more or less away from their authors and progressed almost of their own inevitable nature to logical conclusions of an extraordinary variety. This occurred mainly when the poet started with an external object and tried to draw similitudes from it, as in *The Weeper*, and seldom when, as in the greater portion of Donne, he began with an abstract concept and proceeded into the field of concrete experience. The former method, in general, is the Italian-Spanish, the latter the English-French. It is the difference between elaborate decoration and the intense experience of a complex mind. Vaughan's poem, to return, is worth quoting for comparison with other passages:

'Tis death night round about: Horrour doth creepe
And move on with the shades; stars nod and sleepe,
And through the dark aire spin a fine thread
Such as doth gild the lazie glow-worm's bed.
   Yet burn'st thou here a full day while I spend
My rest in cares, and to the dark world lend
These flames as thou dost thine to me; I watch
That houre, which must thy life and mine dispatch,
But still thou dost out-goe me, I can see
Met in thy flames all acts of piety;
Thy light is *Charity;* thy heat is *Zeale;*
And thy aspiring, active fires reveale
Devotion still on wing: Then, thou dost weepe
Still as thou burn'st, and the warm droppings creepe
To measure out thy length, as if thou'dst know
What stock, and how much time were left thee now;
Nor dost thou spend one teare in vaine, for still
As thou dissolv'st to them, and they distill,
They're stored up in the socket, where they lye,
When all is spent, thy last and sure supply:
And such is true repentance; ev'ry breath
Wee spend in sighs is treasure after death.
Only one point escapes thee; That thy Oile
Is still out with thy flame, and so both faile;
But whenso'ere I'm out, both shall be in,
And where thou mad'st an end, there I'll begin.

To reinforce the quality of this poem, let me quote another, slightly more sublimated but scarely less remarkable, by Richard Crashaw. It is entitled *The Recommendation:*

Those Houres, and that which hovers o're my End,
Into thy hands and hart, lord, I commend.

Take both to Thine Account, and I and mine
In that Hour and in these, may be all thine.

That as I dedicate my devoutest Breath
To make a kind of Life for my Lord's Death,

So from his living and life-giving Death,
My dying Life may draw a new and never-fleeting Breath.

Mr. Eliot has considered in some detail the qualities of the metaphysical poets, and it is an impertinence to attempt to improve upon his studies. I allow myself simply a brief summary of these poets' outstanding qualities: a logical structure (usual but not invariable); a tendency to fuse very precise thought with very intense concrete feeling, not using them alternately, nor using one as a decorative adjunct to the other, but combining both in the same statement; a tendency, especially marked in Donne (as well as in the Last Sonnets of Ronsard and in Baudelaire), to fuse in the same statement intense physical pain and mental anguish—the two become synonymous; and a rhythm, the precision and hardness of which tends occasionlly, as in Donne, even to arbitary brittleness.

These tendencies are, of course, all facets of the same phenomenon—the spiritual unity of the poets. Thought, for these men, was not an academic bypath, but the core of experience, and all their concrete experience remained inextricably bound up in the network of their beliefs, suspicions, and interests. The concrete and the abstract were one; the body and soul were if not one at least hopelessly interfused on this planet; bodily and spiritual suffering were one or at least interpenetrative; and as their thought was precise, their expression was precise, and metre is as

definitely a part of expression—even of the mechanics of thinking—as the meaning-content of verbs and nouns. This tendency
entered dramatic poetry in some degree doubtless, as Mr. Eliot
has suggested, by way of Ben Jonson, and may have reached the
dramatists of the decadence partly through the lyric poets. But
a very interesting alteration took place. This passage from the
Two Noble Kinsmen appears to be by Fletcher, but the author-
ship is not important:

> Remember that your fame
> Knowls in the ear o' th' world: what you do quickly,
> Is not done rashly; your first thought is more
> Than others' labored meditance: your premeditating
> More than their actions: but oh *Jove*, your actions,
> Soon as they move, as Asprays do the fish,
> Subdue before they touch: think, dear Duke, think
> What beds our slain Kings have.

The following passage from the same play is printed as given here
in the Cambridge Edition of Beaumont and Fletcher. Dyce and
most other editors have reprinted the passage as prose. One can,
with a little care, however, select lines and short passages from the
admittedly Fletcherian plays, beginning with the earliest and
running down through to the last, that form a sort of progressive
development of Fletcher's line from the early monotonous eleven-
syllable affair up to passages pretty consistently like this last,
and much of his prose moves to a related cadence. Just where
verse left off and prose began in Fletcher's mind is no great matter—the interesting fact is that, whether through Fletcher's taste
or a printer's error, the following passage is available today as
verse for those who wish to read it:

> I may depart with little, while I live, something I
> May cast to you, not much: Alas the Prison I
> Keep, though it be for great ones, yet they seldom
> Come; before one Salmon, you shall take a number
> Of Minnows: I am given out to be better lined
> Than it can appear, to me report is a true

> Speaker: I would I were really, that I am
> Delivered to be: Marry, what I have (be it what
> It will) I will assure upon my daughter at
> The day of my death.

The reader will observe that, while all the syntactical and verbal machinery of the lyric poets exists in these passages, it is brought to bear in the first passage upon a very slight meaning and in the second upon almost no meaning at all—it is little more than an empty syntactical formula; that the imprecision in thought results in a corresponding imprecision of metre, the second passage being worse than the first in both respects, but neither passage being remotely comparable as successful statements to the poems by Vaughan and Crashaw. It is not that one objects to irregularity of line-length, but that the line wobbles within itself: the poet is trying to get a violin tone by playing on a clothes-line. The line lacks integrity, existence as a unit, and hence cannot have existence as a part of a whole, nor can a clearly defined whole be built around it. Such lyrics as the two already quoted, or as Herbert's *Church Monuments*, or as Donne's Valedictions *Forbidding Mourning* and *On His Name Carved on a Window-Pane*,* form a complete antithesis even to the best verse of the later dramatists.

Mr. T. S. Eliot has been widely regarded as at least in part a disciple of the school of Donne. In so far as his style is Elizabethan, it seems to me entirely, or almost entirely, in the manner of the blurring-out, the decadence, as it occurs in the later drama, a poetry of little or no very tangible value:

> Signs are taken for wonders. "We would see a sign!"
> The word within a word, unable to speak a word,
> Swaddled with darkness. In the juvescence of the year
> Came Christ the tiger
>
> In depraved May, dogwood and chestnut, flowering judas,
> To be eaten, to be divided, to be drunk
> Among whispers; by Mr. Silvero

Of my name, in the window. Ed.

With caressing hands, at Limoges
Who walked all night in the next room;

By Hakagawa bowing among the Titians;
By Madame de Tornquist, in the dark room
Shifting the candles; Fräulein von Kulp
Who turned in the hall, one hand on the door.
Vacant shuttles
Weave the wind. I have no ghosts,
An old man in a draughty house
Under a windy knob.

This is far better work than the second passage from Fletcher, probably not quite so good as the first. But we have here likewise an enormously sententious manner concentrating on a very small meaning—there is an expansion of the subject matter by means of syntactic elaboration that is almost invariably the device of the wary stylist trying to conceal the fact that he is not travelling very rapidly. This poem, easily Mr. Eliot's best, contains what is probably his one passage of major poetry:

I that was near your heart was removed therefrom
To lose beauty in terror, terror in inquisition.
I have lost my passion: why should I need to keep it
Since what is kept must be adulterated?
I have lost my sight, smell, hearing, taste and touch:
How should I use it for your closer contact?
    These with a thousand small delibrations
Protract the profit of their chilled delirium,
Excite the membrane when the sense has cooled. . . .

But the passage, though magnificently precise in itself, and quite terrible, arises from a mass of carefully veiled imprecisions, which, because of their syntax, appear on first glance to have more meaning than is really the case. Mr. Eliot, when he has little or nothing to say, is always careful to leave the issue in doubt; he does not, as does Fletcher above, lay bare his own poverty in the last line; but this scarcely alters the fact of the poverty. In *The Waste Land* the writing is looser, the meter more lax, and the organization of the whole very slight. In *The Hollow Men* even the syntatic disguise is in the main thrown off:

> We are the hollow men
> We are the stuffed men
> Leaning together
> Headpiece filled with straw. Alas!
> Our dried voices, when
> We whisper together
> Are quiet and meaningless
> As wind in dry grass
> Or rats' feet over broken glass
> In our dry cellar

There are few attempts more pathetic than this in modern literature to keep on going, line by line, in spite of everything.

The other modern efforts to rejuvenate the metaphysical school have been on the whole ill-fated—for one thing, the shadow of Mr. Eliot hangs over most of them. Archibald MacLeish has done a few fine lyrics that suggest Vaughan rather than Donne, but because, I suspect, of a certain spiritual limpness, caused by or the cause of Mr. MacLeish's own variety of nihilism, they have not quite the muscularity of Vaughan: Mr. MacLeish suggests a Vaughan in part dissolved in tears and worn away, tears to which he refuses to will even an instant's resistance. His blank verse moves forward heavily, line by line, with practically no organization into larger units of thought or rhythm, a tendency which is, I believe, another aspect of the same state of mind. In his most recent work, *The Hamlet of A. MacLeish*, a great deal of cosmic petulance is expended in his reactions to a theory of art that even a casual perusal of Aristotle should have eliminated and to his more assertive and self-advertising contemporaries; and this, with nothing but his doctrine of human worthlessness as a substructure, leads to a vast amount of undignified and Eliotized exhibitionism. One makes these objections in spite of the fine passages the poem contains—or rather because of them: it is criminal for genius to be so needlessly unintelligent. Louise Bogan has experimented in the metaphysical direction, with, so far as I am concerned, two successes, a *Song* beginning, *Come break with Time*, and one called *The Mark*, which I find among the most startling poems of our period. Mr. Allen Tate, without the skill of either of these poets, or at least their consistent skill, has been completely successful in five or six poems and in part successful in others. And his soul is tougher than that of Mr. MacLeish, wider in its implications than that of Miss Bogan: his state of mind is definitely a "major" state, fully aware and serious, so that his occasional successes in expression are impressive. He does not, however, indulge in the main in a purely logical structure, and when he does his poems usually collapse. His best poems, *Mr. Pope, Death of Little Boys, Light, Ditty, The Subway*, build outward from specific experiences, and do so in an imagery that is wholly concrete, despite the degree of intellectuality behind it. The decidedly metaphysical poetry of Hart Crane, though it presents certain aspects suggestive of Donne, is really based on a very different principle of composition and will be considered later. The brilliant, though little known, poems of Pearl Andelson Sherry, in spite of their "metaphysical" content, or rather background, likewise build out from the specific experience in concrete terms. The two most remarkable poems of Mr. Wallace Stevens, *Le Monocle de Mon Oncle* and *Sunday Morning* (the version in the Monroe-Henderson anthology, *not* the one in *Harmonium*) represent a higher degree of logicalness than most of the poems of our time. It is interesting that, in the contemporary hullabaloo about the metaphysical school of Donne, these poems should be overlooked even by Mr. Stevens' admirers (Mr. Munson, on the basis of his minor puns and jingles, classifies him as a "dandy"); while Mr. Eliot, poetically an anti-Donne, becomes the poetic model of Donne's supposed admirers, simply on the basis of his admirable essays. The logical method in general, however, seems to be very seldom attempted in a pure form today, and it is still more seldom successful: and the reasons for this will be considered in connection with forms that have displaced it.

III. *The Narrative Method*—Narrative, in a simple form, at any rate, is similar to logic in that each successive stage in its development seems to be caused of necessity by the last. It is a sort of concrete logic, and this parallel must be kept in mind while considering it. Narrative, however, frequently tends to concentrate too exclusively upon external data, presenting a dry skeleton, like a geometric formula, rather than an experience in all its fullness. External data may imply much that is not external or they may not; but very often the implications of values beyond the external are not only missing, but the action itself deals with so limited a problem that more profound treatment were impossible. This is especially true of short fiction—the stories of Mr. Ernest Hemingway, in spite of the skill exercised in their composition, or because of the carefully observed limitations of that skill, are a lamentable example. Even more ambitious fictionists are likely to suffer from related limitations. Henry James, an infinitely capable artist, writing of charming but thoroughly mediocre individuals, was forced to deal with the experience of those individuals, regardless of how brilliantly he might percieve it. Now if the work of art is to be especially prized as the organization of all the most difficult aspects of experience in a single dynamic attitude, or is to present some scale of emotional reference or means of evoking such experiences, and drawing them, consciously or subconsciously, into such an attitude, the experience of the characters of *The Golden Bowl* (or of any other work of pure fiction), cannot possibly be as complete or as profound as the experience of, let us say, John Donne. The metaphysical experience is almost completely eliminated, and for the reader—let us say a Donne or a Baudelaire—to whom the metaphysical experience is the central experience, coloring and involving everything else, such a novel as *The Golden Bowl* can be little more than a luxury, exquisite, marvelous, but not necessary or enormously important as a spiritual experience, and on the whole a trifle exasperating. Such books as *Moby Dick*, by Melville, or the novels of Elizabeth Madox Roberts, especially *My Heart and My Flesh*, with their heroic apostrophes, epic descriptions, Elizabethan insanity and excesses, probably come closer to involving the whole consciousness than does the more perfect, wholly sound, and purely fictional work of Henry James.

Poetic narrative, stripped to a bare statement of incident, is likely to suffer from the same defect, though the greater intensity of imagery that sometimes results may overcome it. The English and Scottish ballads are a case in point. Poetic narrative, however, that involves an account of all the mental turnings of Adam, Lucifer, and God, or of a Lear or Coriolanus, are likely to run nearly the entire gamut of experiential possibilities. And the structure, let me repeat, is just as inevitable, just as "logical" as in the case of a lyrical argument by Donne. Dante is perhaps the largest-scale example available of the logical poet, as Shakespeare or possibly Racine of the narrative. To prove that one surpasses the other is very difficult.

IV. *The Psychological Method*—The name of this form is misleading, as any form into which the mind naturally falls or that evokes aesthetic reactions is obviously psychological enough; but the name has been used to describe it, the other names that have been likewise applied—dream, stream-of-consciousness and so on—seem to me still more vicious; and, with the precaution of this brief warning, I am willing to let well enough alone. It consists of a lowering of the connections between the parts of the poem, otherwise of one of the types already described, to or below the threshold of consciousness, so that the progression from place to place, from event to event, from idea to idea, or from sense-perception to sense-perception, is similar to the method of change in dream or in revery. A certain emotional tone is maintained, although it may consist of graduated waves, and may be controlled by subconscious or semiconscious feeling or thought, from and to which the poem departs and returns, but to which its images and anti-images bear no such definite relationship as in the case of the scattered method.

Rimbaud's *Larme* comes near to being the most profound and magnificent expression of the imprecise, wandering, and frequently terrible feeling attendant upon dream, revery, and insanity, that I have ever read. The poem represents in a way two landscapes connected by an event, or, rather one landscape as it appears before and after an event. The details of the landscape and the attendant feelings of the protagonist in each case are instances of the scattered method reduced to a dream-state, and

the event, the coming of the storm and night, which appears to
introduce a narrative element (though not necessitated by anything that has preceded), is in reality merely an intensification
of the mood—the protagonist is suddenly sucked deeper in the
direction of complete unconsciousness, and the terror becomes
more profound:

Loin des oiseaux, des troupeaux, des villageoises,
Je buvais accroupis dans quelque bruyère
Entourée de tendre bois de noisetiers,
Par un brouillard d'apres-midi tiède et vert.

Que pouvais-je boire dans cette jeune Oise,
Ormeaux sans voix, gazon sans fleurs, ciel couvert:
Que tirais-je a la gourde de colocase?
Quelque liquer d'or, fade et qui fait suer.

Tel, j'eusse été mauvaise enseigne d'auberge.
Puis l'orage changea le ciel jusqu'au soir.
Ce furent des pays noirs, des lacs, des perches,
Des colonnades sous la nuit bleue, des gares.

L'eau des bois se perdait sur les sables vierges.
Le vent, due ciel, petait des glaçons aux mares . . .
Or! tel qu'un pécheur d'or ou de coquillages,
Dire que je n'ai pas eu souci de boire!

Baudelaire seems to have had the first glimmering of the abstract principle of this sort of writing. He wrote of Poe:
"Or, il est incontestable que—semblables à ces impressions fugitives et frappantes, d'autant plus frappantes dans leurs retours
qu'elles sont plus fugitives, qui suivent quelquefois un symptome
extérieur, une espêce d'avertissements comme un son de cloche,
une note musicale, ou un parfum oublié, et qui sont elles-mêmes
suivies d'un évènement semblable a un évènement déjà connu et
qui occupait la même place dans une chaine antérierement révélée
—semblables à ces singuliers rêves périodiques qui fréquentent
nos sommeils il existe dans l'ivresse non-seulement des enchaine-

ment de rêves, mais des séries de raisonnements, qui ont besoin, pour se reproduire, du milieu, qui leur a donné naissance. Si le lecteur m'a suivi sans répugnance, il a déja deviné ma conclusion: je crois que dans beaucoup de cas, non pas certainement dans tous, l'ivrognerie de Poe étate un moyen mnémonique, une méthode de travail, méthode énergique et mortelle, mais appropriée à sa nature passionnée."

I have a feeling that Poe's method was in a considerable degree closer to the technique-induced hallucination of Mallarmé than to the method here postulated, though this is purely a matter of conjecture. But what a formula this is for the hallucinated phase of Rimbaud, a poet who was not to appear publicly till 1873! Nothing could be more concise or more comprehensive.

Baudelaire seems also to have been aware of the phase of the "psychological" procedure to which I have just alluded in connection with Mallarmé. He states that, in his belief, technique need not hinder perception but may even facilitate it. Technique, then, is not merely a means of recording perception but is actually a means to discovery, a projection, a refinement, an intensification, of the spirit, created by the spirit to make its boundaries more precisely, to extend them a little farther, to differentiate itself a little more distinctly from the remainder of the universe, from "nature," from that which will eventually absorb it and which is continually endeavoring to absorb and destroy it. Technique so understood not only has a place in the moral system, but is the ultimate development of the moral system; it is the outer boundary of consciousness. The poet with an infinitely subtle technique is as much better-off than the poet with none as the chemist with a fine balance than the chemist weighing with his bare hands. The exigencies of the medium themselves rouse, for a fraction of a second perhaps, to the level of consciousness, perceptions that would otherwise have remained in the "subconscious," undiscovered; and the technique-sharpened sensitivity is able in that moment to seize on the perception and fix it in its place in the general scheme. This method of working has doubtless existed in one degree or another in practically all of the great poets. It is difficult, however, to find traces of its becoming

a definite system previous to Poe, and even in Poe the traces
are slight. They are occasionally more evident in Emily Dickinson, and it becomes quite obviously a system in the later
Mallarmé, is adopted by various minor symbolists in varying
degrees, and is used quite consistently and on a rather more
ambitious scale today by Hart Crane, an American, whose
philosophical foundation is built upon Whitman and Blake.
Here is a specimen of the thing as found in Mallarmé:

> Surgi de la croupe et du bond
> D'une verrerie éphémère
> Sans fleurir la veillée amère
> Le col ignoré s'interrompt.
>
> Je crois bien que deux bouches n'ont
> Bu, ni son amant ni ma mere,
> Jamais a la même Chimere,
> Moi, sylphe de ce froid plafond!
>
> Le pur vase d'aucun breuvage
> Que l'inexhaustible veuvage
> Agonise mais ne consent,
>
> Naïf baiser des plus funèbres!
> A rien expirer annoçant
> Une rose dans les ténèbres.

And here is Crane's *Repose of Rivers*, one of his simpler pieces:

> The willows carried a slow sound,
> A saraband the wind mowed on the mead.
> I could never remember
> That seething steady leveling of the marshes
> Till age had brought me to the sea.
>
> Flags, weeds. And remembrance of steep alcoves
> Where cypresses shared the noon's

Tyranny; they drew me into hades almost.
And mammoth turtles climbing sulphur dreams
Yielded, while sun-silt rippled them
Asunder . . .

How much I would have bartered! the black gorge
And all the singular nestings in the hills
Where beavers learn stitch and tooth.
The pond I entered once and quickly fled—
I remember now its singing willow rim.

And finally, in that memory all things nurse;
After the city that I finally passed
With scalding unguents spread and smoking darts
The monsoon cut across the delta
At gulf gates. . . . There, beyond the dykes

I heard wind flaking sapphire, like this summer,
And willows could not hold more steady sound.

We have here an obvious and commonplace symbol—the course of a river standing for the life of man—and the monologue is presumably spoken by the river itself. The symbolic value of the details, however, is not so precisely determinable—they are details not of the life of man nor even directly referable to the life of man, but are living and marvelous details of a river's course, with strange intellectual and emotional overtones of their own. Mr. Robert Penn Warren has remarked that the life of an allegorical poem resides precisely in that margin of meaning that cannot be interpreted allegorically. As in the poem of Mallarmé, the words are constantly balancing on, almost slipping from, the outermost edge of their possible meaning. Their meaning is defined frequently not by the dictionary, but by their relation to other words about them in the same predicament. Mallarmé, wrote of the poetic line as that which, "de plusieurs vocables, refait un mot total, neuf, étranger a la langue et comme incantotoire." Everything in the line is strangely incandescent, seething, alive. There is not the feeling of muffled bluntness, or experiential

as well as intellectual, uncertainty, to be found in the first
passage from Mr. Eliot.
The psychological procedure has gone still further. In the
work of Miss Gertrude Stein the logical (syntactic) connections
within the sentence have broken down; and in the latest work
by Mr. Joyce, this disintegration has continued even into the
word. Let me quote an article by Mr. Eugene Jolas, called
The Revolution of Language and James Joyce:

"While Mr. Joyce, beginning with *Ulysses*, and in his still un-
named novel, was occupied in exploding the antique logic of words,
analogous experiments were being made in other countries. In
order to give language a more modern elasticity, to give words
a more compressed meaning through disassociation from their
accustomed connections, and to liberate the imagination with
primitivistic conceptions of verbs and nouns, a few scattered
poets deliberately worked in the laboratories of their various
languages along new lines.

"Leon-Paul Fargue in his prose poems creates astonishing
neologisms, although retaining in a large measure the classical
purity of French. He slashes syllables, transposes them from one
word to the subsequent word, builds new words from root
vocables and introduces thus an element entirely unknown
before in French literature. The large place he leaves to the
dream as a means for verbal decomposition makes his work
unique among contemporary French writers.

"The revolution of the surrealistes who destroyed completely
the old relationship between words and thought remains of im-
mense significance. A different association of words on planes of
the spirit makes it possible for these poets to create a universe
of a beauty the existence of which was never suspected before.
Michel Leiris, in his experimental glossaries, departs radically
from academic ideas and presents us with a vocabulary of icono-
clastic proportions. André Breton, demoralizing the old psychic
processes by the destruction of logic, discovered a world of magic
in the study of the dream via the Freudian explorations into the
subconscious strata and the automatic expression of interior
currents.

"Miss Stein attempts to find a mysticism of the word by the

process of thought thinking itself. In structurally spontaneous compositions in which words are grouped rhythmically she succeeds in giving us her mathematics of the word, clear, primitive, and beautiful. In her latest work this compression is of the utmost power.

"Verbal deformations have been attempted by German poets, notably August Stramm and Hans Arp. Stramm limited himself to the problem of taking nouns and recreating them as verbs and adjectives. Arp, more ironic, played havoc with the lyric mind by inventing word combinations set against a fantastic ideology. Certain others went so far as to reproduce merely gestures by word symbols, which, however, often remained sound paroxysms."

And so on. The essay opens with a typically sublime statement, "The word presents the metaphysical problem today." The actual phenomena under discussion as nearly as I can make out are these: The surrealistes and others, including Miss Stein, proceeded with one aspect of the experiments of Mallarmé, but substituted a very lax prose rhythm for the tense poetic rhythm and difficult rhymes of Mallarmé, a substitution which involved another—that of a purely passive state of mind for the taut and nervous intellectuality of the great Symbolist. The technical instrument being therefore practically nil, and the mind entirely receptive, whatever comes into the head is set on paper and, because of the oath of brotherhood or whatever is was, stands uncorrected. The actual poetic result so far as my own preceptions have been able to penetrate, is as shapeless as water spilt on the floor, and of about the same spiritual value. There is neither the genuine psychopathic hallucination of Rimbaud, nor the dynamic control of Mallarmé—they have simply unbuttoned their spiritual vests and stretched out for a nap and called it mysticism.

One can quarrel almost indefinitely with Mr. Jolas's use of abstract terms—it is almost impossible half of the time to determine within a quarter of a dictionary what he really means—but this will not get us far enough to justify the bother. The fundamental point of his argument, so far as his argument emerges, appears to be a belief that it is desirable to submerge the conscious in the subconscious. Now even granting that the subconscious were satisfactorily defined by modern scientists, which it is not; granting that attempts at such definition were purely modern, which they are not (there are some very competent thrusts at it in St. Thomas Aquinas[2]); the subconscious, by any possible definition that justifies the term, remains a mere fringe of one's spiritual existence, in so far, at least, as one is able to enter it and deal with it in art or in life; and any doctrine that would sacrifice the entire remainder of the spirit to that one faint fringe is ipso facto wasteful and subversive. One enters the fringe, furthermore, only by departing from the center of consciousness and only in so far as one departs from that center of consciousness; that is, in so far as one approaches unconsciousness complete, or death. In cultivating the subconscious for itself one's point of approach, or ideal, therefore remains annihilation; in cultivating the fullest possible degree of dynamic and self-directed consciousness the point of approach is the most intense possible state of life. One is alive; one can choose to intensify that condition, dispense with it, or, if one is no poet, vegetate. Mr. Jolas, being a poet, has so far as I am able to discern but one choice, could he penetrate the haze of his own style and actually see what he is talking about; the abandonment of his doctrine or the suicide of a gentleman.

Let me reiterate, however, that I do not wish to deny the desirability of extending the limits of consciousness as far as possible, even into regions previously unexplored—I demand only that the poet keep what he started with and add to it. Rimbaud's hallucinations, according to his own account, were the result of a difficult, even though possibly misguided discipline. And when they were all over, he was able to write that purely logical song perhaps the finest poem he ever wrote, *Éternité*—a poem that, in a sense, sums up all his experience and the wisdom acquired by it; that faces absolutely the most appalling vision, accepts and absorbs that vision, and stands only the more strongly for having faced it; a poem that need lose very little

[2] A fact that was pointed out to me by Dr. W. D. Briggs of Stanford University.

by comparison with the greatest of Blake or even Emily Dickinson. Mallarmé, in his *Faune*, as I shall endeavor to show presently, by starting with a logical argument about the nature of a specific experience, following it as far as possible and then letting the thread run off into revery, jerking it back into logic, and so on alternatively, was able to extend his vision from a logical and dynamic center into regions of the fringe, without losing his bearings. And even in his short poems, as in the poems of Hart Crane, the will remains present in the principle of selection; not everything turned up is found valuable, and only the valuable is kept, and that in the most strenuously imposed of forms. And the principle of selection, though in part formal, is in part based on the logical scheme of values which one feels quite definitely at only a short distance below the surface of the poem. The method determines only the way in which that set of values will function in the particular poem.

Kenneth Burke in his narratives of a few years ago imposed this type of dream-shift in a manner openly arbitrary, and employs the same device more recently (in the *Dial* beginning August 1928) in the otherwise logical flow of his prose-pieces entitled *Declamations*. The narrative in the one case and the argument in the other involve a wider emotional range, in all likelihood, than any American prose of our day save a few things by Dr. William Carlos Williams and some of Elizabeth Madox Roberts; and the arbitrary shift serves as a sort of ironic comment imposed by the author acting almost as if exterior both to himself and his composition. Similarly the brothel-scene in Ulysses employs the mechanics of hallucination without there having been any actual hallucination on the part of the author and without depending on the momentary exigencies of language for its progress or organization. The mechanics of actual hallucination simply form, in this instance, the basis upon which the arbitrarily constructed objective form of the chapter is based. It may be in part for this reason that the chapter does not somehow entirely come off, and this same lack of ultimate fusion is usually to be found in Mr. Burke as well. I should say that to achieve formal perfection the case probably demands either a greater or vastly smaller (as in *Anna Livia Plurabelle*) degree of arbitrary manipulation. But this is almost entirely different from the sort of thing Mr. Jolas is advocating (*Anna Livia*, as he states, is in the main an ideal achievement for him); as is the use of the deformed word in certain poems by Isidor Schneider and E. E. Cummings. The verbal deformation in these poets is ordinarily simply a more compact form of metaphor, frequently a compound of two words; and when their style becomes, as it sometimes does, a mosaic of such words, the result is simply a plethora of figures. E. E. Cummings carries the process of logical decomposition even into typography, achieving a sort of visual—if the reader will pardon me—onomotapoeia. But this normally separates the poem from the last possibility of auditory perception; and as the plastic possibilities of modern type are limited to a small number of arrangements of fixed, limited, and intrinsically uninteresting forms, this variety of plastic perception is a very poor substitute for the infinitely varied and fluid possibilities of sound. The method becomes, by the very nature of its material, trickery—a species of sleight-of-hand—instead of art.

It is very likely that my own short-comings are responsible for my failure to react more than mildly to the work of Miss Stein; very intelligent people admire her greatly, even extending their admiration to her later work. If, however, the reader will attempt by way of experiment the perusal of a little highly abstract prose in a field with which he is unfamiliar, he will find himself almost grasping the meaning from sentence to sentence, but always seeming to lose a little till be goes back to pick it up—there remains constantly the sense of a steady loss of something profound. Now Miss Stein succeeds in giving me precisely this feeling of steady loss as I read her; if I study her carefully I find carefully disintegrated fragments of shrewd wit and observation, but the profoundity neither of Whitehead nor of Joyce. Her work strikes me as thoroughly amusing common sense rendered fragmentary (the act of rendering it so, of course, is part of the method of composition—I do not accuse her of anything so humorless as a postmortem dismemberment) to produce this sensation and profit by it. It is wit subjected to the same process to which the surrealistes subject the metaphysical. My own preference for Pope and Blake remains unshakeable.

In Mr. Joyce's latest work the dream or "psychological" element is unmistakeable. It penetrates the entire texture of the thing. Any attempt to evaluate the new work on the basis of the small part of it so far published is futile, but, momentarily, it is interesting to consider the *Anna Livia Plurabelle* episode as a complete work. It has been published separately, seems complete in itself, and so far as the surface glaze is concerned is unequaled in modern prose save by a few brief passages in the early part of *Ulysses* and by *The Destruction of Tenochtitlan*, of William Carlos Williams. And yet in spite of its richness of detail, its beauty of movement, the piece remains almost purely elegiac, a modern and rather more profound version of Gray's *Elegy:*

Ah, but she was the queer old skeowsha anyhow, Anna Livia, trinkettoes. And sure he was the quare old buntz too. Dear Dirty Dumpling, foostherfather of fingalls and dotthergills. Gammer and gaffer we're all their gangsters. Hadn't he seven dams to wive him? And every dam had her seven crutches. And every crutch had its seven hues. And each hue had a differing cry. Sudds, for me and supper for you and the doctor's bill for Joe John. Before! He married his markets, cheap by foul, I know, like any Etrurian Catholic Heathen in their pinky limony creamy birnies and their turkiss indienne mauves. But a milkidmass who was the spouse? Then all that was was fair. In Elevenland? Teems of times and happy returns. The same anew. Ordovico or viricordo. Anna was, Livia is, Plurabelle's to be. Northmen's thing made southfolk's place but howmulty plurators made eachone in person? Latin me that, my trinity scholard, out of eure sanscreed into oure eryan. *Hircus Civis Eblanensis!* He had the buckgoat paps on him, soft ones for orphans. Ho, Lord! Twins of his bosom. Lord save us! And ho! Hey? What all men. Hot? His tittering daughters of. Whawk?

Can't hear with the waters of. The chittering waters of. Flittering bats, fieldmice bawk talk. Ho. Are you not gone ahome? What Tom Malone? Can't hear with bawk of bats, all the liffeying waters of. Ho, talk save us! My foes won't moos. I feel as old as yonder elm. A tale told of Shaun or

Shem? All Livia's daughtersons. Dark hawks near us. Night!
Night! My ho head halls. I feel as heavy as yonder stone.
Tell me of John or Shaun? Who were Shem and Shaun the
living sons or daughters of? Night now! Tell me, tell me, tell
me elm! Night night! Tell me tale of stem or stone. Beside
the rivering waters of, hitherandthithering waters of. Night!

The elegiac mood and the hallucinated state alike attain here
about their greatest possible achievement. The piece is one of
the best bits of evidence that I know that the cultivation of the
subconscious for its own sake tends definitely toward the elegiac,
because of its passivity, its negative attitude, even on the part
of a non-elegiac writer. Mr. Joyce can afford the luxury so far
as he himself is concerned; but a school of writers that would
attempt to set up this attitude as that ultimately desirable, is
merely the excrescence of contemporary nihilistic tendencies, of
which Mr. Eliot is one of the chief fountain-heads. Mr. Eliot
represents the decadence of an old logic, or rather an attempt to
revive the decadence of an old logic—he is in his poetry, at least,
still trying feebly to prove his own worthlessness, the worthlessness of man. The dream-poets accept this evaluation without a
squirm and proceed on that basis in a state of mind that refuses
to make any distinction between active and passive experience,
between village Cromwells and the real article, between Othello
and Sheamus and Shaun. There is no possibility of the bitter
tenseness arising from the sharply defined anguish of the superior
individual, the active and complex and powerful individual,
awake in all his cells, that we find in the poetry of Donne and
of Emily Dickinson. It is for this reason that I believe the heroic
prose of *The Destruction of Tenochtitlan* to be superior to the
elegiac prose of *Anna Livia Plurabelle*, superior, in all likelihood,
by at least a narrow margin, to any other prose of our time and
to most of the verse.

V. *The Alternation of Method*—A poem may be a development
of a single mood and yet alternately employ two different
methods. Thus in Mr. Eliot's *Gerontion* we have a single mood
developed through an alternating logical and psychological sequence such as I have already described in the *Faune*. Once in

a while the scattered method enters for a few lines, but not for long—it is mainly a way of piling up evidence in the argument. In this particular poem, as I have already said, the logic seems to me more a matter of grammar than of metaphysics, but the poem will do as an example, the better as examples are rare. The method is likely to make for a good deal of obscurity until one has fathomed its more objective aspects, and then the obscurity vanishes. So far as it has been employed as a definitely and carefully developed mode of composition, it appears to be extremely modern, and, on the whole, rather rare. The earliest (and most intricate) example with which I am acquainted is Mallarmé's *L'Après-Midi d'un Faune.*

One may find elsewhere a change of method now and then within a given poem, but it is seldom timed or calculated and hence constitutes a weakness—it usually indicates an inability to continue with that which was undertaken. Also, one often finds one relationship between the stanzas of a poem and another within them, but this is also somewhat different; for here each stanza is a unit, and the poem is another, and each is built upon a certain method throughout, whereas in *Gerontion* or the *Faune* the logical and psychological passages are not units, the only unit being the entire poem.

There are in the *Faune* two distinct sets of alternating movements which overlap in a curious fashion and produce the feeling of extraordinary difficulty and involved implication which almost any reader is bound to have until he shall have read the poem ten or a dozen times. The first set consists in the alternation of the narrative and logical elements, the narrative being indicated by italics. But as this alternation progresses through the poem, it appears to move—at times almost to flicker—back and forth across the dividing line between consciously directed thought and organized recollections on the one hand, and the wandering thoughts and images of revery on the other. The account of the faun's dream ought, one might think at first sight, to produce the subliminal experience, and the commentary the purely conscious; but the faune, in looking back into his sleep, is trying as hard as he is able to organize his dream into some sort of rational sequence, and, for the most part, he succeeds—whereas the preoccupation with the bare facts of his dream frequently causes absent-minded wandering in the midst of his comment. And the fact that both the conscious and the half-conscious hover extremely close to the dividing line throughout the entire poem, makes it very difficult at times so say exactly where one begins and the other ceases. The "psychological" element is here represented not by a state of dream or insanity, as in the poem from Rimbaud or the passage from Joyce, but by a state of revery, which is much closer to organized thought, and which is frequently closely bound up with it; and the organized thought, the comment, is so perturbed by the proximity of the other that it flickers unconscionably.

This form offers, it should be evident, an extremely subtle and complicated instrument of preception, and an instrument particularly adapted to the poet aware to the utmost of the modern philosophic dilemmas. It presents a means of beginning with the concrete experience and working outward as far as one's mentality and sensibilties permit, at a time when no objective scheme of abstract values available will stand very careful scrutiny. Donne, to resort to metaphor, was able to see himself and his experience, in the midst of a definitely mapped and defined scheme of universe and universal values; and by means of lines from that outer skeleton converging inward, he was able to define and locate his own experience in a definite and absolute fashion. Donne's position is now very difficult to assume, as his outline of values to find. The experience only remains; and the poet today is forced to begin with his experience and erect upon it as firm and universal a scheme of values as he is able.

VI. *The Alternation of Mood*—One may have a poem based upon a single method but upon a double mood—that is, the poem shifts back and forth between two or more moods as it progresses. Or two moods may hover for an instant upon a single image, through contrasting imagic and symbolic values, as I have shown in discussing the symbol.[3] Thus Laforgue, using the scattered method, normally alternates rapidly between a sort of tragic nostalgia and a mockery of such a feeling in such a world.

[3] "The Testament of a Stone, Being Notes on the Mechanics of the Poetic Image."

Browning, in *The Bishop Orders His Tomb*, employs a comparatively ponderous double mood running the course of a more or less "psychological" sequence. The double mood appears in a fairly simple form in Villon; is picked up and brought to a remarkable degree of speed and intricacy by Gautier; is occasionally used in a somewhat similar fashion but upon very different material a few years later by Corbière; and it reaches its most complicated development and greatest rapidity in certain poems by Laforgue toward the close of the nineteenth century. In contemporary American work it is prominent in certain poems by Miss Marianne Moore and by Mr. T. S. Eliot, and in a few poems, especially early ones, by Dr. Williams. It appears not to have been used consistently in the lyric before Gautier, and to have been so used first by the French.[1] One occasionally finds a change of mood at the end of an earlier poem, or sometimes within one, apparently for the sake of the shock; but the artistic value of such a shock is doubtful, as it destroys the unity of the poem. The double mood proper consists of a series of such shocks properly tempered and finely timed, which in itself constitutes a new kind of unity. The moods need not appear in identical quantities, but the relationship of quantities and the rate, or rather rhythm, of alternate appearance should be consistent.

The trouble with this form, especially as it appears in the work of Gautier, Laforgue, Miss Moore, and Eliot, is that it tends to an interpretation of the universe in black and white and

---

[1] The aspect of 17th century "wit" in English that seems to approximate this trick is in reality a far subtler phenomenon. Instead of alternate moods one has a fused complex of moods, all being present throughout the poem. Thus the grotesque passion of Donne's *Go and catch a falling star*, or the concentration of religious mysticism in a pun that one finds in Crashaw's poem, *The Recommendation*. If there is real alternation here, in any event, it is between more than two simple elements (usually) and is too rapid to be perceptible—as atomic vibration offers the illusion of static matter. But such an explanation sounds to me like a figure of speech. At any rate this condition appears to me to be approximated in that almost incomparably magnificent poem of Corbiere, *La Rapsode Foraine*; and Miss Moore once in a while would appear to be moving toward it, but her ideational and general experiential background seems to be too limited to let her get quite far enough. In the symbolists and post-symbolists wit is an instrument normally used for the destruction of a positive attitude temporarily assumed in order that it may be destroyed: the whole process is negative. In the metaphysical poets, satire, when it occurs, is a part of a positive attitude.

without prespective—it is an art of silhouette, pure and simple, without sufficient capacity for complication and subtlety. It endeavors to compress all experience into the limits of one arbitrary alternative. To read a few poems only by any one of these writers gives one the feeling that they are complex and sophisticated—their use of language is unquestionably astute. To read all of them reveals them quite simply as arrested adolescents of various degrees of fineness. Life is not to be summed up by mocking at one's weakness for romantic stage-trappings, as in the case of Gautier; at one's sentimentality, as in the case of Laforgue; at one's neighbors' breaches of etiquette, as in the case of Miss Moore; nor at one's moral and metaphysical frustration, as in the case of Mr. Eliot. The program of the last-named poet is easily the most complex of the four, but his sensitivity, unfortunately, the thing that should give his program flesh and blood, is based on altogether too large a degree upon other poets. The actual achievements of Miss Moore on one or two occasions—notably in *Black Earth* and *A Graveyard*—get rather outside her usual formula and approach something very close to major poetry.

The method has a larger field in drama. Drama, as we ordinarily conceive it, is composed of a set, or several sets, of conflicting and alternating moods that are ultimately resolved or brought to a state of balance. The plot is frequently disclosed by an arrangement of events that closely resembles the scattered method. That is, not all the connections are evident until all the gaps are filled, and then the entire situation becomes clear—it is a sort of compromise, of one sort and degree or another, between scattered and narrative procedure. Certain simpler forms may follow a purely narrative method, and other simple forms may be purely lyrical and scattered—that is, in this case there is no plot to be exposed, but merely an emotion of greater or less complexity. Occasionally, as in a few brief modern poetic dramas, there occurs a psychological sequence from time to time. The relation between fragments of conversation is commonly scattered, but may be logical, narrative, or psychological.

In the Japanese Noh play *Tsunemasa*, as we have it in the Pound-Fenollosa versions, there is, curiously enough, but a single mood, in the person of Tsunemasa, himself, supported by a priest and chorus who do nothing but reflect, interpret, and explain him. It is, in reality, a semi-narrative lyric prepared for the stage. In Vergil's first *Eclogue*, there is a very simple example of opposing moods: Meliboeus, who has been dispossessed by the soldiers, complains to Tityrus, who has retained his lands through a special dispensation from Octavian, and compares his fortune with that of Tityrus, who, in turn, speaks of his happiness and good luck. A large part of the mood of Tityrus is here put into the mouth of Meliboeus in the course of his comparison of their fortunes, but it remains none the less distinct. The two moods resolve very gracefully into one in the final speech of Tityrus:

> hic tamen hanc mecum poteras requiescere noctem
> fronde super viridi. . . .
>   iam summa procul villarum culmina fument
> maioresque cadunt altis de montibus umbræ.

This *Eclogue*, in its preoccupation with detached emotion rather than action, and in the remarkable beauty of its movement, reminds one greatly of the shorter Noh plays.

These two plays are of extreme simplicity, however, as compared to most of the world's great drama. A slightly more complex arrangement my be seen in Synge's *The Shadow of the Glen*. Here we have four characters, who seem to fall into two opposing groups—Nora and Michael against Dan and the Tramp. The progress of the play breaks these two groups, scatters them to the four corners of the square, so to speak, and ends with a new grouping—Nora and the Tramp against Dan and Michael. In some of the longer Elizabethan plays one finds a group of minor moods or characters opposed to a major mood, or filling the part of a major mood in some such relationship as that existing in *The Shadow of the Glen*. One may find two or more groups opposed to each other, each containing a major mood of its own and several minor ones working in their own scheme within their own orbits. Another fact worth noting is that a major character may shift from one major mood to another, two major characters, perhaps, changing places for a time. This occurs for instance in the character of Synge's Deirdre. If a major character slips temporarily into a minor mood in the sixteenth and seventeenth centuries, it is very likely to be a humorous one, though not necessarily. It is this complexity of mood and of movement that gives the drama of this period in England, and to some degree in Spain, a great deal of its emotional turmoil—a turmoil that, in the great plays, at least, seethes rhythmically—and its universality, its sense of an entire world experienced and given form.[5]

THE QUESTION OF IMAGISM

In an essay entitled *A Retrospect*, contained in his volume *Pavannes and Divisions* (Knopf: 1918) Mr. Ezra Pound has this to say of Imagism:

"There has been so much scribbling about a new fashion in poetry, that I may perhaps be pardoned this brief recapitulation and retrospect.

"In the spring or early summer of 1912, H.D., Richard Aldington, and myself decided that we were agreed upon the three principles following:

"1. Direct treatment of the thing, whether subjective or objective.

"2. To use absolutely no word that does not contribute to the presentation.

"3. As regarding rhythm: to compose in the sequence of the musical phrase, not in the sequence of the metronome.

"Upon many points of taste and of predilection we differed, but agreeing upon those three positions we thought we had as much right to a group name, at least as much right, as a number of French 'schools' proclaimed by Mr. Flint in the August number of Harold Munro's magazine for 1911.

"The school has since been 'joined' or 'followed' by numerous

---

[5] One might point out here that the tragedies of Shakespeare are no more "chaotic" than those of Racine, nor are they based on a different structural principle—they are simply a degree or two more complex.

people who, whatever their merits, do not show any signs of agreeing with the second specification. Indeed vers libre has become as prolix and as verbose as any of the flaccid varieties that preceded it. It has brought faults of its own. The actual language and phrasing is often as bad as that of our elders without even the excuse that the words are shoveled in to fill a metric pattern or to complete the noise of a rhyme-sound. Whether or not the phrases followed by the followers are musical must be left to the reader's decision. At times I can find a marked metre in vers libres, as stale and hackneyed as any pseudo-Swinburnian, at times the writers seem to follow no musical structure whatever. But it is, on the whole, good that the field should be ploughed. Perhaps a few good poems have come from the new method, and if so it is justified."

A scrutiny of this program in these colder days discloses in the first place a rather amusing lack of actual meaning, and in the second place an absolute lack of innovation, so far as theory is concerned, except in the case of metre; and so far as "free" verse was concerned it assumed almost at once in the work of H.D. and Mr. Pound, as well as in the work of a few more distinguished practitioners not officially of their "school," as great as schematization and rigidity as any of the forms of the past. And had it not, it would have been a failure; it was the discovery of a new metric system that really makes this movement important, not, as the journalists and the more impassioned and younger emigrants would have us believe, an attempt to do without a system. Mr. Aldington's verse became almost at once a sort of limp blank verse, with little or no organization from line to line. The more successful "imagist" poems of H.D. and Mr. Pound— H.D.'s *Orchard*, for example, or Mr. Pound's *Fish and the Shadow*—represent definite rhythmic units based on smaller units, and the line can be scanned.

As to the first and second "principles," number one excludes certain of the more obvious and less valuable species of symbolism; number two is a rather commonplace principle of style which nearly any admirable poet observes and which there was no great need to mention unless the "school" felt themselves particularly haunted by the ghosts of Holmes and Whittier. A. Lowell, of course, forced herself among them in the flesh, but that was later. Mr. Aldington quite obviously obeyed neither of these rules. His most highly praised poem, *Choricos*, is merely a paraphrase of Swinburne's *Garden of Proserpine*, without the latter's metrical firmness and surge. And Swinburne's poem, in turn, is a paraphrase of a rather better poem by Christina Rossetti, toward the concision and simplicity of which Alice Corbin reverts in her revision of Aldington's poem according to imagist principles, which begins, *The old songs die*. Mr. Pound and H.D. obeyed their own rules to a reasonable degree: as Mr. Pound observes, the journalistic camp-followers, Miss Lowell, Mr. Fletcher[6] and others, obeyed neither these dicta nor any other dicta and are chiefly responsible for the current theory that imagist poetry was of necessity concerned with details of sensation registered in rather casual prose.

There is nothing in these rules to preclude the possibility of abstract statement, and such statement can be found both in H.D. and in Ezra Pound. Its scarcity, or rather the scarcity of very profoundly organized emotions, must be laid, I suspect, rather to the intellectual limitations of the two poets rather than to the limitation of their program. Poets of the imagist fringe, who influenced and were influenced by the imagists, mainly because of personal associations, among them William Carlos Williams, Marianne Moore, Mina Loy, John Rodker, and Wallace Stevens, abound in such statements. If, again, one often feels a lack of formulated doctrine behind most of the work of these people, it can hardly be laid to their medium. Mr. Allen Tate in writing of my verse in the book section of the *New Republic* for March 21, 1928, disposes of the matter in rather too high-handed a fashion: "But the imagists were going to make a new language —with a manifesto. They failed. And they failed because language is not merely vocabulary. They failed because a poetry of

---

[6] Mr. Fletcher shortly saw the error of his ways, and abandoned them for a more ambitious, semi-Whitmanian type of verse that he seems to me unable to master. But his reform was honest and based on the very sound critical intelligence that he displays in his prose. Still more lately, perhaps influenced by Hardy, he seems to be moving toward a power and dignity that may prove important.

the image (could it exist) reduces to the parallel exercise of five separate instruments (the five senses) which cannot, without violence done the first principle of imagism, be integrated. For Imagism, as it was set forth in the official dogma, contained its own contradiction. It held out for the fresh visualization of objects—that is to say, for the creation of metaphor—but it ignored the total vision, the imagination, by means of which the raw perceptions are bound together into a whole. The Imagist's poetry lacked meaning; though some of their work, the early poems, for example, of John Gould Fletcher, achieved a kind of success with the merely pictorial and decorative possibilities of the image." Mr. Tate's remark about "the first principle of imagism" is quite simply and obviously untrue; and his remark about the "total vision" is beside the point—the imagist program does not exclude the total vision, it simply never got that far, being concerned with nothing more than a few elementary principles of style. It was a bit naive, but scarcely vicious. I do not go quite so far as Mr. Tate in damning the actual poetic product of the school, but I am willing to admit that it was not major poetry. I believe that some of it is likely to prove rather permanent, and quite justly so.

Mr. Hart Crane, who shares the views of Mr. Tate in this connection, and with whom I have had the good fortune to discuss the matter in private, regards Blake's poem *The Tiger* as one of the supreme achievements of the human spirit. I pointed out to him the fact that there is not a single statement in the poem not embodied in concrete terms, that it is purely a "poetry of the image," and he was forced to acquiesce. The same is true of Mr. Crane's own poem *Repose of Rivers*, as of nearly all of his most perfectly fused work—in Mr. Crane's work, indeed, the degree of imperfect fusion is in almost direct ratio to the degree of abstract statement, and I believe is closely related to it. *The Tiger* and Mr. Crane's poems alike spring from a definitely organized and rather complicated doctrine. This, however, forces me to offer a brief classification of "imagistic" procedure in connection with ways and degrees of symbolization.

We have in the first place, the poem dealing with a simple concrete experience that has no ulterior significance—that is, its meaning is purely literal, regardless of the amount of related but not obviously included experience that may be awakened by it. These "correspondences," needless to say, function quite as definitely when one is sane and sober as when one is not, though the element of strangeness is less noticeable, as we are more or less accustomed to the former condition. H.D.'s *Orchard* is such a poem; likewise the magnificient address of William Carlos Williams *To Mark Anthony in Heaven*, or Browning's *Serenade at the Villa*. One has the diametrically opposite procedure of the poem in which every detail has an allegorical interpretation. This sort of thing lends itself chiefly to obvious generalizations of no very permanent interest. In the later stages of Symbolism we often find "l'hièroglyphe enfantin," to which Baudelaire objected in general at an earlier date: the blue-birds etc. of Maeterlinck, and other such sleight-of-hand paraphernalia. If the work of art merely "stands for" something, let us by all means have the thing it stands for, instead of bothering with the art. But if it *is* something, related to but different from experience, and organizing experience into something finer more accurate than it was, then the art is worth having. Whitehead says somewhere that the trouble with abstractions is that by the very nature of things, they are incomplete, they are abstracted from something; and that something is then discarded, though in many circustances it may be all-important. Allegory at its weakest, and to some extent in all of its manifestations, is merely an attempt to give concrete body to an abstraction, *while preserving the limitations of the abstraction*. It does not attempt to redissolve the abstraction into the original body of experience and then concentrate the experience, for then the whole process would be self-destructive—there would be no allegory. The sound work of art, however, is as far as possible (allowing for such obvious facts as that language itself represents a degree of abstraction, which a poet overcomes in so far as he is a poet) not an abstraction from experience but a concentration of experience, and the universality of its scale of emotional reference is pretty much in proportion to the degree in which one *cannot* draw from it abstract conclusions.

But Blake's *Tiger* is a case in which pure allegory is completely successful. The reason probably lies in the fact that Blake was not himself an allegorist, but a visionary, and that the allegorical interpretation is in a large part our own addition. That is, the God of this Universe was doubtless for Blake a supreme Tiger, and the vision simple and direct. He described the Tiger in the sky as a less fortunate mortal might describe a tiger in the jungle.

In between these two types of imagery lies the poem of some degree of allegorical purport, but which cannot be interpreted allegorically in every detail. Nearly all of Mr. Crane's work falls in this region.

The value of a poem of the first type depends upon two things: the intensity and universality of the original experience and the intensity and integration of the details of perception and expression. That integration may in many—very likely in most—cases require a degree of abstract statement sprinkled along the way, and if that be the case, it is vanity to do without such statement. *The Tiger*, however, does without it quite successfully, as, I believe, do certain other poems. If, as may be the case, the value of the concrete image is evident without additional statement, the integration or lack of it is almost purely a matter of musical integration—of proportion and metre. When Mr. Tate writes that much of my poetry "hobbles along on the necessary limitation of the imagist technique" he is, I am convinced, misplacing the blame—the trouble was that I was struggling with a half-mastered metre, which only occasionally came through. To create a new metre is a more difficult task than is commonly admitted by those who have never felt the need to run the risk. And for Mr. Tate to explain his liking for the poems that pleased him by the presence of a few abstract statements really strikes me as simplifying the poetic problem almost to the point of the ludicrous.

The three poems just mentioned as entirely unallegorical are about equally well-written; their magnitude, depending upon the range and depth of emotion involved, corresponds inversely to the order in which they are named. And this range and depth of emotion has nothing to do with the aspects of the "subject matter." Browning, addressing an orchard in bloom might have written as great a poem as his *Serenade at the Villa*. H.D., with

Browning's theme, might produce an exquisite but would surely produce a minor poem. Anything may serve to crystallize experience, whether the spirit to whom that experience belongs be frail or gigantic. "A certain slant of light," entering the consciousness of Emily Dickinson, was sufficient to produce one of the most profoundly beautiful poems in English.

The value of the poem of either the pure or mixed allegorical types depends again upon the range and depth of the concept of which the "image" is the concrete symbol, and upon the intensity and integration of expression. The chief difference would seem to be that this type of thing has a better chance of being a "pure poetry of the image" because the concrete symbol is fitted a bit more arbitrarily, and hence may be fitted more neatly, to the necessarily very schematized ideation. Such things as *Serenade at the Villa*, for instance, or most of Hart Crane, implicate entire ranges of ideation and feeling that cannot be reduced to any formula save the poem itself. The purely allegorical likewise presupposes a clearly schematized set of abstract values, a luxury which we no longer possess. Blake endeavored to create one of his own, for lack of better, and in that particular activity was at best but in part successful. Hart Crane, by means of his semi-allegorical method, continually and most often successfully attemps to evade an unequivocal statement of this sort by constantly running his allegory ashore on the specific. He is an example of a soul with a natural taste for the schematized and abstract being forced by his milieu toward the specific; and it is on the specific that by far the greater part of the important poetry of the last eighty years has been based in the main. Personally, I believe that the greatest poetry will be possible if this fact is realized and admitted as a basis of procedure: it is the poetic equivalent of the humanistic attitude defended by Mr. Babbitt in the *Forum* for January 1929 (and elsewhere). Mr. Babbitt writes: "In direct proportion as one develops the critical temper, one is forced to base one's convictions, not primarily on any tradition, but on the immediate data of consciousness." This "critical temper," as Mr. Babbitt insists, is the outcome of education and other strenuous discipline—it is utterly the reverse of the humanitarians naive faith in his own natural rightness. In

Rousseau and Romanticism, Mr. Babbitt stresses the moral effect of example at all social levels. This I believe to be sound; and the most valuable example is the poet, because, through the experimental contagion of his form, he dynamizes the consciousness of the individuals at the highest levels. The poet is face to face with his own soul: if he fails, as Mr. Eliot has done, it is a case of personal inadequacy; and it becomes the duty of the critic to disinfect him, lest the contagion spread indefinitely. Mr. Eliot's plaintive search for a dogmatic religion is a begging of the question.

The poetry of the specific experience still makes possible that most important of artistic phenomena, the relation of the balanced and unified individual to the facts of existence. It admits not only of adventures in the mystical dimension, such as those of Mr. Crane, but also in the more purely human or ethical. William Carlos Williams functions a little too completely in the latter, as Mr. Crane in the former; there is a certain incompleteness about both of them. The limitations of Allen Tate, to complete the trio of living American poets who excite me most, are, in so far as I feel them and as far as I can penetrate, inadequacies of style, which he ought eventually to overcome. *L'Après-Midi d'un Faune* offers the most ambitious method I know for making most of the modern situation, but it is so elaborate that it is likely to be used very seldom by lyric poets and may too easily tend to diffusion rather than concentration. The Imagist School, so far as its practice was concerned, and for the most part as regards its first two principles, was nothing but a superficial recognition of this tendency on the part of two exquisite minor poets and one indifferent poet; and inasmuch as their recognition was inadequate and their contribution in no wise definitive, the name Imagist had better be dropped from the critical vocabulary. The contribution of these poets to modern poetry in general, aside from certain individual and admirable poems, was mainly metrical, and if they must have a name, and some one can think of one, they had better be named for their metres.

SUMMARY AND CONCLUSION

I have endeavored to define and evaluate the possible modes

of literary expression, with especial reference to those that have appeared or been revived during the past seventy-five or eighty years. My conclusions, in brief, are that the song or "scattered" lyric may function now quite as effectively as at any time in the past, and for evidence one need look no farther than Hardy and Corbiere; that the poem of the specific experience is the modern equivalent of the logical structure of the metaphysical school, being essentially the same thing and possessing potentially all the same virtues—it simply works out from instead of working in toward, the center, the experience; that the modern attempt to revive the Metaphysical School is almost purely syntactical, and is necessarily syntactical, as no adequate metaphysic exists unless one is able conscientiously and individually to find his way back to Rome; that the psychological or dream method is definitely subversive unless modified by a strong intellectual substructure as well as a rigid technique; that the alternation of method provides a variant, subtle and perhaps of great value, upon the poem of the specific experience; and that the alternation of mood as a consistent system is a trifle childish. The drama of Shakespeare is a species of poem of specific experience developed to a high degree of detail and complexity, and if certain secondary difficulties could be overcome, I see no reason why such a drama should not reappear. One difficulty is purely technical—the problem of metre—and the other is partly so. Blank verse as the metrical instrument is inconceivable at the present time, and rhymed verse will always be inconceiveable in English. There remains the free verse of such writers as William Carlos Williams or perhaps Ernest Walsh as a possible medium. The verse of Ezra Pound moves too slowly for the purpose, and uses almost invariably a closed line, being thus a bit inflexible for dramatic purposes. The other difficulty is the mating of a style capable of containing the necessary high points of emotion with a type of character capable of them. In, say, the Racinian drama, the use of royalty as the subject matter of tragedy dispensed with this difficulty. Royalty was theoretically the highest point in humanity and hence capable of the greatest possible range of emotion. Kings and queens lived amid a great deal of formality, exterior solemnity, and consequently the rhetorical style in their mouths did not seem ridiculous when the emotional point was not high, and the poet was able to use the same stylistic tone throughout. To create a type of character at the present time that should offer comparable conveniences would unquestionably be very difficult, but might be possible. It would also be necessary to create a character with sufficiently strong (and unprovincial) moral feelings for some sort of dramatic motivation to be born in him. This might still be possible, but unless the lyrical poets establish attitudes of greater dignity during the next few decades than most of them seem inclined to establish at present the possibility may vanish. That the logical —Dantesque or Miltonic—epic is scarcely possible at present is a misfortune, but, if the drama could be reestablished, need not be a catastrophe. The low emotional level of prose, and the fact that the novel is essentially a democratic form, dealing with individuals of slight intrinsic interest, both make it seem unlikely that the novel will ever attain to the piston-pure magnificence of Racine.

The only poet in England who has in my opinion achieved major work since Thomas Hardy is D. H. Lawrence, whose attitude and genius in general were always unstable, abnormal, and fragmentary, and who now seems to have collapsed completely. In France, I can think of no one since M. Valéry, a poet of unquestioned genius, but who, like Hart Crane, is blind to all values save those affecting himself as an absolutely isolated phenomenon: he is unaware of the wider range of ethical phenomena arising from the interaction of human beings. In America there is the comparably classical figure of E. A. Robinson, less interested in the purely metaphysical, more in the ethical, but with sensibilities a shade too chilled for him to rise to the level of Hardy. Of the next generation we have, as I have said, Dr. Williams; and among the young men Messrs. Tate and Crane. Mr. Yeats suffers from defects similar to those of Mr. Robinson, but almost more benumbing. Aside from the prose of Mr. Joyce, Mr. Burke, and of Miss Roberts, the works of these men remain, however, the chief major efforts of our century. No one of them will bear comparison with Thomas Hardy or Emily Dickinson, but their achievement is great, and accomplished in the face of considerable odds. It remains to be seen whether they can make sufficient headway so that seventy-five years hence it will be possible for a dramatist to think in terms comparable to those of Phèdre or Anthony.

ROBERT BRIDGES AND
ELIZABETH DARYUSH

It has long appeared to me that Bridges and Hardy must be regarded as the two most impressive writers of poetry in something like two centuries, perhaps since Milton; if Hardy is likely to appear the greater of the two on the first consideration, by virtue in part of the greater number of his highly successful lyrics, in part of the simpler and thus more directly accessible richness of his feeling, Bridges may gain on more mature consideration, as a result of greater intellectual scope and soundness and of a wider diversity of artistic mastery. Bridges is certainly the more mature, complex, and, morally speaking, the more rich of the two men. Hardy at his best offers a kind of summation of folk wisdom: it is his power and his limitation. Bridges, though he may not be invariably the most sound of thinkers or of critics, is the heir of the universities, the descendant of Arnold and of Landor, of Herbert and of Milton; his subject-matter is the full experience of the civilized man.

Similarly, it appears to me that the daughter of Robert Bridges, Mrs. Elizabeth Daryush, is one of the few first-rate poets to appear in the British Isles since the generation which produced her father and Thomas Hardy; aside from Yeats, T. Sturge Moore, and Viola Meynell, I can think of no poet now writing in England or in Ireland sufficiently interesting to bear

From *American Review,* VIII no. 3 (1936-1937) pp. 353-367.

comparison with her. She has been, as was her father for the greater part of his life, severely neglected and underestimated; and now that her father's reputation is beginning to increase, she runs the risk of being neglected, actually because of the purity and plainness of her best style, but on the explicit plea that she is a mere imitator of her father. She learned a great deal from her father: he was one of the greatest preceptors of the art, if one really understands, in some measure, his accomplishment, to be produced in England; she had the good fortune to grow up beneath his hand; and she appears to have profited intelligently by circumstances that can only be a source of envy to others. But she is not an imitator; and though a less great poet, she is an equally original poet, and frequently equally a master. It is interesting to consider them together in order to define the similarities and differences.[1]

Mrs. Daryush has disowned her first three books, published in 1911, 1916, and 1921, and wishes them destroyed. I have seen only the last of the three, and am willing to agree with her, though the book is deficient in virtue rather than positive in vice. Her mature career may be said to have begun with *Verses*, published in 1930, to have reached its most perfect achievement in *Verses, Third Book*, published in 1933, to have reached a crisis and collapse of form in *Verses, Fourth Book*, published in 1934, as a result, it would seem, of the discovery of new matter to which she found her style ill adapted, and to have begun the mastery of this matter, or of a few aspects of it, in *The Last Man and Other Poems*, published in 1936. Her talent, then, although it was obviously formed by her father's influence, appears to have borne fruit only after his death, and to have developed very rapidly within a very short period, after a long period of stagnation.

In the first three of the mature books, we have a poet much

---

[1] Poetical Works, Excluding the Eight Dramas by Robert Bridges (Oxford, 1936). This title is misleading, however, for *The Testament of Beauty* is likewise excluded. It is regrettable that there is not an inexpensive edition of the dramas, for four of them—the two on Nero, *Achilles in Scyros*, and *The Christian Captives*—are as great as anything Bridges ever wrote. The five volumes by Mrs. Daryush discussed in this essay are issued by the same publisher.

closer in spirit to Robert Bridges than in the last two, but still with important differences: the style of both poets, at their best, is pure and free of mannerism, whether of poet or of period; it represents the finest development of the intellectual, and anti-romantic, tendency of the nineteenth century, a tendency illustrated by the Wordsworth of the "Ode to Duty," by Bryant, by Landor, and by Arnold; but the greatest work of Bridges is relatively impersonal in theme as well, whereas most of his daughter's best work is in this respect intensely personal. The more personal lyrics of Bridges tend to become graceful and mild; the more impersonal lyrics of Mrs. Daryush tend toward vagueness in conception and in execution. The distinction is not absolute, but it is nevertheless obvious.

To illustrate the point I will quote four poems, two of the best poems by each, and two inferior specimens. The following poem, which is by Robert Bridges, is entitled "The Affliction of Richard":

> Love not too much. But how,
> When thou hast made me such,
> And dost thy gifts bestow,
> How can I love too much?
>   Though I must fear to lose,
> And drown my joy in care,
> With all its thorns I choose
> The path of love and prayer.

>   Though thou, I know not why,
> Didst kill my childish trust,
> That breach with toil did I
> Repair, because I must:
>   And spite of frighting schemes,
> With which the fiends of Hell
> Blaspheme thee in my dreams,
> So far I have hoped well.

>   But what the heavenly key,
> What marvel in me wrought

Shall quite exculpate thee,
I have no shadow of thought.
   What am I that complain?
The love from which began
My question said and vain,
Justifies thee to man.

The next poem, which is by Mrs. Daryush, is number XXXV
of *Verses, Third Book*, and appears without a title:

Fresh Spring, in whose deep woods I sought,
   As in your cool abodes I played,
The phantoms of my childish thought,
   The spirits of the faery shade;

Warm Summer, in whose fields I met
   My fancy's every found device,
Where small imagination set
   The very scenes of Paradise;—

Now are your forests high the hall
   Of shades more surely fugitive;
Now raptures lost beyond recall
   In your unsunned recesses live;

Now to your cloudless meadows come
   Forms lit with longing's fiercest flame;
Now truly are your haunts their home
   Eternal, whom with tears I name.

These are, I believe, two of the most nearly perfect, and two of
the greatest, short lyrics to be found in English. The poem by
Bridges deals primarily with the apprehension of an experience
more complex, and, if not more general, certainly more generalized; it is the experience of the intellectual who has progressed
beyond the disillusionment of "Dover Beach", but who has not
forgotten his scepticism or its bitterness. The poem by Mrs.
Daryush deals with a simpler experience and in a sense a more

personal one, an experience universal only in the sense that all of the basic experiences are universal; the theme is the intense realization of personal loss. It is characteristic of the more personal and emotional approach of Mrs. Daryush that, when she discovered the inadequacy of her earlier style to her later subject-matter, she would have turned on her earlier work in a manner little short of savage. There is a note appended to *The Last Man and Other Poems*, which offers numerous revisions, most of them excellent, of her earlier poems, and which requests the complete deletion of a great many other poems, most of which should certainly be retained; the poem which I have just quoted is one which she would like to destroy. It appears not to have occurred to her that her early convention was adequate to her early matter, and she appears to have small conviction of her mastery of that convention.

The disrupting influence in the last two books by Mrs. Daryush appears to be twofold. She appears to be moved, momentarily, at least, by a view of a kind of mechanistic destiny, without being able to surrender the inherited and traditional morality which has its origins in a very different view of destiny; and she appears to be increasingly conscious also of social injustice, of the mass of human suffering. The first difficulty, in so far as it enters her work, seems to the present writer to be a matter of confused thinking. The second difficulty is one of adjustment of style to matter, and, in some measure, at least, a difficulty of settling the emotions inspired by new matter to the point at which it may be scrutinized and comprehended. Her father might thus have made this transition more easily, for he was the more balanced and the more intellectual of the two temperaments, but the fact remains that he never attempted it. In any event, it is in connection with these subjects that one finds in Mrs. Daryush the extreme of the emotionalism which, when one compares her at least to her father, appears to be her differentiating quality. It is interesting at this point to compare two of the less successful poems by each poet, for at the lower levels of achievement the differences between the two are accentuated and the difficulties with which each is dealing become more clear.

The following sonnet is number thirty-five, of "The Growth

of Love", by Robert Bridges:

> All earthly beauty hath one cause and proof,
> to lead the pilgrim soul to beauty above:
> Yet lieth the greater bliss so far aloof,
> That few there be are wean'd from earthly love.
> Joy's ladder it is, reaching from home to home,
> The best of all the work that all was good;
> Whereof 'twas writ the angels aye upclomb,
> Down sped, and at the top the Lord God stood.
>
> But I my time abuse, my eyes by day
> Center'd on thee, by night my heart on fire—
> Letting my numbered moments run away—
> Nor e'en 'twixt night and day to heaven aspire:
> So true it is that what the eye seeth not
> But slow is loved, and loved is soon forgot.

The poem is clear and sound in its conception; in its rhetorical execution it is not only faultless but brilliant; yet it moves almost with too great rapidity and ease; it does not display that struggle with, that concentration upon, its subject-matter, which results in deeply moving detail. In these respects it is typical of the lower levels of Bridges.

The following sonnet is from "The Last Man" by Mrs. Daryush. "The Last Man" consists of a blank-verse monologue, spoken by the last survivor of the human race after the final destruction brought on by the warring oligarchs, the monologue enclosing a sonnet sequence which might better stand alone, since it is primarily a personal meditation on various aspects of the ethical conflict which I have already noted in connection with the author's work.

> There is no Eden now; the central tree
> Is dead, and with it all that once was mine
> Of shapely growth. . . Gone is the clear design
> Of gardens, vineyards, all my orderly
> Inheritance, gone even the forest black

Beyond, from which I hewed my happiness,
And, in its place, only the featureless
Lush green, untended and without a track.
"Knowledge of good and evil." . . . Rather, this:
Sight of some known, some living, weal or ill
Worth even my very life to aid, to kill,—
That was the precious guarded tree of bliss;

Now it has vanished—there's nothing to say:
Go here, Go there . . . not even *Go* or *Stay.*

This poem is more interesting in some ways than the sonnet by
her father; there is probably nothing, for example, in her father's
sonnet as striking as the last line and a half of the octave of this.
But the most obvious thing about this sonnet is the lax despair
of the tone, a despair familiar enough to anyone who knows the
twentieth-century Americans, with whom one suspects that Mrs.
Daryush is very imperfectly acquainted, and, corresponding to
this despair, the shockingly bad writing. Mrs. Daryush relies
heavily upon italics for emphases, a plea, merely, to the elocu-
tionist to do what the rhetorician has failed to do; instead of
concentrating her matter, she diffuses it, especially in the octave,
through a repetitious series of visual images, and these images,
save possibly the last, are more or less stereotyped; she employs
very weak stereotypes of phrasing, "the clear design", "any
orderly inheritance", and of these two the second repeats and
includes the first; she repeatedly employs weak run-over con-
structions, which leave the first line involved inconclusive as a
perceptual unit, and which break the second line into two weak
units, these occurring in lines four to five, five to six, and seven
to eight, the last of these not being so bad that it might not stand
if not preceded by the others; and in the next to last line the
accentuation is unpardonably faulty, this fault being common in
her most recent work, and the result, apparently, of certain
habits acquired in the practice of syllabic meter in some of her
other poems. Mrs. Daryush, here as in many poems on social
injustice, is overcome by her subject-matter and experiences a
collapse into uncritical emotionalism, a collapse of a kind com-

mon indeed among the late romantics but surprising in the heiress of Robert Bridges. It is not that the orderly inheritance of Mrs. Daryush is inadequate, but, I believe, that she has not sufficiently understood it; she has acquired habits without justifying them, and in the fact of a new orientation of experience, she has not at command the ideas which might reorient her habits and help her to maintain them. She may succeed in doing this; or it may prove that the habits are sufficiently strong to re-establish themselves, as, in fact, they appear to be doing, if one compares the improvement of the best poems in the most recent volume with the work in the volume preceding it.

In an age of much-publicized amateurs in metrical experiment, these two poets have rather unobtrusively accomplished some of the most brilliant metrical innovations in English poetry. Bridges wrote excellent poetry not only in traditional English meter, but also in classical meter, and in accentual, and in some of his later lyrics and in *The Testament of Beauty* he experimented—with no great success, in my own estimation—with syllabics. Mrs. Daryush has done nothing with accentual or classical meter, but she has perfected her father's experiments with syllabic meter, and has brought it to as high a degree of perfection, I imagine, as it can be brought. I cannot illustrate the extent of their experiments by quotation here, but I can at least illustrate the quality. The following lines are the opening stanza of Bridges' famous poem, "A Passerby":

> Whither, O splendid ship, thy white sails crowding,
>   Leaning across the bosom of the urgent West,
> That fearest nor sea rising, nor sky clouding,
>   Whither away, fair rover, and what thy quest?
> Ah! soon, when Winter has all our vales opprest,
> When skies are cold and misty, and hail is hurling,
>   Wilt thóu glíde on the blue Pacific, or rest
> In a summer haven asleep, thy white sails furling.

Now it frequently happens, especially in the work of a subtle and cautious experimenter, that a poem may be scanned more or less successfully by more than one system. Robert Bridges in his life-

time frequently expressed great scorn at the unsuccessful attempts of critics to describe his meters. I do not know how he
personally scanned this poem, but it appears to me to scan perfectly if we regard it as a variation from an iambic norm: we thus
get a preponderance of pentameter lines, with two hexameter,
the second line being the sole hexameter in this stanza, and being
so by virtue of a very light but nevertheless recognizably iambic
foot, consisting of the last syllable of *bosom* and the subsequent
preposition; we get a good deal of trisyllabic substitution, the examples in this stanza being the fourth foot of the fourth line, the
third foot of the fifth line, the fourth foot of the sixth line (unless
we elide the light syllables), the third and fifth feet of the seventh
line (the second foot of this line being monosyllabic), the first
and third feet of the last line—and if one chooses to read *bosom*
in the second line as a monosyllable, thus reducing this line to
pentameter, the fourth foot of this line becomes trisyllabic, unless indeed one reduces it by elision (the only other hexameter
in the poem, the first line of the second stanza, can likewise be
reduced by vigorous elision); and in the seventh line we get a
specimen of accentual sprung rhythm, in the two syllables carrying accent marks.

Sprung meter, to which I have just referred, is of two sorts,
accentual and syllabic. Accentual sprung rhythm occurs when a
light syllable is dropped from a foot, so that the remaining and
accented syllable at once carries the whole weight of the foot (as
occurs frequently in accentual meter) and is brought into juxtaposition with another accented syllable, this juxtaposition of
accents by other means than normal inversions being the characteristics of sprung meter. Syllabic sprung meter occurs when
the unaccented syllable of a foot is heightened in accent till
it equals its neighbors, so that we have two or three (or if more
feet are sprung, more) accented syllables in sequence. In syllabic
sprung meter, the accentual measure of the line is destroyed, and
only the syllabic measure remains. Wyatt employed accentual
sprung meter; Barnabe Googe employed syllabic sprung meter;
Robert Greene employed both; Gerard Hopkins who defines
sprung meter carelessly, commonly employs the accentual variety, but his intention is frequently obscure. It is characteristic of

Bridges that when he employs the accentual sprung meter in the second foot, he should follow with a trisyllabic foot to render the effect a little smoother and more ambiguous, though there are one or two bolder specimens later in the poem. As my description of the other metrical effects in the poem indicated, nearly every experimental effect in the poem is compensated by a suggested alternative interpretation, the result being a meter at once unusual, learned, and very subtle.

The following poem, "Still-Life," by Elizabeth Daryush, is number XVIII from her most recent volume. It is one of her most brilliant successes in syllabic meter, and exemplifies syllabic sprung meter in a good many of the lines. There is, in my estimation, nothing approaching this or some half dozen other syllabic lyrics by Mrs. Daryush among the syllabic lyrics of her father, or in *The Testament of Beauty.* One reason is, perhaps, that Robert Bridges worked mainly with the twelve-syllable line, either whole or broken in two, which appears to be too long a unit for a meter unbound by accent; whereas, Mrs. Daryush, in working with the ten-syllable line, whole or broken, seems to have struck a natural rhythmic unit. Technically, there is probably only one truly accentual poem by Robert Bridges as good as this, the one beginning, "The hill pines were sighing". On the other hand, "A Passerby", at least by a narrow margin, is probably firmer in its rhythm, since the accentual syllabic norm accounts not only for the number of syllables, but for the number and placement of accents so that we have true variation in movement, and of the richest and most learned kind: in the syllabic poem we can have no variation from the syllabic norm, and within that norm we have only variety of rhythm, variety from which there can be no variation. Granting this difficulty, however, we can scarcely read the poem without being greatly impressed:

> Through the open French window the warm sun
> lights up the polished breakfast-table, laid
> round a bowl of crimson roses, for one—
> a service of Worcester porcelain, arrayed
> near it a melon, peaches, figs, small hot
> rolls in a napkin, fairy rack of toast,

butter in ice, high silver coffee-pot,
and, heaped on a salver, the morning's post.

She comes over the lawn, the young heiress,
from her early walk in her garden wood,
feeling that life's a table set to bless
her delicate desires with all that's good,

that even the unopened future lies
like a love-letter, full of sweet surprise.

If we regard the subject-matter of this poem, we find something rather curious: the matter explicitly described implies, largely through the ominous and melancholy tone, a social context which is nowhere mentioned, yet from which the poem draws its power, a power which is not only real but great. This implication probably reaches its most intense impression in the two lines, unforgettable in the melancholy of their cadence, which open the sestet; but was never absent. The poem thus represents a successful handling of the social material with which the two last books have been obsessed, and an indication of continued development.

The greatest poems by Bridges are probably those beginning: "Joy, sweetest life-born joy", "Love me too much", "Sad sombre place", "The birds that sing on autumn eves", "The southwind strengthens to a gale", "Wherefore tonight so full of care", "Whither, O splendid ship", "Why hast thou nothing in thy face", "Beautiful must be the mountains", and "How well my eyes remember"; but there are other great poems and many others that are excellent. The greatest by Mrs. Daryush, I believe, are numbers XVIII, XX, and perhaps XXVIII of *Verses*, VIII of *Verses, Second Book*, V, IX (a highly "generalized" lyric, and hence a violation of my initial proposition), XXVI (an imperfect but powerful poem, stating explicitly the mechanistic preoccupation to which I have alluded), XXVIII, XXX, XXXIV, XXXV, and XXXVIII of *Verses, Third Book*, I of *Verses, Fourth Book*, and V and XVIII of *The Last Man and Other Poems*; though again there are other excellent poems, per-

haps a fair number as good as the poems mentioned in *Verses*.
The quality which I personally admire most profoundly in both of them is the ability to imbue a simple expository statement of a complex theme with a rich association of feeling, yet with an utterly pure and unmannered style. Thus Bridges:

> Unbodied presences, the pack'd
> Pollution and remorse of Time
> Slipp'd from oblivion re-enact
> The horrors of unhouseled crime. . . .

and Mrs. Daryush:

> Anger lay by me all night long,
>   His breath was hot upon my brow,
> He told me of my burning wrong,
>   All night he talked and would not go.
>
> He stood by me all through the day,
>   Struck from my hand the book, the pen;
> He said: "Hear first what *I've* to say,
>   And sing, if you've the heart to, *then*."
>
> And can I cast him from my couch?
>   And can I lock him from my room?
> Ah no, his honest words are such
>   That he's my true-lord, and my doom.

Such work represents, I believe, and in spite of the italics, which could easily in this case be dispensed with, the perfection of English poetic style; something of the same quality is reached here and there by Shakespeare, Jonson, and Donne at the end of the sixteenth century, and earlier, in a few passages, by Gascoigne, and by a few poets on a few occasions—notably Herbert in "Church Monuments"—in the seventeenth century. A few poets, such as those whom I have already mentioned, achieve something comparable in the nineteenth century. There is much other great poetry in English, but poetry of this type, at its best, is probably the greatest, and in its purity of style and richness of meaning it defines the norm, the more or less clear consciousness of which probably gives much of their identity to the variant types. The virtues of such poetry are nearly forgotten in the twentieth century.

DONALD STANFORD'S
NEW ENGLAND EARTH

I have known the poetry of Don Stanford from its beginnings, for a period, now, of approximately ten years; and as the poetry has improved, and as I have become increasingly familiar with its total quality, the conviction has grown on me that Stanford is one of the finest poets of our time.

His subject matter is all related: on the one hand he deals with sensual beauty, and on the other hand with the moral and intellectual powers which give order to the sensual, or which endeavor to do so; and as sensual beauty requires ordering, so it has its converse of chaos and ugliness, with their attendant terrors, and of these subjects Stanford has made use as well as of the others. His poetry almost invariably has sensory richness; it displays a moral sweetness and firmness unusual in the poetry of our time; and it has a measure of profundity.

The matter of the poems requires little explanation; on the other hand, the quality of the sensibility is of a kind none too popular. Since the sensibility lives in the style, and since Stanford has been preoccupied with problems of style, one should call attention to a few of the more important aspects of what he has done.

In the poem called *Rhesus*,[1] we may observe in a state nearly resembling that of chemical purity the type of rhetoric at which

From *New England Earth and Other Poems* (Stanford, 1941), pp. 5-8.

Stanford is aiming consistently. The allegory is a cliché, a generality of the coldest sort. The detail of the poem escapes the formulary throughout by virtue chiefly of an almost formulary, yet finely managed, hyperbole. This reduction of feeling to extreme generalization suggests the 18th century; the hyperbole (which becomes, as in *The Grand Mesa*, genuine passion whenever the substance fully supports the tone) and much of the diction suggest the late 18th century. Like much of the romantic poetry of that period of similar qualities, the poem is remarkably vigorous in spite of its deficiency of individual experience; and, as I have said, it gains its vigor primarily through its author's mastery of a rhetorical convention. When that mastery is enriched, as in many of the poems, especially the later poems, by a variety of individual experience, the result is frequently something of remarkable power.

And if Stanford resembles the 18th century romantics in a few poems, the resemblance should be more carefully described, and it should be related to another and more obvious resemblance, a resemblance to the metaphysical poetry of the 17th century, especially as it appears in the late and relative ethereal masters such as Dryden and Rochester. When he resembles the 18th century romantics, it is chiefly in the combination of certain rhetorical habits, which they took over from the classicists, with the extremely formalized assertion of a high pitch of feeling. He differs from them in what is probably their chief characteristic, however, their tendency to isolate feeling from motivation, or meaning, though like Collins he has written a few poems (among his earliest) of the disembodied passions. It is not unnatural that a modern with some historical training should chance in his efforts to retrieve a classical sensibility to retrace in some sort the path by which that sensibility was lost; this in spite of the fact that he will probably carry with him, as Stanford appears to do, much of the knowledge accuring from that very experience of loss.

With the complexity of Donne and the suavity of Dryden as his ideals—ideals the second of which, at least, he appears to me surely to have realized within the limits of the forms which he has employed; with an historical sense of the processes by which those ideals were lost and the sensibility of his own period produced, he has made a deliberate effort to master himself and to find his personal bearings with relationship to history. The result is the poetry which I have described: a poetry polished, precise in its statement, complex in its associations; a poetry highly civilized, and deceptive in that its claims are far more modest than its scope; a poetry in which the nostalgic otherworldliness of such writers as Vaughan and of Traherne, and in which a large part of the disillusioned worldliness of Dryden and of Rochester, would appear to have been replaced by an obsession with which those writers were unfamiliar, the fear of that particular disintegration of the spirit with which the race has become familiar during the romantic period, the disintegration of which Collins' *Ode to Evening* is one of the first considerable symptoms, and of which Baudelaire was the first considerable critic. This obsession is expressed with particular power in *The Grand Mesa* and in *The Seagull*; and in the later nature poems there is an older and simpler subject which is nevertheless related, love of the sensory universe, and grief inspired by an acute awareness of its transience, a subject, I suppose, as old as the Stone Age, certainly far older than Herrick, Horace, or the Greeks, and expressed here with a beauty which I, at any rate, cannot expel from my mind.

RHESUS

I sing of Rhesus. All his vision whirled
While at the flood his naked limbs he hurled.
He rose, in greeting to his angry grave
Drank of the huge crest of the blanched wave,
So wide the swath his steely body sheared
The bottom through the severed sea appeared.
Then as a canyon moved by earthly shock
Seals the dividing stream in jaws of rock
So Rhesus clove the towering ocean brim
'Till watery walls had thundered shut on him.
Hail quiet Rhesus in the clasp of death!

If a perfected and immortal breath
Could leave that body by the roaring sea
In scorn of heaven it would dwell with thee.
Howl on you unseen and blood-shaking blast!
The windless deep dissolves his flesh at last.
Yea, though his soul disperses with the flood,
Who braves the sea may taste hardier blood.

RELIGIOUS AND SOCIAL IDEAS IN THE DIDACTIC WORK OF E. A. ROBINSON

It is with some hesitation that I broach the subject of Robinson's religious and social ideas in a separate essay. The ideas are few and vague, and they are embodied in Robinson's weakest poetry, most of which is very weak indeed; but they are a part of the product of a great poet, and they are bound to receive a good deal of attention as time goes on. There is already, in fact, especially in the learned journals and in certain graduate schools, a discernible tendency to look for a philosophy in Robinson, and at all costs to find it and to admire it. It is dangerous to admire a great man for his sins: we may too easily adopt his sins for our own out of admiration for his genius; and when the inevitable reaction occurs, the great man's reputation is likely to suffer unduly.

To understand Robinson's mind, we must recollect the essential outlines of New England religious history.

The early English settlers in New England were a carefully selected group, in the main. Their religious tenets, Calvinism in theology and Congregationalism in church government, were disliked by authority in England to the extent that it was unsafe to profess them; whatever the defects of these tenets, the men who held them in the face of danger were men of moral integrity and intensity; those who risked the desperate venture in New

From *Arizona Quarterly*, IX no. 1 (1945), pp. 70-85.

England were even more obviously so. It is not surprising, therefore, to find a certain consistency of character in the New Englanders or to find certain New England strains which produce men of unusual ability with remarkable frequency. The Adamses and Holmeses and Lowells are well-known examples of such families, but if one studies pedigrees one is impressed with many examples likewise of descent through the female line, where the relationships are obscured by changes of name. Ann Bradstreet, for example, may be called the mother of American poetry in more senses than one; and Robinson, though not descended from her, was descended from her sister. The original settlers, then, were people who were drawn toward certain religious ideas and who had sufficient moral energy to risk life and wealth for their convictions; they must have had certain characteristics in common, and the characteristics must have been strong ones. But once the settlers were established in New England, these characteristics were strongly reinforced by the ideas themselves and by the isolation in which the ideas and the process of breeding to a type were then able to function.

The most important Calvinistic doctrines were the doctrine of man's utter depravity (as distinct from the Catholic doctrine of man's corruption), the doctrine of God's Decrees, and the doctrine of Predestination. According to the first, man was wholly lost in sin and abominable in the sight of God; according to the second, God had ordained from eternity every detail, no matter how trivial, in the history of the universe; according to the third, God had selected, out of his infinite goodness, a few souls for salvation, the selection having been arbitrary and irrespective of any virtues which those or other souls might appear to have. The last doctrine is merely a subsidiary heading of the second, for if all events are decreed, then the fate of each soul is decreed; and it is closely related to the first, for if man is wholly depraved, he is incapable of true virtue, and if God chooses to save him, it is for inscrutable reasons. These concepts, and others related, tended to encourage a highly allegorical frame of mind in the public at large; it became customary to read all events for their significance as part of the divine plan. They tended also to reinforce the moral nature of the Puritan indirectly; logically, these doctrines should have relieved the Puritan of moral responsibility, but actually there was an assumption that election would show itself in conduct, so that the Puritan studied his own behavior assiduously to discover the signs of his election, and it was only human that he should study his neighbor's behavior even more assiduously than his own. Life was incredibly hard, moreover, in early New England, and only the energetically moral were likely to survive.

There was a central contradiction in the Calvinistic doctrine, however, which over a century and a half led to the gradual abandonment of the doctrine: man's acts were decreed, yet man was damned for his sins. The New Englander's moral sense in the long run proved stronger than his loyalty to Calvin, and little by little the doctrine of Predestination disappeared; what was ultimately left, at least in the more intellectual society, was Unitarianism, a doctrine which emphasized morality and minimized theological dogmas. Robinson appears to have come from Unitarian stock, to have inherited the traditional moral sense and moral curiosity, which are the sources of his better poems, and to have broken easily with the few remnants of theology which Unitarianism retained. Like a good Unitarian, however, he seems to have remained unconvinced of the need for precise definition of general ideas.

But the early Calvinism of Europe contained another element, originally the most important of all. It taught that one might be reasonably sure of one's election by virtue of inner assurance, a more or less mystical communion with God, frequently very violent in its emotional form. The first generation of Calvinists in New England found this doctrine dangerous to society, and substituted for it the concept that one might believe oneself of the elect if one entered the Church and conformed to its principles, a belief which strengthened the allegorizing habit, for it made every act symbolic of man's spiritual state. But the mystical element in Calvinism was not suppressed by this modification; it merely remained more or less beneath the surface; and it was revived in the eighteenth century by Jonathan Edwards, who taught a highly evangelical and emotional kind of religion, whatever the learning and ingenuity with which he expounded it.

The mystical tendency in New England was very strong, and Unitarianism gave it no nourishment; in the nineteenth century, when Calvinism was dead so far as the man of intellect was concerned, Emerson gave a new form and a new impetus to the tendency. Emerson took the essential doctrines of European romanticism and restated them in the terms of Edwardian Calvinism. He taught that God and the universe, mind and matter, are one; that emotion and instinct are not only the true guides to virtue but the voice of God, the operation of Grace; the surrender to this guidance is equivalent to the experience of the mystic. In fact, he went farther than this, for he taught that through this surrender one not only communes with God but becomes God. Emerson himself was a product of New England and a man of strong moral habits. He seems to have mistaken habit, or second nature, for nature; since his habits were good, he believed that his nature was good. He gave to American romanticism, in spite of its irresponsible doctrine, a religious tone which it has not yet lost and which has often proved disastrous. He gave also a kind of moral and religious sanction to mere eccentricity, to self-satisfaction, and to critical laziness. The type of mind which follows its first guesses in matters of opinion and perception, with irritated contempt for opposing arguments, and which finds any kind of careful thinking beneath the dignity of a gentleman, is his legitimate heir and can find explicit justification in his writings. This kind of mind is common in modern New England (and no doubt elsewhere); and commingled with the New England moral sense and moral curiosity, there is a good deal of this intellectual laziness in Robinson; and as a result of the laziness there is a certain admixture of Emersonian doctrine, which runs counter to the principles governing most of his work and the best of it. This tendency does not result in stylistic eccentricity in Robinson, as it does, for example, in much of Emerson and of Frost; but it results in loose thinking and in a good many failures of structure, and it shows itself in nearly all of his openly didactic or philosophic pieces except *Hillcrest*, a great poem which states an ethical doctrine which is counter-romantic and counter-Emersonian. His greatest poems, with which I am not at present concerned, are in the moralistic tradition: they deal with individual human dramas; the terms in which he understands the dramas are mainly those of traditional Christian morality, terms which have come down to him as folk wisdom or common sense and which he applies directly to the individual experience as a matter of course.

But it is with the explicitly didactic and expository work that I wish to deal here.

There are a good many poems which treat the subjects of God and immortality, but they are not remarkably clear. The most ambitious of these is *The Man Against the Sky*, a fairly long contemplative poem, of which the versification is generally similar to that of *Dover Beach*. The poem opens with a description of a solitary man crossing a hilltop into the sunset. This man is symbolic of man in general approaching death. Robinson says that his symbolic man may have progressed through great anguish to a triumphant death; or that he may have proceeded easily in the light of an uncritical faith; or that he may have been disillusioned, a stoical artist or philosopher, passing indifferently to extinction; or that he may have been disappointed in life and fearfully unreconciled to death; or that he may have been a mechanistic philosopher, proud of an intellectual construction which gave him no personal hope; but in any event that he represents all of us in that he approaches death alone, to face it as he is able. Robinson asks, then, whether we may not have some expectation of a future life, even if we doubt the existence of Heaven and Hell; and why, if we believe in Oblivion, we are guilty of perpetuating the race. He replies that we know, "if we known anything," the existence of a Deity, a Word, which we perceive fragmentarily and imperfectly, and this knowledge is our sole justification for not ending ourselves and our kind:

> But this we know, if we know anything,
> That we may laugh and fight and sing
> And of our transience here make offering
> To an orient Word that will not be erased,
> Or, save in incommunicable gleams
> Too permanent for dreams,
> Be found or known.

The nature of this Deity, and the nature of our knowledge, are not defined further than this; the crux of the poem is thus offered vaguely and in a few lines; and the greater part of the concluding section is devoted to describing the desolation which we should experience without this knowledge. Philosophically, the poem is unimpressive; stylistically, it is all quite as weak as the lines I have quoted; and structurally, it seems to defeat its purpose— for while it purports to be an expression of faith, it is devoted in all save the few lines which I have just quoted to the expression of despair.

Credo, from *Children of the Night*, perhaps expresses a similar concept and in an equally unsatisfactory manner, but the connective *for* which introduces the second half of the sestet is confusing:

> I cannot find my way: there is no star
> In all the shrouded heavens anywhere:
> And there is not a whisper in the air
> Of any living voice but one so far
> That I can hear it only as a bar
> Of lost imperial music, played when fair
> And angel fingers wove, and unaware,
> Dead leaves to garland where no roses are.
>
> No, there is not a glimmer, nor a call,
> For one that welcomes, welcomes when he fears,
> The black and awful chaos of the night;
> For through it all—above, beyond it all—
> I know the far-sent message of the years,
> I feel the coming glory of the Light.

In the following sonnet from the same collection, there is a statement of a belief in God based on the evidence of human love and the beauty of nature that, as far as it goes, might be Christian or Emersonian or neither:

> When we can all so excellently give
> The measure of love's wisdom like a blow,—

Why can we not in turn receive it so,
And end this murmur for the life we live?
And when we do so frantically strive
To win strange faith, why do we shun to know
That in love's elemental over-glow
God's wholeness gleams with light superlative?

Oh, brother men, if you have eyes at all,
Look at a branch, a bird, a child, a rose,
Or anything God ever made that grows,—
Nor let the smallest vision of it slip,
Till you may read as on Belshazzar's wall,
The glory of eternal partnership.

I do not quote these poems for their poetic virtue, for they have little; the language is vague and trite, the fifth line of the poem just quoted is rhythmically very flat and is guilty of a needless and clumsy use of the progressive form of the verb, and Belshazzar's wall is a curious place on which to read the glory of eternal partnership. But the poems are characteristic expressions of this phase of Robinson's thought; they are characteristic, in fact, of his efforts to express generalized thought on any subject— thought, that is, for its own sake, not for the light it throws on a particular human situation, such as the situation in *Eros Turannos* or *The Wandering Jew*; and they may perhaps serve as some justification of my failure to come to definite conclusions with regard to the precise form of Robinson's theology.

In the *Octaves*, from the same collection, we have a sequence of poems for the most part on the experimental evidence for a belief in God; the evidence is defined very vaguely, in spite of the effort to achieve a gnomic style, but the writing in certain lines achieves a strength greater than any in the three poems which I have just been discussing. The ninth of these is clearer than most; it deals with the disappointment which we feel when a person of high character displays weakness, and the disappointment is offered as evidence of the real existence of the impersonal standard:

When one that you and I had all but sworn
To be the purest thing God ever made
Bewilders us until at last it seems
An angel has come back restigmatized,—
Faith wavers, and we wonder what there is
On earth to make us faithful any more,
But never are quite wise enough to know
The wisdom that is in our wonderment.

The eleventh octave is one of the best written, but offers no solution to the problem posed; it deals merely with the unsatisfied search for the solution:

Still through the dusk of dead, blank-legended
And unremunerative years we search
To get where life begins, and still we groan
Because we do not find the living spark
Where no spark ever was; and thus we die,
Still searching, like poor old astronomers
Who totter off to bed and go to sleep,
To dream of untriangulated stars.

The language applied in these poems to the evidence for a belief in God, language, for example, like "spirit-gleams of wisdom" in the eighth, is likely to be both vague and more or less romantic in its connotations; such a phrase as the one just quoted, in fact, would perhaps appear to indicate a belief in the discovery of God through pure intuition and lend some support to those who find a strong trace of Emerson in Robinson; but there is not sufficient evidence in the poems to prove that the intuition is Emersonian intuition or that the God is Emerson's God. The worst one can say of the poems is that in general they are carelessly thought and carelessly written. Emerson used language reminiscent of Edwards without being a Christian; Robinson could easily have used language reminiscent of Emerson without being an Emersonian. Robinson, especially in his earlier years, might well have resembled a good many learned scholars of my acquaintance who claim to admire Emerson and who quote him by phrases, but who fail to understand or for sentimental reasons refuse to admit the total effect of his work. This kind of thing is fairly common and seems merely to indicate a normal and healthy opacity on the part of superior minds. *The Sage* appears to be a poem in praise of Emerson, but it does not define his doctrine. One could adduce a little more evidence of this kind from the shorter poems, but I believe that all of it would be similarly inconclusive.

The evidence scattered through the longer works is even less conclusive. Captain Craig and his friend Count Pretzel von Würzburger the Obscene both talk as if they were paraphrasing Emerson; but *Captain Craig* is a character sketch, not a philosophic poem, and although these two characters are treated with affection, they are likewise treated with irony, and it seems unlikely that Robinson admired them without reservations. The men are represented as helpless failures, and Pretzel as "a vagabond, a drunkard, and a sponge," and their words are perfectly in character. It might seem the part of wisdom to receive their pronouncements as one receives the pronouncements of Falstaff rather than as one receives those of Dryden in *Religio Laici*. Robinson said to Nancy Evans: "If you want to find out about my 'Transcendentalism,' read *The Man Against the Sky* and *Matthias at the Door*—it's in those poems." And Nancy Evans adds to the quotation marks around the word "Transcendentalism": "The quotes were in his voice."[1] We have considered *The Man Against the Sky;* the philosophical comment in *Matthias* is found in the last ten or twelve pages, in the long conversation between the protagonist and the dead Garth. The gist of the conversation is simply this: that one must be born—that is, achieve spiritual life—before one has a right to die; but the nature of the spiritual life to be achieved is not even suggested. There is the same difficulty in *Lancelot*, the greatest of the long poems. The main theme of this poem is the birth of understanding through error and suffering. Lancelot and Guinevere sin, become involved in tragedy, and then because they become aware of a better way of life, they renounce their love to achieve

[1] Nancy Evans in *The Bookman* (November, 1932).

wisdom. The drama of sin, disaster, and renunciation is handled with great power; but the nature and virtues of the contemplative life are merely implied and hinted through the use of sentimental terms such as "the Light" and "the Vision."

As against the vagueness and the traces of romantic mysticism which I have been discussing, there is the one great expository poem, *Hillcrest*, which does not go into theology but expounds an ethic which is somewhere between the Christian and the stoical and which in its last four stanzas is explicit in its disapproval of romantic optimism and romantic mysticism; and there are many poems on individual experiences which seem to be governed very largely by the principles expressed in *Hillcrest*.

One appears to have in Robinson, then, a poet too little equipped for speculation, too much at the mercy of tradition, though less at its mercy than were many of his contemporaries; and the tradition which affects him is a complex one: the tradition of Calvinistic moralism on the one hand, and on the other the tradition of Unitarian aversion from thought, this latter qualified to an uncertain extent by the more positive Emersonian glorification of pure intuition and impulse. These tendencies are not in rational agreement with each other, but they have existed side by side in New England since the time of Emerson or earlier, and frequently in the same mind.

Robinson's poems on social ideas are similar to his other didactic works. Most of them are poor and none are of his best; in general they indicate the abilities and disabilities to which I have already pointed: the best adhere most closely to the case of the individual man, the worst adventure farthest into general theory. *The Master*, a poem on Lincoln, and *The Revealer*, a poem on Theodore Roosevelt, are primarily poems in praise of their respective subjects; but they indicate, perhaps not very clearly, Robinson's distrust of the common man and his belief in the superior leader as the only hope for democracy.[2] They are the best poems which I shall mention in this connection, *The Master*, especially, standing well up among the best of Robin-

---

[2] Hagedorn, in *Edwin Arlington Robinson, a Biography*, tells us that Robinson early conceived an admiration of Carlyle. The fact should not be pushed too far, but it is worth mentioning.

son's secondary poems. *Cassandra* is a poem warning the nation against the naively enthusiastic commercialism of the early part of the century:

> Your Dollar, Dove, and Eagle make
>   A Trinity that even you
> Rate higher than you rate yourselves;
>   It pays, it flatters, and it's new.

The admirable sharpness of such satirical statements as this is not equaled by his statements in praise of the virtues which he defends:

> Think you to tread forever down
>   The merciless old verities?
> And are you never to have eyes
>   To see the world for what it is?
>
> Are you to pay for all you have
>   With all you are?—No other word
> We caught, but with a laughing crowd
>   Moved on. None heeded, and few heard.

He does not tell us what old verities he has in mind nor how old they are—whether, for example, they are the verities of Emerson or those of Aquinas. Nor does he define the nature of the price in the last stanza, and a good many divergent definitions would be possible. He is quite as vague here as in his references to a positive theology; yet the force of a didactic poem depends precisely upon the clarity and validity of the ideas expressed.

Demos, a double sonnet, warns us that "the few shall save/ The many, or the many are to fall;" but Robinson is again too vague. Does he mean, for example, that democracy cannot survive unless it is regularly governed by great men? If so, there is small hope for it, for great men rise to power in a democracy only occasionally and as a result of their being incidentally great politicians or as a result of some other chance. Robinson may mean that the common mass should be improved little by little by the teachings of great men as those teachings after many years reach them and become a part of their tradition. I should place my own modest hopes in this latter formula, and in the belief that for the immediate present the common man is guided in some measure by such traditional wisdom, imperfectly as he may apprehend it and profit by it, and by a fairly acute sense of where the economic and social shoe pinches; this is not the formula for an Utopia, but I think it works reasonably well. But Robinson unfortunately does not say what he means, and he seems at times to be recommending a Carlylean leader-worship, or a doctrine of an elite class, either of which in practice would result in a Hitler or in an oligarchy.

On the Way is a dialogue spoken by Hamilton and Burr at a time when they were still superficially friendly with each other. Burr expresses the personal jealously of a politician for a man greater than himself—that is, Washington—and Hamilton expresses an admiration for Washington similar to that expressed elsewhere by Robinson for Lincoln and for Theodore Roosevelt:

> It was a man, Burr, that was in my mind;
> No god, or ghost, or demon—only a man:
> A man whose occupation is the need
> Of those who would not feel it if it bit them;
> And one who shapes an age while he endures
> The pin-pricks of inferiorities;
> A cautious man, because he is but one;
> A lonely man, because he is a thousand.
> No marvel you are slow to find in him
> The genius that is one spark or is nothing:
> His genius is a flame that he must hold
> So far above the common heads of men
> That they may view him only through the mist
> Of their defect, and wonder what he is.
> It seems to me the mystery that is in him
> That makes him only more to me a man
> Than any other I have ever known.

With the admiration for Washington one cannot quarrel, nor

can one quarrel with the unkind but essentially true statements about the common man; but again one is at a loss to discern the relationship of Washington to the common man, the way in which he may be said to guide the common man or be of value to him. In the nature of this relationship lies all the difference between barbarism and civilization, however halting; for Washington will be merely a menace to the nation if the common man depends upon him blindly. Unless the influence of Washington can outlast Washington, can teach the common man a few truths and give him a few perceptions, so that he can hope to survive the intervals between Washingtons, then the common man is lost.

Dionysus in Doubt deals immediately with the prohibition amendment of the 1920's, but more generally with the impropriety of legislation upon questions which are matters of personal morality rather than public:

> Also I marvel at a land like yours
> Where predatory love
> In freedom's name invades the last alcove;
> And I foresee a reckoning, perforce,
> That you, not eager to see far
> From where your toys and trumpets are,
> Make nothing of.

With this as a starting point, he deals sketchily with common personal attitudes which finds a menace to society; for example:

> Wherever the dissension or the danger
> Or the distrust may be,
> All you that for timidity
> Or for expediency capitulate,
> Are negative in yourselves and in the state;
> Yet there are worse for you to see,
> As everywhere you may remark:
> Some animals, if you see them in a manger
> And do not hear them bark,
> Are silent not for any watch they keep,
> Nor yet for love of whatso comes to feed,

> But pleasantly and ineffectually
> Are silent there because they are asleep.
> There are too many sleepers in your land,
> And in to many places
> Defeat, indifference, and forsworn command
> Are like a mask upon too many faces.

These attitudes, and others which he attacks, are, as he says, a danger; but they are no more common in democracies than elsewhere. Robinson appears to have confused the vices of humanity with the vices of his country. The writing, moreover, is lax and indolent, whereas satiric and didactic poetry above all other should be compact and sharp; the confusing of the trite figure of the watchdog with the equally trite figure of the dog in a manger is an especially bad example of this laxness. Dionysus goes on to meditate on the dangers of the standardization of the human mind implicit in the kind of legislation to which he is objecting:

> "Sometimes I wonder what machine
> Your innocence will employ,"
> He said at length,
> "When all are niched and ticketed and all
> Are standardized and unexceptional,
> To perpetrate complacency and joy
> Of uniform size and strength . . ."

But once more he seems to read into his own age and country a danger common to all times and countries: Socrates, Galileo, Abelard, and Columbus suffered from this vice in human nature no less surely than anyone has done more recently. The tendency for the mediocre norm to impose itself and for the superior individual to combat and escape this norm or to be sacrificed to it have always existed and I imagine always will; and as for the prohibition amendment, we eventually got rid of it. I have no objection to the castigation of vices, and the vices which Robinson castigates are real; but unless they are rightly located, the poem suffers and there is the possibility that society may suffer. The reader may assume, for example, that there was less standardization and more individual freedom under the reigns of Louis XIV of France or Philip II of Spain; the reigns of those monarchs may have been marked by important values which we lack, but freedom was not one of them, and it strikes me as doubtful that the values in question would be recovered by the re-establishment of comparable political systems. Before we blame our spiritual defects on a political system which it has cost blood and centuries to establish, merely because the defects and the system coincide in time, we would do well to make a careful study of historical causes. And this issue is not irrelevant to the issue of poetry; a poem which embodies so careless an outburst is not an adult performance—that is, it is not a good poem. *Demos and Dionysus* develops much the same argument, and with no greater distinction.

King Jasper, a long allegorical narrative, and the last poem Robinson wrote, takes up social themes again. King Jasper, the modern industrialist, has erected wealth, power, and civilization (civilization is represented by his charming but ineffectual son, young Jasper) on treachery to Hebron, who represents the common man. King Jasper's wife, Honoria, loves him for what he has accomplished and for his love for her, but at the crisis of the poem she is forced to abandon him and kill herself; Honoria, in so far as she represents honor, seems to represent it in a limited and conventional sense, except in her final act—she is, throughout, in jealous conflict with Zoë, who, according to Robinson, represents intelligence and who, according to Miss Estelle Kaplan[3] and more plausibly, represents intelligence and vitality or (my own suggestion) vitality mistaken for intelligence in a traditionally Emersonian manner. The reasons, on the allegorical level, for the conflict between Honoria and Zoë, are not wholly clear. Young Hebron, his father's successor, who comes in the role of the avenger, is represented throughout as a hard, grasping, and imperceptive barbarian; he destroys civilization in avenging the wrong on which it was founded. Zoë alone survives; she alone understands and cannot be wholly possessed by anyone. As a social allegory, however, the poem is defective with relation to

[3] *Philosophy in the Poetry of Edwin Arlington Robinson*, by Estell Kaplan (New York, 1940).

Zoë. Capitalistic democracy, as represented by King Jasper, fails; the revolutionary democracy, as represented by Hebron, contains no elements of potential success—it is represented as the end of civilization. Now Zoë, as the allegorical representative of intelligence, cannot exist in a vacuum; she has to be possessed by someone, even though imperfectly, yet the only forms of social activity shown in the poem are incapable of possessing her. Either Zoë should have been destroyed or there should have been a solution. To tell us that there is no hope for civilization and then at the end:

> Nothing alive
> Was left of Jasper's Kingdom. There was only
> Zoë. There was only Zoë—alone.—

This is merely outrageous balderdash; it is the final substitution of irresponsible sentimentality for thought. It is fair to remember that this poem was composed during Robinson's final illness and was finished on his deathbed; yet the thinking is essentially similar to that in his earlier work.

Too much of the writing that has been done on Robinson, especially in the forms of books and of long articles, has been done in the spirit of devotion rather than in the spirit of criticism. It is foolish to speak of the Total Vision of a man who could write the poems that I have been discussing. Robinson was in no sense a philosophical thinker. He was a man with a great gift for writing certain kinds of poetry and with a stubborn common sense which prevented a large number of his poems on themes of the sort which he understood from being corrupted by the weaker side of his nature. His inconsistencies are serious if one is bent on being misled by them; and had he been a better thinker, he would certainly have been a greater poet. But his inconsistencies are no worse, and his bad thinking is no worse, than one can find in Wordsworth or Hardy or Bridges; and his great poems place him in the company of those poets.

THE POET AND THE UNIVERSITY: A REPLY

In poetry for November last, Mr. Hayden Carruth objects to some of my remarks on the subject of the poet and the academic career. Any reply is bound to be a kind of *ad hominem* (and *ex homine*) affair. In the first place, Mr. Carruth knows extremely little about the academic career. I do not know whether he has done any teaching, or, if he has, how much; but I know that in the nature of things he can have done very little, for I have met him, and he is very young. On the other hand, I am forty-nine years old (to my sorrow), and am now beginning my twenty-second year as a teacher of English, my twenty-fourth year as a university teacher, and my twenty-sixth year as a teacher. Most of the contempt for the academic career, and for the academic character, is expressed by young men who did not get much beyond their B.A., either for lack of interest or for lack of ability, or by young men who when forced into close contact with mediocre academic figures lost their equanimity and decided that all professors were stupid. Most professors (of language and literature, at any rate) are more or less stupid, to be sure, but so are most other people. Seven or eight of the most brilliant men I have ever known have been professors of one literature or another; and if I were to search for their equals among the non-academic literary men of the past twenty years, I could count

From *Poetry,* LXXV no. 3 (1949) pp. 170-178.

them on the fingers of one hand, and probably without using my thumb.

In the first place, I assume that we are discussing ways of earning an honorable living. No poet is likely to do that with his poetry, though a few scattered cases can be found of poets who have: even Shakespeare, presumably, would not have been very successful had he not been likewise an actor and a producer. The system of patronage as it flourished in the eighteenth century is for the most part ended, though we have had a few generous patrons of the arts in our day, and we have various fellowships offered by institutions and foundations. The patronage of governments is largely at an end: the man of letters can seldom hope to be made Consul at Liverpool, or Ambassador at Madrid. These changes may be lamentable, but I do not believe that they are. As to patronage, one might read Samuel Johnson; and political patronage is no more desirable than personal. Patronage in any of its forms may be valuable to a young man who is beginning his career, provided the form of the patronage enables him to get into a position to take care of himself; but a life-long reliance on patronage produces the type of character commonly referred to as the literary bum, and the literary bum will never have enough personal character or enough self-respect to produce great art. Personally, I would rather abandon my art than my self-respect: without my self-respect I could not write decently, in any event.

I am glad that Mr. Carruth discarded the common objection to the academic career, that it dissociates the practitioner from real life. I am no more restricted to the materials and the activities of my profession than is the average barber, real estate salesman, or insurance lawyer, and the materials and activities of my profession are intrinsically more civilized than are those of theirs and have a much wider range of spiritual implication. I meet men daily at Stanford University, some of them faculty members, many of them students, whose interests and experience are much wider, I suspect, than those of the men met in the normal course of business by Wallace Stevens or by W. C. Williams.

As to extra-curricular connections, they are not only not impossible but as often as not they are impossible to escape. My spare time and energy for two years went to an effort to help defend a man who was unjustly accused of murder, and who was persecuted by a hysterical community and prosecuted by one of the most corrupt political organizations ever to flourish in the West. During the war I was too old and otherwise undesirable to be of interest to the Armed Forces, with the result that I found myself presently in charge of Civilian Defense in Los Altos (before the battle of Midway, at any rate, C.D. was a serious matter on the coast, and for good reason). At one time I must have had at least 400 people working under me, and I suspect considerably more than that. I, like my wife, have been a member of groups combatting racial and religious discrimination, and though we have been far less active than we should have been, we have tried to do what time and energy permitted. My wife was once Commissioner of Girl Scouts for the Los Altos area, and has at various times (totalling at least five years) been active in the Girl Scout organization and in the Cubs (baby Boy Scouts). I do not wish to sound as if I felt myself unduly virtuous in connection with these matters; I am merely a trifle tired of being told two things: (1) that I have retreated to an ivory tower and removed myself from the community; and (2) that the academic profession of necessity absorbs all of my energy, as if it were some sort of incubus. As to my spiritual communication with the proletariat I might mention this, which is a matter of record: I was one of the few people in the nation who knew that Harry Truman would win the last presidential election, and I won a five dollar bet on the matter.

As to purely amoral extra-curricular activities, these also are possible, and may, as they say, extend one's acquaintance enormously and profitably. For example, I breed and exhibit Airedales. My young dog, Champion Buckthorn Black Jack, was best of breed and second in the terrier group the last time I showed him; and he has been best of breed many times before and has been twice third in the terrier group. His mother, whom I bred and showed throughout her entire show career, once managed to go best in show. His litter brother and sister are both champions and have records almost as good as his own. I get to about seven or eight shows a year. I get to the Los Angeles area at least once a year: a week from the day of this writing I show at Chico, in the northern end of the Sacramento Valley, and the day following I show at Sacramento, and I get home from Sacramento about 3 A.M. Monday morning and start correcting papers for my Tuesday class in The Theory and Practice of the Criticism of Poetry. Alas, the Ivory Tower.

Mr. Carruth says that writers today have little choice as to profession, yet he ends by advising them to take up navigation, or sheep-herding, or ceramics—something, in other words, as far removed as possible not only from writing but from community with mankind. If we set aside the temptations of patronage, I do not believe that the choice of writers is any more limited now than it ever was. As to choices regarding the manner of *earning* a living, Wallace Stevens chose to be an insurance lawyer, and rumor has it that he has been a good one; W. C. Williams chose to be a physician, and I have heard reports that he also has done very well; so far as I am aware, neither man has complained of his choice. Both men, of course, have written beautiful poetry, but I sometimes suspect that both would have done better if their professional careers had concentrated their minds on their arts instead of on other matters. Poetry cannot be taken lightly; it is not a party girl to be met on an occasional evening. On the other hand, it is quite possible that both men would have made bad teachers (and equally bad preachers) for temperamental reasons. It is possible, however, that both passed up the academic career because of the sentimental prejudices against it which were prevalent among the bright young literary men of their generation. The choice of neither was restricted however: a degree in law or a degree in medicine is almost as arduous as a Ph.D. in literature, both intellectually and financially, and it would be uncharitable to suppose that either of these gentlemen could not have overcome so slight a difference in difficulty.

What are the hazards of my career as compared to the hazards of others? In the first place, let us recollect that it is a career, and not a system of dependency or of panhandling. The careers of Williams or of Stevens (I suspect) would have left me far less than my own, and they would have directed most of my energy away from the matters which most interest me instead of toward them. The careers recommended by Mr. Carruth—ceramics, the maritime service, or janitorial service (I know a young poet who has gone into this last, apparently on theories akin to those of Mr. Carruth), would be a genuine retreat to an ivory tower. I have not, unfortunately, either the tall and willowy frame or the fragile temperament which would enable me to engage gracefully in that kind of retreat, and the men who do engage in such retreats seldom have the toughness of spirit to produce anything worth looking at. If one's blessed little immortal soul cannot take a certain amount of roughing around, it probably is not worth preserving anyway.

In comparing the career of the teacher with that of the priest, Mr. Carruth says that the priest has (or had) fewer practical duties than a university teacher. He is dreaming: I suggest that he get acquainted with a few priests.

Mr. Carruth says that as a teacher the poet will dissipate his poetry by talking about poetry to his classes. This is something that neither he nor any psychologist can prove. So far as my personal history is concerned, it was the necessities of teaching which forced me to clarify my ideas about literature, and it was this clarification of ideas which enabled me to write the only poems which I am interested in preserving. Had it not been for my academic career, it is quite possible that I should still be a minor disciple of W. C. Williams, doing little impressionistic notes on landscapes. It is true that I have written less and less poetry as I have grown older, but I believe that there is in the main a preceptible improvement in the quality of the poetry. As to the reasons for the decrease in quantity, they are perhaps several: in a period of critical muddleheadedness such as our own, I have had to divert a good deal of my energy into prose, if only to keep my own ideas in order; as I have risen in the Stanford English department, and as the university has grown, my duties have increased (this situation, however, would hold in almost any career); as I have grown older, my energy has diminished—I mean my nervous and physical capacity for working instead of sleeping; as I have grown older, I have become more critical of my own work and am less easily satisfied with simple or casual themes than I once was; and beyond all this I do not like to repeat myself. I can see no reason to leave 1,500 pages of mediocre verse behind one, with a few good poems lost in it all. I would rather let the few good poems stand alone; they will have a better chance of surviving if I do my own editing, if I do not leave the editing to editors.

Mr. Carruth apparently regards teaching as odious drudgery. I have not found it so. I enjoy teaching, simply as a day-to-day activity. I should be lost without it, even if I did not have to earn a living. It is true that I teach in a good university, one which draws a superior body of students, but there are other good universities, and a good man ought to be able to get into one. If I were to name the thirty most intelligent people whom I have met in the past twenty years, some seven or eight would be colleagues or former colleagues, close to fifteen would be students or former students, and the rest (perhaps) would be chosen from other groups. I have close to twenty students working under me at the present time who can write better critical analyses than any New York or Chicago book reviewer (or than almost any New York or Chicago "critic"), and with whom it is a genuine pleasure to be in daily contact. And my contact with them is not merely a pleasure; it is also a serious professional activity.

In the university life, as in business, law, medicine, or the army, there are inferior men, and worst of all there are the career boys, the glamor boys, the smoothies, the professional phonies. At some period any department and any university are weakly administered, and the phonies acquire a good deal of power; they do some damage, and they attempt more. But this situation is merely one of the hazards of our fallen mortality; it is not peculiar to the universities.

The university life as I have known it is varied, active, serious, and conducive to intellectual growth. It wears one out, more or less, but so does life in general. The university life is not, God knows, a form of escape, nor is the university a sanctuary. The life that Mr. Carruth recommends for the poet, however, is unquestionably a form of escape. It is a life for fairies and fantasists.

INTRODUCTION
TO THE EARLY POEMS

I publish this book to provide an authorized edition of my early and "experimental" work. Some one would do this in any event, and probably one who would sweep all of my uncollected work into a single volume, with no indication of what I had considered my best work as I was writing and publishing it. I include three small books, a group of four poems previously uncollected from magazines, and two later groups of some size. The first of these later groups, the *Fire Sequence*, appeared in *The American Caravan* of 1927; the second formed the first section of my volume *The Proof* (1930). The *Fire Sequence* contained two poems written later and about another landscape, and these will be found in the final group where they belong; they are *Incandescent Earth* and *Orange Tree*. The final group originally contained a few other poems reprinted from the *Fire Sequence*, and these I have left in the *Fire Sequence* and have omitted from the final group, which is miscellaneous. Except for these few details of arrangement and the inclusion of a group of four poems previously uncollected, I have done no editing and I have revised no poems. Any other uncollected material is rubbish. I wish to be clear on two points: I regard this work as inferior to my later work; I regard it as very good of its kind, quite as good as any of the "experimental" work of this century. In any collection as

From *The Early Poems of Yvor Winters* (Denver, 1966), pp. 7-16.

large as this and written within so few years, there will be some
bad poems; I think that I can identify these, but I do not believe
that the incidence is high. In order to present the record, I have
retained them. These poems can be best clarified by a little autobiographical
detail; I will try to keep it to a minimum.

I became interested in poetry and the writing of poetry at the
age of fourteen. In my last year of high school, at the age of six-
teen, I discovered Miss Monroe's magazine, then called by its
original name: *Poetry: A Magazine of Verse*, and I became a sub-
scriber. In McClurg's Book Store in Chicago I discovered copies
of *The Little Review* and of *Others*, and began purchasing them,
and it was at this time (and place) that I bought a fair number
of books by Yeats, Pound, Williams, and other moderns. I became acquainted with the work of Stevens in high school, long
before the publication of *Harmonium* in 1923. I entered the University of Chicago in the fall of 1917, and became a member of
the recently formed Poetry Club. This was a very intelligent
group, worth more than most courses in literature; among the
new members were Glenway Wescott, a year younger than myself, who, like myself, had discovered most of the unknown
moderns in high school, and Elizabeth Madox Roberts, about
twenty years our elder. Janet Lewis, later to become my wife,
joined the group the following year, but after I had left the university. Through this group I made the acquaintance of Miss
Monroe, who encouraged me to visit her in her office. She was
usually busy when I called, and I read old issues of *Poetry* and
books in her large collection of modern verse and criticism; occasionally other visitors came by, some of them interesting.
Shortly before I left the university in the following winter, Miss
Monroe, who had been sorting out her files in the hope of finding
more space on her shelves, gave me a complete set of duplicates
of the first six or seven volumes of the magazine, enough to bring
me up to the point at which my subscription began. At the end
of the autumn quarter of 1918, I discovered that I had tuberculosis and was taken to California, the home of my childhood, for
a few weeks and then to Santa Fé, New Mexico, where I remained
until late October of 1921, most of the time in bed in a sana-

torium. I took my files of *Poetry* and my books of modern poetry with me, and I subscribed to *Others* and *The Little Review*, and, as occasion permitted, to a few later and similar magazines. These magazines and a few books were my chief sources of education during a period of five years. Alice Corbin Henderson, Miss Monroe's assistant, had preceded me to Santa Fé with the same disease; I shortly made her acquaintance, and she lent me books and advised me. Late in 1921 or a little after, I made the acquaintance of Marianne Moore by mail; she was then a librarian in the New York Public Library, and she sent me books, very kindly but I am sure illegally. The books sent me by Miss Moore were all books that I needed to read, but they were chosen with a typical disregard of historical or other classification; I remember reading *The Golden Bowl*, at the age of twenty-one and with no preparation, while I was a teacher in a coal-mining camp. And there was a French priest in Santa Fé who gave me a few, and my first, lessons in French, lessons which set me to work at a frustrating effort to decipher Rimbaud, a poet of whom my friend the priest thoroughly disapproved.

The *Immobile Wind* and nearly all of *The Magpie's Shadow* were written while I was at the sanatorium in Santa Fé. I believe that two poems in *The Bare Hills*, "The Impalpable Void" and "The Fragile Season," were written toward the end of the same period. There was no French influence on these poems except as it might have filtered through the Imagists or perhaps through Stevens or Sturge Moore. I had been reading Bridges and Hardy, whom I admired but who did not influence me at this time, and Emily Dickinson and Adelaide Crapsey, who may have influenced me. I was familiar also with many translations from the poetry of the Japanese and of the American Indians; the Indians especially were an influence on *The Magpie's Shadow*.

In October of 1921, I left the sanatorium and went to Ranchos de Taos, where I stayed with friends for a few weeks. I then went to Madrid, a coal-mining camp about twenty miles south of Santa Fé, where I taught in the grade school for a year. The name of the town was not pronounced as we would pronounce it; it was *Mad*-rid. That is, in English; the Mexicans, when speaking their native language, gave it the correct Spanish pronunciation.

Madrid was in a long, narrow, and deep valley, a shark's-mouth, about three miles into the mountains from Los Cerrillos, the railroad outlet for the mines. Los Cerrillos had been a Mexican village before the mines came; the houses in Madrid were frame shacks, all of them painted a light harsh blue, the houses of Cerrillos were adobe. The coal was mined in Madrid; the brothels and dispensaries of illegal liquor (this was in the days of Prohibition) were in Cerrillos. The high school also was in Cerrillos, and I taught there the following year; there were six boys in the high school and I think two girls. Accidents, many fatal, were common in the mines, from which union organizers were vigorously excluded and sometimes removed; drunken violence was a daily and nightly occurrence in both towns; mayhem and murder were discussed with amusement. Yet I was treated with deference: I was able to keep order at the public dances on Friday nights merely by my presence until ten o'clock, but after ten, because of the consumption of liquor, I needed (and received) the assistance of the marshal. The miners tipped their hats to me when they passed me in the street; the Mexicans addressed me as Maestro, the others as Professor.

In the spring of 1923 I left for the University of Colorado at Boulder, where I enrolled as a second-quarter sophomore for the summer quarter. After nine consecutive quarters, including three summer quarters, I received a B.A. and an M.A. in Romance Languages, with a minor in Latin. My training in the languages, and especially in philology, was excellent; my training in literature was nil. Before the end of the first year I was reading extensively in French literature and was making a beginning on the Symbolists, who were not in the curriculum; by the end of my second year I read French and Spanish very easily, including Old French and Old Spanish; I was a fair Latinist and had read a good deal of Vergil, Ovid, Horace, and Catullus and less of a few other poets, and knew some Italian, but I could not speak French or Spanish well enough to teach them. Nevertheless, in my ignorance, I went to the University of Idaho at Moscow, in the northern end of the state, where I taught French and Spanish for two years. Boulder was a big enough city to have a streetcar line, and it was an hour or so from Denver; Moscow was too small for a street-car line and the only cities were at least half a day away and were small besides. The library at Moscow was almost nothing, but it contained a couple of standard sets of Iberian literature which enabled me to read extensively in Old Spanish, Old Portuguese (Galician, gallego), and in the Spanish poetry of the Renaissance. I read all of Proust, most of Flaubert, and other French prose, and continued my reading of the Symbolists. By the end of 1927 I knew French literature fairly well and had a passable knowledge of Spanish. My knowledge of English and American literature before the modern period was very slight.

In the summer of 1926 I was married to Janet Lewis in Santa Fé. She also had gone there because of her health, and she was not well enough to return to Moscow with me, so I went alone. The following summer we both went to California, and I entered Stanford University as a graduate student in English in the autumn of 1927.

The first poems in this collection were written early in 1920, when I was nineteen years of age; the last were written early in 1928, when I was twenty-seven; they are the work of eight years or a little less, and are the work of a young man. They deal with my experience in the places which I have named, and were written with the knowledge which I have indicated. The *Fire Sequence* was written during my last winter at Moscow, but dealt with Madrid in retrospect. In the 'twenties I was not in Paris, nor even at Harvard. After a year as a student at Stanford, I became a full-time instructor of English, but continued my studies and completed my doctorate; I have remained on the same English faculty since, but retire in June of 1966. I had no opportunity to study English literature before coming to Stanford, nor the history of criticism, nor the "history of ideas" generally.

Early in 1928 I abandoned free verse and returned to traditional meters. This was not due to the influence of Stanford nor to any sudden intellectual or religious conversion. It was becoming increasingly obvious to me that the poets whom I most admired were Baudelaire and Valéry, and Hardy, Bridges, and Stevens in a few poems each, and that I could never hope to approach the quality of their work by the method which I was using. I changed my method, explored the new method, and gradually came to understand the theoretical reasons for the change which I had made as a practical necessity. I perhaps should point out also that my theory of the scansion of free verse was worked out toward the end of my last year at Moscow, when most of my free verse had been written. There are a good many critics today who believe that all of my poetry has been governed by principles worked out in advance and then put mechanically into practice. Actually, I wrote as anyone writes, with what intelligence I could muster at the time, improving my intelligence as I went along. During my first year at Stanford, I took the usual courses in Old and Middle English; I discovered that for me English poetry began with Chaucer, although I was grateful for such knowledge as I acquired of earlier poetry and even for the poor training which I received in English philology. I read Chaucer and the Scots Chaucerians systematically and began a systematic reading of English poetry from Skelton onward to Bridges and Hardy, and of Americans as well. I missed few poets of importance, I am sure, during the eight or nine years in which this was my principal occupation, and I have reread many a good many times. This reading disclosed two more poets, Fulke Greville and Ben Johnson, who have remained with the five already mentioned, among the poets who move me most profoundly, and the passage of time has produced two more, both to much younger than myself to have influenced me, but very great poets, J. V. Cunningham and Edgar Bowers. And there have been isolated poems by other men: *Church Monuments*, for example, by George Herbert, and *The Cricket*, by F. G. Tuckerman.

One final word of warning. My shift from the methods of these early poems to the methods of my later was not a shift from formlessness to form; it was a shift from certain kinds of form to others. I was aware of form (when it occurred) in the work of other writers from an early date and was always preoccupied to achieve it in my own work. Form is something in itself is insufficient. But theory is helpful as a guide, and some persons can acquire a measure of perception with the help of theory, and this fact provides an excuse for the existence of critics and teachers. When I say that these poems had form, I refer not only to the possibility that the free verse may be scanned by my method, perhaps with difficulty; I refer to the fact that these poems are rhythmical, not merely from line to line, but in total movement from the beginning to end, and that the relations between the meanings of the parts is an element in the rhythm, along with the sound. In the long run, however, the free verse and the associational procedure in the use of imagery and in the interrelation of images and other passages proved severely restrictive. In the last two groups, especially, in this collection, the movement, and consequently the diction, were often violent; form dictated the state of mind and often the subject, and these were not always intelligent. Sometimes the subject justified the state of mind and the form, but not always, and some poems are exceptions to what I have just said. Some of the best poems in the collection and some of the worst are in these two groups. But I had pushed this method past the limits of its efficaciousness, and for reasons which I have discussed in my criticism I found myself unable to write what I wished, and I therefore changed my method.

From first to last, most of my favorite poets have been relatively modern, and my matter and my methods have been modern. At no time in my later work did I try to emulate the Elizabethans or the poets of the eighteenth century or to revive their methods, despite the theories of various critics. My aim for the first poem in this collection was a clean and accurate diction and movement, free of clichés; in other respects my methods have altered with the years.

INDEX OF POETS AND CRITICS